OF FICTION AND FAITH

Of Fiction and Faith

Twelve American Writers Talk about Their Vision and Work

W. DALE BROWN

WILLIAM B. EERDMANS PUBLISHING COMPANY
GRAND RAPIDS, MICHIGAN / CAMBRIDGE, U.K.

© 1997 Wm. B. Eerdmans Publishing Co.
255 Jefferson Ave. S.E., Grand Rapids, Michigan 49503 /
P.O. Box 163, Cambridge CB3 9PU U.K.

Printed in the United States of America

02 01 00 99 98 97   7 6 5 4 3 2 1

Library of Congress Cataloging-in-Publication Data

Brown, W. Dale.
Of fiction and faith: twelve American writers talk about their vision and work /
W. Dale Brown
p.   cm.
ISBN 0-8028-4313-1 (alk. paper)
1. American fiction — 20th century — History and criticism — Theory, etc.
2. Religion and literature — United States — History — 20th century.
3. Novelists, American — Interviews.
4. Religious fiction, American — Authorship.
5. Faith in literature.
6. Fiction — Authorship.   I. Title.
PS374.R47B76   1997
813′.5409382 — dc21   97-17558
                                                          CIP

Contents

OF FICTION AND FAITH

Introduction

In an era that prizes individual choice and private opinion, book reviewers and teachers of English are fast becoming anachronisms. The very idea of any arbiter of public taste is threatened by our faith in "You see it your way and I see it mine." Why should anyone presume to tell us what books to read, what films to watch, what music is good for us? Personal pleasure has become the central guiding principle behind our trips to the bookstores and the cinemas.

Book publishers argue that they simply give us what we want as they fill the shelves with O.J. tomes, celebrity biographies, and self-help manuals. It is unfortunate, as Barbara Kingsolver says, that "there is no Hippocratic Oath for the professionals who service our intellects."

But another view persists. Without regard to the market or the talk shows, many artists have continued to say what they think we need to hear. Even when we are not listening. These writers hark back to the old-fashioned notion that books can make us better. Such a view might be summarized in the words of Franz Kafka:

> If the book we are reading does not wake us, as with a fist hammering on our skulls, why then do we read it? Good God, we would be happy if we had no books, and such books as make us

happy we could, if need be, write ourselves. But what we must have are those books that come upon us like ill-fortune and distress us deeply, like the death of one we love better than ourselves, like suicide. A book must be an ice-ax to break the sea frozen inside us.

Ezra Pound says it more succinctly: "A book is a ball of fire we hold in our hands." And William Carlos Williams understands the seriousness of it all: "It is difficult to get the news from poems, but everyday men die miserably for lack of what is found there."

This is not to erase the value of popular literature, those books that leave us where we were. It is simply to suggest that we also need those books that take us where we have not yet been. Twinkies and Snickers Bars are tolerable in moderation, but a steady diet of such fare finally fails us.

But you have been to the bookstores. In Waldenbooks you may be able to find Henry David Thoreau on a shelf labeled "classics," near the back of the store. In the Family Bookstore you discover the newly popular Christian thriller. Both venues feature formula and glitz, cliché and simplicity, in ways that frustrate readers who are serious about the furniture of their minds. If we are to locate those books that "come upon us like ill-fortune," we are forced to search carefully.

This interview project began with Frederick Buechner. I wondered about this fine writer whose name I had to spell for bookstore clerks so they could look it up on their computer screens to try to figure out where I might find a copy of *The Sacred Journey* or *Godric*. I knew people who looked forward to each of his new books, but he never seemed to get bookstore space equal to that of John Grisham, Danielle Steele, or Frank Peretti. I wondered why. I decided to ask him.

I discovered a writer oddly between two worlds. He was, as he put it, "too religious for the irreligious and too secular for the religious." And I was to learn that he had company. Traveling around the country, I met Peggy Payne in her log house up a gravel road in North Carolina and Will Campbell in his chicken coop study in a Tennessee holler. I talked with Jon Hassler in a motel lobby in Ann Arbor and listened to Doris Betts over the clinking of forks on plates in a restaurant in Chapel

Hill. Walt Wangerin let my tape recorders into his living room and Robert Goldsborough invited me into his offices at Crain Publications in Chicago. Garrison Keillor gave me bread and cheese in his apartment on the west side in New York City. Robert Olen Butler and Elizabeth Dewberry met me at the old Seelbach, the *Gatsby* hotel, in Louisville. Clyde Edgerton met me at "Dusty's Flying Taxi" in North Carolina, and Denise Giardina welcomed me into her West Virginia home. How gracious they have been, and what fun.

They talked to me with great friendliness about their careers, their audiences, their approaches to writing, and their attitudes toward issues of faith. The rejection of easy piety has excluded most of these writers from the family bookstore, and the avoidance of popular cliché has sometimes left them on the discount table, if anywhere, in the mainstream bookstores. But they persist. These are writers who will surprise and dismay; they may disturb and puzzle. But they finally offer insight into the lives we live.

I want to thank my wife, Gayle, for her patience with the tapes and the trips; my children, who had to settle for T-shirts from Boston and New York and Durham; the many student assistants, especially Amanda Van Heukelem, who labored over the transcriptions for hours and hours; and my colleagues at Calvin College who have supported the project with their encouragement. Finally, my thanks to the dozen writers here, whose books have entertained or shaken and sometimes both.

Grand Rapids, Michigan   W. Dale Brown
June 1996

DORIS BETTS

1954 — *The Gentle Insurrection*
1957 — *Tall Houses in Winter*
1964 — *The Scarlet Thread*
1966 — *The Astronomer and Other Stories*
1972 — *The River to Pickle Beach*
1973 — *Beasts of the Southern Wild*
1981 — *Heading West*
1994 — *Souls Raised from the Dead*
1997 — *The Sharp Teeth of Love*

DORIS BETTS

Learning to Balance

*"I have never found life, faith, or art really so neat. I continue
to outlive many days surveying this world with the suspicion
that Deus has really absconded. With the funds."*

Doris Betts is an elder, a Sunday School teacher, and a part-time
organist in the Presbyterian church. A former chairperson of the faculty
at the University of North Carolina–Chapel Hill, she has taught in the
English Department for more than twenty-five years. From 1978 to
1981, she served on the Literature Panel of the National Endowment
for the Arts and since 1980 has occupied the position of Alumni
Distinguished Professor of English. Mother, grandmother, and wife,
Professor Betts lives on a farm near Pittsboro, North Carolina.

Since 1954 she has produced three collections of short fiction and
five novels. *Souls Raised from the Dead* appeared in 1993. Betts has been
accused of being a gloomy writer because she is preoccupied with the
spiritual and with death. She likes William Saroyan's comment, "I
began writing in order to get even on death." "That's not a bad reason,
really," says Betts, but her Calvinist roots lead her to more than the
predictable bleakness of many contemporary novelists. "Deny the

3

metaphysical and the trivial will triumph," says one of Betts's characters, and, although she mourns the visible emptinesses of our time, she continues to believe that "there is a moment in every day that the devil cannot find."

In August 1992 we spoke over lunch and in her office at the University of North Carolina, a place where she is clearly at home.

▼   ▼

WDB: I remember a review you did in *Southern Quarterly* on an Anne Tyler novel. You said something about a missing philosophical dimension in her work. You wish she had done something more with spirituality?

DB: But she isn't going to. She has a Quaker outlook on people, and that will be maintained, but she doesn't want to get into theology and philosophy. And in a way I suppose that's prudent.

WDB: But you do get into theology and philosophy?

DB: Might as well.

WDB: I'm interested in those writers who write out of an awareness of Christianity, who write seriously, even satirically, perhaps, and certainly not simplistically. Fred Buechner, for example, has been very important to me.

DB: I've always thought his job must be even harder because he is a minister. I mean I play up against a kind of secular profession. He plays up against one in which orthodoxy is at a premium with parishioners who have views. He has done what Graham Greene did — write books that are obviously theological but without proselytizing in them. His motives are aesthetic, but they are in that light. I really admire that.

WDB: David Holman says, "Doris Betts's characters are always asking unanswerable questions." Serious writing by Christians often, I fear, shies away from the questions. You say somewhere that "Christian spoils to a rancid adjective." Yet we speak of the Christian publishing industry, Christian bookstores, Christian novelists. Over a year ago, I attended a church service at a small congregation meeting just off-campus at the University of North Carolina. As it turned out, one of your colleagues was doing the sermon that day. He talked about when you were chair of the faculty and Billy Graham had been invited to campus, and you became embroiled in a controversy over whether or not you should introduce Graham. The speaker quoted from the speech that you apparently did eventually deliver. And it was pungent with wonderful phrases. You spoke of "the tribe of Thomas" into which you were born. Do you remember that speech?

DB: I do remember that speech because it was a kind of turning point on this campus for me. I was not only faculty chairman but very conscious that in a secular, tax-supported institution where you represent everyone from the atheist to the agnostic to the Jew to the Hindu to the Christian to the nothing, that some neutrality was required. Also, I am not a particular fan of Billy Graham, although I liked him better after he was here. He handled faculty questions superbly; I did not know he could do that. But two students came and told me that there was going to be this big thing in the gym, an audience of ten thousand, and they wanted people before he spoke each night — and this is the word they used — "to testify." You can just imagine! At first I refused; I just shuddered. At the same time it's very hard to say no to two excellent students, students who had never asked me to do anything before. I began to feel guilty. Was this what Paul meant about being ashamed of Jesus Christ? Am I afraid to just come out and declare myself a Christian? Am I worried that I'll lose the respect of the faculty that has elected me? This is not a campus where one hears much about religious faith. Bill Friday, who was then president of all sixteen University of North Carolina campuses, called and said, "Doris you have to do what you want to do and I want you to know that I'm going to be on the platform, and I think you can do whatever you want to do." I said, "Well, if they won't introduce me as chairman of the faculty, if they will just allow me to be a person, a writer, I will do it." And so I did. Everything that I had thought would happen didn't. On the contrary, two things happened that I found interesting. One was that I did talk about doubts and of being of the "tribe of Thomas," and I said that for me faith was always going to be a pilgrimage. And then Billy Graham spoke after me about how he'd

5

never had a doubt in his life. He had swept through the revolving doors and come out on the other side. It was a large crowd and people whom I had never met before would come up for days after and say, "I'm a Baptist." It was as if everybody was revealing some shameful secret. That was not the reaction that I had expected. I'm sure there were people who disagreed and didn't like it, but for me it turned out to be a very rewarding experience. That little talk has been reprinted more than anything I ever wrote. Isn't that bizarre?

I did come to like Billy Graham. It was interesting to watch him give a speech. Sitting on a platform, I could see his method. I would never be able to do it. He has small cards and he talks off one of them and he'll glance down and maybe move two or four. He's really saying "Uh-huh, they didn't like that, I'll skip this." It's all a kind of patchwork.

WDB: He's reading an audience?

DB: Yeah, that's right, and sometimes he'd go for a long sequence and sometimes he'd just shuffle ahead, and I believe he could have given maybe ten speeches out of those cards. The other thing was that he had a faculty luncheon here in one of these big banquet rooms — a question and answer session. I came to that also. It was an almost antagonistic audience and the questions were loaded. And he was superb. As a fellow teacher, I thought, "My gosh, that's good work." He was neither defensive nor dogmatic. He was thoughtful, he was generous, and he was intelligent. He was, in fact, an intellectual. It was another side of him. So I did come to understand something about how much audience means to him and how he adjusts to that. As a writer I don't adjust, but I did not find it contemptible in him. I could see that that was a matter of principle for him, and it was consistent and reasonable.

WDB: You have a character in *The River at Pickle Beach* — I think she's a nun — who says, "Deny the metaphysical and the trivial will triumph." Is that happening in contemporary fiction and contemporary culture?

DB: I think that's a very great risk. It seems to me particularly evident in, say, the brat pack writers of New York City who have had big successes and are very young. They are extremely clever; not a thing wrong with those brains. But they don't really have very much to say, and you can strike only so many poses. After you put them down, you have nothing left on your mind. As the years pass, such writers flicker and go out or they change. I read so much material like that; it's partly just a function of being young and clever and impressed with technique. If you decide to have something to say, you go at it in the worst way and have two people sit down at the bar and discuss life — incredibly boring. But I miss that quality because I'm not going to get it in eighteen-year-olds, and it is not popular now. So most of the reading that I enjoy doing comes from writers who at least are still questioning.

WDB: I seem suddenly to be coming upon a raft of writers who are, at least, interested in religious questions. Gail Godwin in *Father Melancholy's Daughter* or John Irving in *Owen Meany*. There does seem to be an interest in religious issues.

DB: I think that's true. It seems to me that even if it's not conscious, part of it may be a rebellion, not just against what I might call certain superficial fictions, but against the prevailing mode of deconstructionist criticism. Sooner or later most writers begin looking at that and think, "These people are not on my team." At the end of that is a real nihilism and it will all go down. I suspect that a great many writers who keep up with what's going on have begun to look again at deconstruction. How long can you go on telling stories if human beings don't matter, and how long will you be read, because there is also a great shift to preferring nonfiction? Biography has become almost more rewarding than fiction, because it appears to look at a whole life and perceive some kind of pattern. Some have made a determined effort not to perceive pattern, but I think that is hard to sustain. You can do with only so much razzle and dazzle.

WDB: Then there's the romance novels.

DB: Yes. People are clearly reading those in the same way they look at television. They are looking to be entertained. Yet those books are almost piously moral for all of the soft pornography in them. I mean the evil get their just deserts. It's pretty much like literature for children in which the villain is always punished and there's not much complexity. More interesting, I think, among writers who are serious,

7

would be disagreements between writers like John Gardner and William Gatz. Gardner got so much flack over that book *Moral Fiction*, and William Gatz, who is his good friend and a good friend of mine too, is a writer who really does think of writing the way you might think of musical painting. He puts together objects in a way that they haven't been put together before so that the glittering surface is an end in itself. He always says that what he remembers from reading a novel is not the content but the sentences. I think that's the real disagreement in writing. It's the same thing that has happened in art and in music; it just has been slower to get to literature because we still think words are what we use to make sense to one another. I'm inclined to think common sense is not willing to let go of that presumption. I do think that at the other end is an abyss and you need not write at all if you really think that through. But I like content wedded to an excellent style. I think content alone can be like it sounds, like the religious publishing you were talking about, like preaching to the choir. The sentences set your teeth on edge.

WDB: I want to ask you about the Associated Reform Presbyterian background. "All the Right People." This is what you were born into and grew up in?

DB: Yes. And it's a shrinking denomination. The whole denomination has twenty thousand to thirty thousand members. It is not as fundamentalist as I perceived it when I was a rebellious adolescent. It is leavened by some kindness and by the songs, by the good songs. At the same time, a woman may not be an elder. Its reading of the Bible is still quite literal. Do you remember a while ago when there was a little paper that was going around the Sunday School classes that said that scientists had discovered that the sun really did stand still? Remember that?

WDB: So Joshua was right? The missing day.

DB: I just loved that. And that's the sort of literalism I mean. You may as well not say "I don't believe this is correct; where did this come from?" You just may as well not bother with that. Hook, line and sinker. You have to take the whole thing.

WDB: So you grew up in this. Did you reach a stage where you began to wonder where Cain got his wife, and all that?

DB: Yes, when I was very young, in fact. At the same time, I was devout and pious but up and down, up and down — worrisome. As soon as I got away from it, I really went all the way away. I thought people like Jean Paul Sartre and Albert Camus had the real answer.

WDB: Your age of Enlightenment?

DB: Yeah. As C. S. Lewis said, if you are not going to be a Christian, the next best thing is to be a Stoic. I think he's quite right. Those are the only real options. Everything else strikes me as being whiney.

WDB: And now you've returned to mainstream Presbyterianism?

DB: Yes. I'm in a small church near Pittsboro — fifteen miles south of Chapel Hill. Pittsboro is beginning to become a big community, but it still is a small southern town. There's maybe one other person in the church who has anything to do with the university. Most of these people are farmers or people who do public work or work in factories or are school teachers. They are not fundamentalists in a way that would have driven me away. The Sunday School class I find thoughtful. I find comfort in that asking questions is not thought a falling away from grace. Nobody has to come up with exactly the same answers. It's really a very loving, small church and I have been very happy there. I'm very involved. I'm an elder, I'm a Sunday School teacher, I serve on several committees, and I'm an organist, but I play poorly. In a small church everybody has to pitch in. This Sunday is the opening of Sunday School for the season. My job is to cut up fruit for the fruit bowl and help clean up the dishes afterwards.

WDB: When you're writing and think of audience, do you think of some particular person or group of people? Or from whom do you hear? Who writes you letters?

DB: I had a wonderful letter today from a woman in New York state who sounds about my age. She just made my day. But I've always agreed with Eli Evans, who says that when he wrote a book, he had a mental jury for each book of maybe about twelve. They were the people he wanted to please. Pleasing them would be enough. And he says that these juries change. He wrote one book that involved his family history; he wanted his mother and father on that jury. But he removed them from the next one. I've always had a sort of a jury. Hugh Holman is a professor here whom I admire very much. He is someone with

9

whom I've never discussed religious matters, but I know that he is a Presbyterian, an elder, and that fact affected his work. He took that duty seriously. He was an excellent teacher. So on my jury there are people like him whose opinions I respect. Many of them are fellow writers but not all. Most of my family are not bookish. So if they are pleased and proud, it has to do with their affection for me. That's not to be sneezed at, but it's not the same thing. They're not critics. They think that if you get anything printed, it must be good. Would that it were true.

WDB: I'm interested in this business that you mention with Hugh Holman. What does being a Christian have to do with being a writer?

DB: For me, the relationship increases. *Souls Raised from the Dead* is more overtly engaged with these questions than anything else I have written. Religion is literally in the plot. The book is full of moments when people actually go to church and bury their dead with ritual and argue in anger that God, if he is a loving God, should not have done this. I hope, however, that it is possible to read the book if you do not share my preoccupation with religion.

Increasingly, I find that someone I like is Graham Greene. And not only for the overt books like *The Power and the Glory*. Once you have listened to what he says, even the thrillers have those little moments when something ticks into place. Some guy stands in front of a shop window and there's a cross in it, and that's all he says. He just moves on. What I see in that is exactly what I think the book of Job says — that there really is no way to prove the existence of a Divine Creator who oversees the world. If you see it, you will see it. If you don't see it, no one can persuade you. It is not an argument in nature or events. It is an overlay that you place on things or don't. Once you place it, you are in an impossible situation for persuading modern people. So I write with that consciousness. My overlay is there, but I have in my books people who do not have that overlay, who do not see it and who will never see it. The ending of *Souls Raised from the Dead* will seem to some to be ambiguous. The man's child has died; he is in despair; he has just rescued a child from a wreck. The reader is supposed to feel a sense of coming out of that despair. He rides on the way to the hospital to see if she is going to recover; he rides by his mother's house

— she seems to him a shining Christian who has always been convinced. He does not know that she is in utter despair. So he rides by this dark house, having made this turn in himself, and is convinced that she has just said her prayers for him and gone to sleep. But the reader knows something different. He rides on ahead through the rain with his lights out, and the reader is supposed to sense that his movement is the movement of the novel, and maybe we even suspect that his mother is not going to be in despair forever, but the book isn't going to say that. It's going to leave you with the scene in which you have your options. You can have either despair or hope. And the hope is not supported by very much evidence if you're going to approach it with the scientific method.

WDB: That reminds me of many of your characters — Homer Beam at the end of "The Astronomer," not having understood Scripture very well. He struggles so much, but he keeps asking. And the wonderful character in "The Very Old Are Beautiful" who has the sort of faith you're calling an overlay. There's so much in your books about faith and about living well. For me one of the most memorable images in *The River to Pickle Beach* is Jack Sellers watching the bird in the birdbath. The bird comes and every day, every day, stops up there and looks and takes a long time before he sticks his foot in the birdbath. And you suggest that's the way a lot of us live our lives. And you have another character who talks about "trickling out our days," just living, as opposed to living well. John 10 stuff. Abundant life. Is that a big concern for you?

DB: Yes. "Life in all its abundance" — that's a biblical quotation I love. That may be one of the differences between my attitude toward fiction and, say, Flannery O'Connor's way. She literally wanted at some moment in her story to have the eternal break through. There is a moment in which the veil goes thin and you see the pines and the sun breaks through as a wound. I guess I am not as confident as she. I also don't see that it breaks through very often. If it does break through for me, it's apt to be in something that some person does. I am more interested in the fact that, with this overlay, the pilgrimage can be now. We can be en route to the kingdom now, though that may be as much as we are expected to be able to do without apparent miracle, without apparent intervention, certainly without an intervention that you can justify to anyone else. I suspect that we've all had moments when we thought, "Yes — uh-huh," but if you explain it, it's like trying to explain why you're in love with somebody. There is no transference; you have to have been this person who has been hit by it. I concentrate very much on redeeming the time, this time; this time is what we've got.

WDB: And "Lord I believe, help thou mine unbelief." Isn't there a constant tension that you're very aware of?

DB: Always, always. I don't think most modern people can proceed, if they are honest, without that tension under their feet. It's all about learning to balance that. That's what I love about Walker Percy's *The Second Coming*. Most of the scholars tell me that's not his best book, but it's my favorite.

WDB: Yes. Even though he sort of accidentally won the prize for *The Moviegoer*, I've always liked the later works more.

DB: I think a lot of it was better. I think the fact that he won that prize was a moment of grace that brought him attention that he wouldn't have had otherwise, and that brought him an audience.

WDB: Will Campbell says that he won the National Book Award accidentally. A woman, one of the judges, picked it up during the time when they were having trouble picking a winner.

DB: I think it was the wife of one of the judges. She's a writer herself and her biography is just out. Jean Stafford is the one. Her husband had come home and told her they couldn't decide on a winner, and she said, "Have you read this? I really like this a lot."

WDB: This matter of how a writer gets noticed or neglected certainly relates to your work. I prowl around in the work of several writers who seem to me to be undervalued — Will Campbell or Fred Buechner. I think it's Jonathan Yardley who says that you've never gotten the attention you deserve. But you seem, like Emily Dickinson, to enjoy your anonymity. Is there a way in which a writer like yourself, preoccupied with the meaning of things, winds up as the odd one out? I remember your characters saying things like "It's dying that really makes us wonder." Your characters are caught up in that sort of introspection. Does that put you out of the mainstream? Are there ways in which your stories are uncongenial in contemporary publishing?

DB: I don't think I'm as entertaining a writer for people who like excitement in short bursts, who like MTV, who like action. In fact, I read those books; I'm a great fan of detective stories; I think P. D. James is splendid. She has existentialist ideas herself. But again, really good detective stories are stories about good and evil too; that's what intrigues you. But I'm not a flashy writer.

WDB: For a recent course in short fiction, I used your stories: "The Sympathetic Visitor," "Gentle Insurrection," and others of those very early stories. I found the students' responses quite remarkable. We had fine conversations.

DB: I wrote those when I was a sophomore in college.

WDB: I have a colleague who is much impressed with "The Ugliest Pilgrim" and wants to use it in an anthology. It seems to me that when people do discover you, they marvel at never having known about you before.

DB: Well, this popularity business, it is a difficult thing. For example, right now most people doing an anthology, when they come to a woman's name, they really are looking for a story that illustrates feminist values. The publishing industry is all about relevance, and relevance passes, it seems to me, very quickly. Like fads. I think that has a lot to do with many of the anthologies which focus on short-term issues. I have thought that perhaps *Souls Raised from the Dead*, since it does deal with medical ethics, a hot topic to some degree, might plug in. But I'm not much interested in medicine; I'm only interested in the fact that human beings can find the same questions that Peter and John and Mark do.

WDB: It seems to me, ironically, that your books are full of the big issues: race, for instance (who could forget Jube in *The Scarlet Thread?*), and feminism (so many strong and interesting characters like Nancy in *Heading West*).

DB: I don't know. But it's just as well. I have a busy enough life anyway. I do a lot of public speaking in my small pond here, and I find travel tiresome. I need time to read, and think, and teach. That's more important.

WDB: What about *Heading West*, one of your more recent books. Has anyone ever asked you about possible connections between that novel and *Thelma and Louise*, the film?

13

DB: No, what they did ask me about was Patty Hearst and Anne Tyler's book *Accidental Tourist*. There are some similarities there, I think, even though that's not my favorite style of book.

WDB: Have you sold film rights to *Heading West*?

DB: Yes. That was the only real money I have ever made. I built a house with the money from it; I am very happy with it. However, I was happier until I found out that long after I had taken my one-time amount, somebody, whose name is a legendary Mafia kind of name so you might as well have the legend, bought the rights and has been collecting a thousand dollars per week ever since, without producing it. Don't ask me who is paying the money; it doesn't make any sense to me, except that Hollywood is another strange world. So I have the dubious realization that somebody is making more money off my novel by doing nothing with it than I am making at the University of North Carolina. This strikes me as so funny. Only in America, right?

WDB: A film version of your short story, "The Ugliest Pilgrim," won an academy award?

DB: It was a very good film. It sometimes shows up on educational television. It was made by a young woman who picked the story for feminism, not religion. She picked it because Violet Karl, my character, is a young woman who takes her life into her own hands; that's what interested her, and so the religious issues become stylized and a bit stereotyped. The young man that Violet meets at the Oral Roberts headquarters is extremely good looking, not at all as I had viewed it, and she lets Violet go off and leave her Bible on the desk, which Violet would never have done. That was a mistake. There are little things that bother me. But it's still good; I like to watch what film can do that words cannot. Film makes things fast. There is a moment in there in which they do in one quick picture what took me a page to do. They have Violet looking at the Bible, and it's underlined with yellow highlighter, and they have Monty looking at the motorcycle magazine, and he looks over and swaps the Bible for the magazine. He gives her the motorcycle magazine and takes the Bible, but he gets it upside-down at first. That's all that happens, but it's a very nice scene. I thought at the time, "Yes, I like that."

WDB: Have you read Annie Dillard's novel, *The Living*?

DB: Yes. I do have small reservations I guess. I love the sweep of it, the descriptions, and I do think the overlay is there. The value she puts on people is there. She's wrestling with evil as I am. She has a manifestly evil character, and she doesn't do what you'd do in theology where you have evil really being good all along — a failure to miss the mark. It's a different ball game than just having someone that's born kind of evil. What you sense is that she sees human beings the way she sees natural history. And in that you can lose track of which person is which. The book is so dense, and it sort of levels out for me. On too big a scale, maybe. Yet, I admire the book.

WDB: You consider yourself a short-story writer and not a novelist; I might say of her that she's an essayist and not a novelist. But it is wonderful how she can get such wonderful gems, "The gift of seeing is the pearl of great price," for example.

DB: She came through here some years back and I had lunch with her. She had mentioned me in one of her books — a great compliment. But I did not understand until the lunch was over that one reason she wanted to meet me was that she wanted to talk about miracles. I didn't know it, and it didn't occur to me to bring it up; evidently that was at the time that she was turning to Catholicism. She did bring up things that I took to be touristy. She wanted to see some fundamentalist revivals while she was down south. But I realized later that I misunderstood entirely. She's very likable, very bright.

WDB: Another topic I'd love to hear you tackle is education. Your books take an occasional shot at education. In an interview last year with William Walsh, you talked about the secular education of your students. With Farley in *The River to Pickle Beach,* you criticize the overspecialization of today's academy. How do you feel about your students and the job we are doing in higher education?

DB: Well, higher education is hurting in so many ways that I don't want to contribute to the hurt. We're hurting financially, of course. Students are not as well-read as they used to be maybe, and I don't want to just blame television. It's more the whole culture which has shifted away from reading to visualization. What I have objected to sometimes about higher education is that, in an attempt to separate church and state, we have removed from our textbooks the religious impulse which actually caused a great many historical activities, literary works, and so forth. I don't think that was the intent in the supreme court decision.

WDB: Yes. There's an irony in our moving opposite to the spirit of the rulings that actually encouraged conversation about religious issues.

DB: I teach a course in recent literature, and because I thought it reasonable to include books that presented various views of life, various philosophical answers, I included a religious one, not because that was a way of persuading someone, but to leave it out struck me as false. I think we do our students a disservice, because often they see nothing about religious faith except the lowest common denominator. They see nothing but TV evangelists and fools, and it doesn't occur to them that intelligent people might find this religious business worth living their lives by. We leave them to make up their own faiths, and they do try. A touch of Buddhism, a touch of drugs, and the New Age stuff, but they really ought to have clearer options, even if they say no. And they are entitled to say no. So that is one of my criticisms about American life. I think becoming so secular that you are antireligious is not a favor to human beings in a very difficult world. My experience with higher education here has been very good. It's a good school. I like it. It's a big institution still with people staying away from home for the first time. It is exciting. I can't think of a place I'd rather be.

WDB: We've talked a lot about your taking religion seriously. At the same time there's a kind of suspicion of the church or the institution. I remember Bebe, who becomes "an everythingist," and Rosa, who can no longer believe in Romans 8:28. And Nancy, who says, "Nobody gets past age 13 and believes any of this anymore." The sense of the institution as numbing, as mere ritual. Do you feel some of that?

DB: Yes. Yet, if it were all that I felt, I wouldn't be in the church myself. I would be on the outside. It seems to me we have a responsibility to continue to make the church more of what it was meant to be. But I don't think my objections are any different from the ones Dostoyevsky makes with his Grand Inquisitor. The church is a human institution; its hierarchy is human. We have this treasure in earthen

16

vessels, so there is a great deal that is quite unsatisfactory about the church, and it has very little to do with what God said. Even so, I don't know an institution any better. In a cold-blooded sense, as I say to students, who else are you going to get to marry you, to name your child, and to bury you? And why do you want the church to do it? Legalistic institutions do not substitute for our demands at those moments, those important moments, in our lives. We long to be allied with two things: with all the people who came before us — tradition — and also with our hope, so we can transcend life. The church is indeed often a failure, but we don't have anything any better. It isn't fair just to walk away from it. I meet often with a group of colleagues with whom I talk about such things. When I started meeting with them on Fridays, I thought I would have to be another Dorothy Sayers. We almost never talk about theological matters, although occasionally we do. Nonetheless, we share the same assumptions, so we tend to discuss everything under a rubric that remains unspoken. Including the criticism of the church. It's like criticizing your own family.

WDB: It's legitimate because you're part of the family?

DB: Yes, because you love them.

WDB: We've talked about abundant life and paying attention. Do you mean to suggest that maybe God is making patterns that we're just not noticing?

DB: Exactly. I do believe that. If you see it, you see it. It is biblical, of course. "He who has eyes to see, let him see."

WDB: That life is not going just anywhere but somewhere?

DB: I think so. If it isn't, it's still better to hope for it and to put your energies into that.

WDB: In "The Fingerprint of Style," you say, "I have never found life, faith, or art really so neat. I continue to outlive many days surveying this world with the suspicion that Deus has really absconded. With the funds." And many of your stories contain such preoccupations with the personality of God. You've said, for example, that the yearning for religious faith and the difficulty of having one nowadays is what "The Astronomer" is about, and *The River to Pickle Beach* certainly has that feel. But all of the reviews I read seemed to avoid such questions. Do any of the critics of your work pick up on this at all?

17

DB: Not much. A few at least address the question, but they address the question because I mentioned it, and so they feel they have to. It seems obvious to me, but evidently it is not obvious. What I'm saying to you about overlay pertains to what you read as well. If you expect it to be there, you will see it. But nowadays, if you are not obvious, if you're not writing for the Logos Bookstore — and I'm not so sure I want to get categorized that way — you can have a problem. And I don't think the job of literature is preaching. It's something else, but it is literature's job not to ignore the fundamental questions everybody lives with.

WDB: Say a word or two about *Souls Raised from the Dead*.

DB: I had already written it and chosen that title when I found a poem by Czeslaw Milosz which actually says, "Raise me from the dead." It's a wonderful poem about the death of the poet's mother who was apparently a victim of World War I, and he comes out of European suffering that for us is hearsay. The suffering gives his poems and his faith a resilience that he doesn't have to mention; he exudes it. I got the title from a note that was sent up to me when I was reading at the university in Charlotte. I didn't have a title then, but read a section in which a woman goes to Durham into this seedy neighborhood where they make keys and stuff. A woman sent up this note on the back of a supermarket slip. She suggested the title. She said there used to be a plate-glass window in Atlanta that has now been torn down for urban renewal, but it had painted on it: "Keys Made, Palms Read, Souls Raised from the Dead." I thought — that's a gift — so I took it, and the fact that there was a poem with the same theme and almost the same phrasing was ideal. But the soul that is raised in the novel is not the child who dies, because dying is dying. It is the question of whether the father is to be raised from despair.

WDB: Is there a preacher in the novel?

DB: There's a preacher, and I'm afraid he's a satiric figure — he's deaf, he's deaf.

WDB: You're often very tough on preachers. I remember the one in *Tall Houses in Winter*. Nasty man. And there's the preacher in "The Ugliest Pilgrim."

DB: This one is bad too, but it may not matter. You know what

Percy does at the end of *The Second Coming*, with the priest who just says the same old things over and over again but it may not matter. O'Connor does that too, and I have a priest who is deaf, but it may not matter.

WDB: Like Greene's whiskey priest?

DB: Exactly. It may not matter; one may be a channel nonetheless. I am going to finish a novel that is under way that is about a preacher — a serious, Presbyterian preacher from Piedmont, North Carolina. But that's another story. But in *Souls Raised from the Dead*, the soul to be raised is that of a highway patrolman. I've always felt that to work with the big questions, you don't have to use only archbishops and kings. Surely it can be done with middle-class workers and farmers and beauticians. If not, then the Good News is not true, and so he is a highway patrolman whose daddy was a shoe salesman. These are lower-middle-class southern people who happen to live in Chapel Hill and don't understand the university at all and find the professors rather puzzling. It is his daughter who dies, and it is his despair we wonder over. Will it lift?

I've done several readings from the manuscript in different places, and it's amazing the people that come up out of the audience. They'll come up terribly upset, because something has been touched there. One is that they have either had or cannot get kidney transplants, one of the issues in the book. The other is that they have lost a child, often through an automobile wreck, and they confirm for me that nothing is worse. If you're ever going to have to forgive the universe for anything, that's the hardest, that you should live on with your child having been ripped away. They all say one thing. "Don't you have it just get better. It never gets better." I believe that, and I don't want to be false to that, so I don't have him end up with a miracle, because he's going to grieve all of his life. I do, however, believe it can be mitigated, that there is a context for that.

WDB: There's lots of Bible in your books, isn't there? I mean, you talk about being "raised in a snow storm of biblical illusion."

DB: Aren't you glad you can read the Bible as literature now? I didn't know it was a gift; I thought it was a nuisance. Turns out to be very useful.

19

WDB: I remember Homer Beam in "Astronomer" and his problems with Scripture. And I remember that wondrous woman, Wanda Quincy, in "The Glory of His Nostrils," who memorizes Job.

DB: Yes. That's a story about abortion, by the way. Look how quickly that got dated; when I wrote the story, abortion was illegal. And Homer's story goes back to a series of sermons I once heard on the book of Hosea.

WDB: I wonder if people notice that?

DB: No. They never have, and it doesn't matter to me. Until then I had never been able to read all the way through Hosea; I just didn't really like Old Testament prophets, especially the minor ones.

WDB: You say writing is "a gift the church gave you." Is that what you're referring to: a seriousness, an attitude toward words, taking words seriously?

DB: Yes. Both the seriousness about what the issues were and the beauty of the language. I know I should like the Good News Bible, but I never will. I will read it, and it has its uses, but I will not prefer it. It has been translated by people with tin ears. It may be more accurate, but it's not as beautiful.

WDB: You also frequently get into observations on popular culture. You refer somewhere to our culture as "an open wound." That reminded me of a Bobbie Jo Mason image; she labels it "an oil slick." Now you have Wal-Mart and Hardee's and Kmart in the South. Just like the rest of us. Is there some shift here that you mourn?

DB: I do. But then I live far away from it. The farm is not more than two miles outside of Pittsboro, but it's really very far. You can't see the road, but the airplanes come over. We have horses and dogs and trees, and I find that essential. I don't believe I could live in New York City; I really think that the scale is weighted too much toward the human beings.

WDB: I have to talk about one of my favorite books — *Tall Houses in Winter.* I suspect you don't like it?

DB: Dreadful. I'd like it burned! It's morbid. It's melancholy, and very young.

WDB: But there's something even there about love and how it validates your characters. And other stories like "The Ugliest Pilgrim" and "Astronomer," or even Jack and Bebe in *Pickle Beach*. If someone were to say to me, "What are Doris Betts's books about?" I would have to say something about that.

DB: I think that is true, but I would avoid saying that because it seems so sappy. There isn't any way to say that.

WDB: But does that suggest a religious core?

DB: It seems to me it does, because if you don't have it grounded in something larger than touchy-feely California love, it goes sappy very quickly. It goes sentimental. There's a big difference between sentiment and sentimentality and it seems to me that that's the great risk when you say love conquers all. It doesn't conquer all, but it is the best thing of all and, at least in Christianity, it is rooted in the belief that that is the metaphor of the New Testament. God is love.

WDB: I'd almost call that optimism in your books.

DB: It is kind of an optimism. It's what I mean by hope. I mean not only do we survive after this life, which to me is not crucial, but it would be nice, so I have a hope. But there is a hope in Christianity that comes through the suffering. That does seem to me to be the message of the gospels, that on the other side of it all, in fact overarching at every moment, there is optimism, there is love, there is hope. That's the good news after all. You don't get that, or I don't get that when I listen to the TV evangelists, and I don't want to get it when I listen to the guy in the glass cathedral saying God Loves You. I shrink and wince: I don't want a little brass harp to hang around my wrist.

WDB: Yet despite the affirmation, there's sadness too. What is that line in *The Scarlet Thread* about the sparrows? "God knows the sparrows fall, but they keep falling. Ain't creation just one dead bird after another?"

DB: Well, look at Flannery O'Connor. Remember that story where the boy goes in the river and is baptized and presumably passes through. She sees that moment of passing out of this life into the next as the achievement, the promotion. I'm a little less confident; therefore, my inclination is to pull that boy out of the river and go give him a haircut and something to eat. Live as well as you can and leave the rest to the Father. Maybe that's a difference between Catholicism and Protestantism.

WDB: I haven't said much about *The Scarlet Thread*. There's the "sins of the father" business, and Thomas, the villain, is the one who survives. A Jason Compson sort inheriting the new world. And the people the reader really likes either die or, like Esther, take off.

DB: But she still is alive; you know she'll be okay.

WDB: The most remarkable character, I think, is David and that extraordinary relationship with Bungo. Did you do a lot of research into gravestones and all that?

DB: It's probably the best thing in the book. I did get interested in that. We were living in Sanford then, and there was a lot of sandstone. I actually tried to carve out some faces. Then I found out how hard stone working is. You sort of need to know where the bruises are to write about it. This goes back to what the Bible teaches. The Bible teaches you, I think, that if you want to talk about the spirit, you have to get to it by way of the body, and hence Job. If you really want to talk about art, you have to talk about where you mash your finger.

WDB: Beyond the amazing stuff about tombstone carving, the book shows a deep incompleteness. And you are often on that subject. Elizabeth Evans says of your story "Dead Mule" that it's a story where "laughter turns into sardonic grimace."

DB: Isn't that what being grown up is about?

WDB: Frederick Buechner talks about the tragedy and the comedy.

DB: That's right, and the way that they link. It is what I look for in mature writers. They may never talk about it out loud, but their characters will. It's so often what I miss in contemporary fiction. There's vitality and passion and great sex and all that, but they haven't arrived at that sense of doubleness and cannot be hurried to it. It has to be earned. It cannot be imposed.

WDB: What's a part-time Calvinist?

DB: Well, it's hard to read Calvin or read about him very long, especially as a female, without having a certain wince.

WDB: You mean what he says about his wife and all that?

DB: Yes. That's right. He says she never interfered with his work. Dreadful! I do ascribe to much that is called Calvinist, I suppose, but it seems that we're back to balance. We still don't understand sin and failure. It would have been better for the church as an institution if it had plunged right into that and got that digested and stopped being self-righteous.

WDB: So, how do you feel when the Republicans are talking about "family values" and the whole world pushes toward a notion of Christianity that is everything but David and Noah and Lot.

DB: That's right. All those nutty people that God loved. I like all those nutty eccentrics that God chose, even Calvin.

WDB: Given your ARP background, do you sometimes feel a passionlessness in liberal Christianity? These folks we call fundamentalists, at least they have passion.

DB: Yes. I guess both extremes are equally bad. I have a woman friend who is a minister, but she really has a mixture of various California religions. After a while I can't sit through any more about my child within, or about my anima and animus; I can go read anywhere about all that. But that is not what I come to church for. I come to church to learn whether this thing is really true and what difference it really makes to me. I don't come to it with some Kiwanis club ethics or behavior, so I agree that we have lost something in losing the people who are committed to something. We've tried to be all things to all people so that anybody can come in. Just believe any little ol' thing, you just come right in and smile, have a little sunshine. So we're back to balance, to the risks of spelling it all out very clearly and becoming Pharisees. It's very interesting the paradox that's involved. It's like a dance.

WDB: Where should people start with your work? You think they should leave out *Tall Houses in Winter* entirely?

DB: They should start with the next one.

WDB: So you're never satisfied?

DB: Never satisfied. It's sort of like saying, "If you wanted to get to know me, would you start five years ago?" No, you'd start right from now.

WDB: What about labels? I know you dislike "Christian novelist." How about "southern novelist" or "gothic novelist?" Louis Simpson used the term *gothic* to classify you in his introduction to the anthology that included *Beasts of the Southern Wild*. But I must say that his definition surprised me; it seems that anything concerned with spirituality would be labeled gothic.

23

DB: Yes. I never thought of myself as a gothic writer. That in itself shows the age we are living in; it's very peculiar. And Simpson's introduction surprises me because it's not typical of his criticism. Repeatedly, you're confronted with some kind of stereotype. Clyde Edgerton, now, has always played into the stereotypes about southerners more than I do. He'll do the takeoff on Senator Flaghorn or somebody and have a good time of it. I don't enjoy it. The stereotypes annoy me, so I tend to resist all that. I don't read writers because of such labels. I read them for something else. Right now, for instance, to be a woman writer means to be a writer supporting the radical feminist cause. I think I am a feminist, but I don't believe the label would suit me. I write about the South, but I'm not really into the mall fiction that people talk about so much. So I resist the label.

WDB: As to the feminist issues, I was struck by the one review that says you finally made it with *Heading West*. The reviewer argues that you've been experimenting with strong female characters but now you've finally arrived. You've written a work where the woman emerges triumphant or whatever.

DB: Yes, but I even caught flack for that because in the end she finally marries. She likes men. I hadn't felt one had to trade that off.

WDB: My students very much like "The Gentle Insurrection," the story where Letty, like Eliza in John Steinbeck's "Chrysanthemums," learns about the beauty of one's daily obligations. It seems to me there's a powerful woman there, or Bebe in *Pickle Beach,* or Jessica in *Tall Houses.* I find it strange to suggest that you've just begun to get to strong women characters.

DB: Everybody reads these things differently, I guess. That doesn't make much difference to me, except it does have something to do with how you are read and whether you are read.

WDB: Do you still think that "there's a moment in every day that the Devil can't touch?"

DB: Yes, I guess I do think that, though sometimes I don't find it.

WDB: There's that romantic sense in some of your books, a sense of that possibility that keeps coming back.

DB: That story you've mentioned, "Astronomer," certainly has that.

It was written when I'd been reading William Blake, and it has that translucent universe. At that moment I believed it very strongly. It's hard to sustain. There are waves.

WDB: What do you find most galling and most pleasing these days? Do you have students who come back and say, "You've helped me"?

DB: Yes, lots of those, and in fact, right now most of our students are doing very well, so we have a lot to be proud of. I'm to get a little North Carolina award, and the speakers will include two former students who have done well as writers. It is good to teach students who then go out and do something, especially because they are all so different. They are not cookie cutter people who write like me. We have a good program in which they are exposed to enough writers so they do not become anyone's disciple. And they are doing well. *Esquire* magazine recently had one of their red hot summer kinds of spreads. This one was a piece on writing programs, in which we were applauded as one that does turn out writers. And we do; that's very rewarding. These are my other children, they really are.

WDB: Have there been times when your writing has disturbed the peace, gotten you in trouble with some group or another?

DB: Yes. In North Carolina some of it has been the straightlaced reaction. Many people feel that you can't be religious and write about sex too, that it's automatically beyond the pale. So I've had some letters like that. If they sign them, which they don't always do, I always try to write back and raise those issues and talk about them. I don't believe you persuade those people, but it would be an act of arrogance not to try. My duty is to continue to speak of such things, because God made the pleasures.

WDB: I know Clyde Edgerton has gotten embroiled in several controversies.

DB: Yes, and his Christian readers, many of them, seem to miss what he is doing altogether.

WDB: Right. I mean, how can they misunderstand so completely?

DB: Some people don't know how to read, and they read the way they pick out a verse and apply it.

WDB: So you're suggesting their approach to the Bible has affected their approach to all books.

DB: Yes. Since they haven't learned to read the Bible and notice when it was metaphoric, when it was literal, when it was poetry, when it was history; they can't bring that kind of flexibility to other books.

WDB: On the subject of controversy, what about your treatment of race? You use the word "nigger," for example.

DB: Yes. And now people are down on Twain. I guess the rest of us go with him. Well, I haven't had too much controversy. The one thing you mentioned, "The Sympathetic Visitor," was the only story I was ever sued for. I was a sophomore in college, and we received a letter threatening a suit from Thurgood Marshall, from his law firm. He did view the story as racist, and he was acting on behalf of the real black people in Statesville upon whom I had based the story. He was viewing it as an invasion of privacy. It was a shock to me because they were all friends of mine and because we had no money; my husband and I were struggling students. I look back on that now and realize I made an extremely bad decision. I was eighteen and very stupid. I used one of the person's real names. That was stupid. It never occurred to me to remember how people read. I never thought about her reading it and being hurt. But she did and she was. So I went to see her and explained that I never meant to hurt her and that the story was meant to make her and her family heroic, not the other way around. We had a personal reconciliation and ultimately the whole business of the suit was dropped. It did teach me about my responsibility as a writer. I would never again invade privacy in that way. I do not have the view that Faulkner had when he said one good poem is worth any number of little old ladies. I think that's not true. I think there's a number of good poems already, and little old ladies do make a difference. That was a bad moment in my writing career in which I saw something that I had been blind to. I do try to get students to cope with these issues when they write, too. What will their mothers think, for example, is an important question. They can't be limited by that, but they do have to think about whether or not their story will do damage in the world. If so, is it important enough to do that damage? I think that's a genuine question.

WDB: You're always aware of the depravity business, aren't you? I wonder if *Heading West* isn't a study of evil. Doesn't Nancy Finch become fascinated with the abomination? Aren't you trying to figure out what makes Dwight Anderson so evil? Or is it finally about Nancy's realizing, as she says at the end, that she is capable of evil herself?

DB: When I autograph books for people, I often write something like, "To one pharisee learning to be a publican," which is what I think happens. There's a moment when Nancy realizes that she didn't kill Dwight purposely but she could have. In that moment her whole notion of evil is altered and with it her easy judgment of all the people she left behind. She sees them differently when she comes back home. They are not really any better than they were — Faye is just as frivolous, Momma is just as domineering — but her view of them has been altered by the fact that she is not superior. She realizes that she cannot judge them.

WDB: That's almost Flannery O'Connor again. Like the grandmother in "A Good Man Is Hard to Find" who realizes the Misfit is one of her own children.

DB: That again strikes me as being part of the growing up process. Nobody is more judgmental than adolescents. They know who the good guys and the bad guys are. It's a tiresome attitude.

WDB: Carolyn Gordon, talking about Hemingway, says that "a good writer should never be more than six years old." It seems to me that you're up to something like that. You don't start off with some thesis nailed up on the wall; you are simply trying to tell the story.

DB: Yes. Trying to find a character. Two is better, but if you can get one real character, you will get a story.

WDB: But you're not starting out with some idea to demonstrate, some thesis to prove?

DB: Once I've done the first draft and the thing is there, I might go back and sharpen it. I didn't write *Souls Raised from the Dead* because I wanted to write something about theodicy. I was driving and I saw this highway patrolman beside the road. Apparently, a chicken truck had run off the road and broken apart. Chickens were running loose, and the way they are raised now, you know, they'd never been loose before. So you have a scene of mixed horror and humor, and you have this man trying to bring some order out of this chaos. It was just fabulous. I was both laughing and appalled because there was chicken blood all over the place and people were trying to steal chickens. This is a scene Jean Paul Sartre would have gotten something out of; indeed you can get that on a highway in North Carolina just as easy. The whole novel started from that. Later I realized my character's daughter was like the chickens. He had protected her, kept her in a heated and cooled place, but you can't protect like that. Then the idea developed. I think that's true with most storytellers. You get an intersection, a moment that for some reason is a spark. You start from there and whoever you are.

FREDERICK BUECHNER

1950 — *A Long Day's Dying*
1952 — *The Seasons' Difference*
1958 — *The Return of Ansel Gibbs*
1965 — *The Final Beast*
1966 — *The Magnificent Defeat*
1969 — *The Hungering Dark*
1970 — *The Entrance to Porlock*
1970 — *Alphabet of Grace*
1971 — *Lion Country*
1972 — *Open Heart*
1973 — *Wishful Thinking: A Theogical ABC*
1974 — *Love Feast*
1974 — *The Faces of Jesus*
1977 — *Treasure Hunt*
1977 — *Telling the Truth: The Gospel in Tragedy,
Comedy, and Fairy Tale*
1979 — *Peculiar Treasures: A Biblical Who's Who*
1980 — *Godric*
1982 — *The Sacred Journey*
1983 — *Now and Then*
1984 — *A Room Called Remember*
1987 — *Brendan*
1988 — *Whistling in the Dark: An ABC Theoligized*
1990 — *The Wizard's Tide*
1991 — *Telling Secrets: A Memoir*
1992 — *The Clown in the Belfry*
1992 — *Listening to Your Life*
1993 — *The Son of Laughter*
1996 — *Longing for Home*
1997 — *On the Road with the Archangel*

FREDERICK BUECHNER

Doubt and Faith

"The worst isn't the last thing about the world. It's the next to last."

Critics have often broken Frederick Buechner's career into two parts. The phenomenally successful first book, *A Long Day's Dying*, and the less successful *The Seasons' Difference* are placed on one side. Then came conversion and ordination, to be followed by forty years of books written directly from a Christian consciousness. Such a view unfortunately reduces the spiritual longing in the early books and the struggles for faith in the more recent ones.

Especially since his nomination for the Pulitzer Prize for *Godric* in 1981, Buechner has attracted growing attention from critics and readers. Out of his career as novelist, apologist, teacher, essayist, and preacher have sprung thirteen novels, eleven works of nonfiction, three volumes of autobiography, an award-winning short story, some poetry, and numerous essays and sermons. Two book-length critical studies about him are already available. Charged with the tension of faith and doubt and infused with a longing for spiritual consolation, his writings find an audience among those who struggle for honest belief. He stands

31

as one of the foremost among those artists whose works ring with an insistent summons to Christian faith.

I joined Buechner for a few days in October 1989 on a tour of Iowa, where he gave lectures and readings to church and university groups, to preachers, and to book lovers. The following conversation offers a taste of what this profoundly quiet yet direct man says through the words of his books and the words of his life.

▼   ▼

WDB: How would you introduce yourself as a writer? I know you are uncomfortable with the phrase "Christian writer."

FB: The reason I shy away from the phrase "Christian writer" is that it always suggests Christian in a limited and clubbish sense. Often when someone says their neighbor is a Christian, I know they mean a Christian like them. And there are lots of other kinds of Christians, so I shy away from it. I don't know if I'd want to put any adjective to myself as a writer. I'm a writer like anybody else. I do the best I can. Somebody said the other day that I was a religious writer in the sense that I was trying to make religious points. I'm really not. I'm like any other novelist. I'm trying to listen to what goes on in the lives of my characters and to the interesting things that happen to people; and, because I am a religious person, I always listen for the religious things that go on. But I can't think of any adjective that I would want to be known by.

WDB: You have spoken a good bit lately about fairly recent changes in your life and especially about your children leaving home. As you have dealt over the last few years with your children suddenly being adults, your own aging, family sicknesses, and all that sort of thing, has your perspective on your writing changed?

FB: I don't know how it has changed my perspective on my writing, but it has greatly changed my perspective on myself. Since the children grew up and left, it has really been another ball game. You read about the empty nest syndrome and all that, and it really exists. You can imagine ahead of time the changes that come into your life when you have children — those are obvious — but I never anticipated the changes that come when you don't have them anymore. It leaves an enormous empty place for me, especially because I am alone most of the time as a necessity of writing books. You can't write books with someone else. So I don't have any colleagues or any "outside" life, so when I finish my work it's just my wife and myself, and we can't be everything for each other. You've got to have something else. That is why I am doing more lectures and readings, just to try to fill in the empty place. I don't think my writing has really changed. You change, your writing changes, but you're not particularly conscious of the shifts.

WDB: You've talked a few times about being driven to justify your early success in the first novel, *A Long Day's Dying*. Is that still an operative thing?

FB: Certainly it was the most successful book I've ever written. It's sort of pathetic, because I wrote it when I was twenty-three years old or something like that. I don't think it plays much of a part anymore. I would certainly love to have more readers. I would love to have a book as successful today as that book was then — not for the sake of fame or fortune so much as just for the sake of having more readers to share my thoughts with.

WDB: How do you explain the lack of readers?

FB: I don't know. It's depressing to me. I really can't explain it. I've just accepted it. John Irving, whom I had in class at Exeter, sent me the manuscript of *A Prayer for Owen Meany* and asked me to read it. I read it and loved it. I told him what a really good book I thought it was and how it was, in a good sense, a very religious book. And I asked him to think what would have happened to it if it had been written by the Reverend John Irving.

WDB: So you think that your profession as a minister has hurt your success as a novelist?

FB: I'm sure of it. Yes, I am between two worlds. And also there's no question that I stand awkwardly with the mostly secular literary establishment. Alfred Kazin, for instance, wrote a review in the *Oxford Companion to American Literature* in which he said, out of nowhere, "Eyebrows will be raised in certain quarters by the amount of space

33

given to Frederick Buechner." I wondered why, in his mind, eyebrows would be raised. Because I have the credentials. I've written a long time, and I've been fairly well reviewed. I think what he meant was, I'm not really a writer of literature. I'm a writer of propaganda, somebody with a special ax to grind. A lot of reviews assume this. There was one of them in the *New York Times*. I've forgotten the name of the writer, but he was talking about religious writers, and he said one of them is Frederick Buechner, "whom I wrongly," he says, "did not read because I thought he was a propagandist." And I think that's what a lot of them think. For instance, when the *Bebb* books came out, I thought and my publishers thought that this could be kind of a breakthrough; they're sort of racy and fun, and colorful things happen in them. Much more money was put into advertising. I put my royalties into it, and it didn't make any difference at all. The same faithful group went out and bought them — five, six, seven, eight thousand people and that was it. Nobody really knows what makes a book sell anyway. Even people who sell books don't know; even publishers don't know. So there is always a mystery about it. My guess is that it is being known as a minister; I think that's the kiss of death for a lot of people, and with good reason — that's the sad part. I mean, you can imagine the kind of books most ministers would write. If they were writing novels, there would be a lot of bad ones.

WDB: It's strange to me; the Bebb books were my introduction to you. I would never have guessed they were written by a minister.

FB: No, I don't think so either; I don't think anybody would.

WDB: Do you know John Davenport, the critic in *Spectator* who did a review in 1965 or 1966 of *The Final Beast*, a very good review, in which he said, "Mr. Buechner has put his foot in it."

FB: Yes. I remember that review. A very good one.

WDB: He said you "write from an unfashionable centre," suggesting that your Christian faith would be a barrier for some readers. I suppose there's no way to address such a problem.

FB: I don't see any way of doing it. No. But the interesting thing is that I have often thought to become ordained was the stupidest thing I ever did in terms of my writing career. But on the other hand, I must remember what my ordination has meant. It gave me my subject and my passion, and if I hadn't been ordained, who knows how things would have turned out. I would have been a writer, but I would have written the same kinds of books everybody else writes and on the same kind of subjects. And there is really nobody else I know of writing the kinds of books I'm trying to write.

WDB: Let's talk about the Christian side of that audience. Do you see a problem in that you are, to use the overworked word, a liberal in a time when that is just not popular among many Christians?

FB: Yes. Sure.

WDB: We have talked about the sensational sales of Frank Peretti's book *This Present Darkness* — a so-called Christian bestseller. To hear such news must be discouraging in some way or frustrating.

FB: Well, no more than lots of other things, I suppose, but I think the kind of Christians who find his books appealing would be horrified by my books. After all, my books have bad words in them and people do naughty things.

WDB: And there are no easy answers in your books.

FB: No, that's right. What I had always hoped was that, since I come so much from the same kind of world as those people who don't touch Christianity with a ten-foot pole also come from, maybe I could be a bridge, one of their own who had gone over to the other side, saying things in a language they would understand. And there have been some of those, but for the most part, people I get letters from are people like you. Quite a few are teachers and ministers and people who are in the church; not in the fundamentalist church, but in some other.

WDB: So your imagined audience is still what you have called "believing unbelievers" or the "nego" or doubter that you talked about in *Now and Then*.

FB: Yes. Exactly.

WDB: When you sit down to write a book, do you consciously think of that audience, that somewhat skeptical searcher?

FB: I think I do. I lean over backwards not to give sentimental, fuzzy, simplistic views of anything.

WDB: In that leaning over backwards or that attempt not to resort to quick answers, do you ever get criticized for being too tolerant?

FB: You mean those who think I have sold out to the other side?

WDB: Yes. Those who want you to be more specific. Do you get letters that say you didn't go far enough in this book or you weren't explicitly Christian enough?

FB: I picture this one young man; he may not be young at all, but he sounds young. He has written me three or four times, taking me to task for making my saints have feet too much of clay. Why can't I write about a real hero of the faith? I answered one of his letters; then he wrote another wanting to keep the argument going. I just dropped it because I didn't have time. My answer to him the first time was that any saint I write about would always have feet of clay, because they are the only saints I know anything about or that I could imagine. I don't think there is any other kind. I can't imagine a hero of the faith in the sense that he or she did not have shadows and darknesses. But that's the only instance I can really remember. Another thing, slightly relevant, was that years ago an article of mine on the Bible taken from *Wishful Thinking* appeared in *Readers Digest*. And I got an enormous amount of mail, and some of it would have to be called hate mail. I remember one letter especially. In the article I had said that all sorts of things jostle each other in pages of the Bible, the sublime and barbaric for instance. And I mentioned the 137th Psalm where it begins, "By the waters of Babylon we sat and wept," and ends up "happy is he who takes the little ones and bashes their brains out against the rock." Here, I said, is an example of the unspeakable next to the gorgeous. And I got this letter written in a clumsy, semiliterate hand, saying that, disparaging the Bible as you have, I can only wish that somebody would take your little ones and dash their brains out against the rocks. At first I was horrified, and then I thought, "Who is this person?" So I wrote a letter back and said, "If you could see my little ones playing in the house right now, you couldn't dream of dashing their brains out against a rock. Whatever way we disagree, we both believe in a God of love, and we can't think in those violent terms." And I got the most touching letter back saying simply, "I've written lots of people; I've written Billy Graham and Oral Roberts, and you're the first person ever to answer. Thank you so much." Just someone lonely, wanting attention.

WDB: I did a review of *Whistling in the Dark*, and as I was doing that I asked a good many people their opinion on several of the entries. Some of those I asked wanted more specificity. They wanted you to be more forceful on such issues as homosexuality or abortion, for instance. They wanted a stance, a position. That's the kind of pressure I mean.

FB: Well, the same *Readers Digest* friend said he thought I waffled on the subject of abortion, where I don't take a stand. I don't know what stand to take because they're both so imperfect. I know if I had to choose, I would choose for a woman's right to abortion, but at the same time I'm appalled at destroying life.

WDB: Everybody wants the simple answer.

FB: Yes, that's right.

WDB: And now you've added a third volume to your autobiography?

FB: Yes. *Telling Secrets* is a sort of autobiographical romp, reaching back over the last ten to twelve years. The earlier autobiographies [*The Sacred Journey* and *Now and Then*] dealt with more or less the headline news in my life, getting born, the death of my father, going to school and seminary, getting ordained, getting married, and all that sort of stuff. But these new lectures have more to do with the back pages of my life. It's the more interior things that I talk about. And I also talk about secrets. I talk about my father and the fact that he had a drinking problem. I talk about my experience with ALANON, and I also for the first time talk about my mother, who just died a year ago in July. She really survived all the bad things that happened in her life by simply denying them, and she couldn't bear to touch on anything painful. I remember some years ago I wrote a book called *The Return of Ansel Gibbs*, where in a very fictionalized and disguised form I touched upon my father's death. She read it and she was so angry that she almost wouldn't speak to me. I was still so under her spell at the time that it never occurred to me to say what I had every reason to say, which was that I had as much right to tell my father's story as she had a right not to tell her husband's story. But the rule in families like that is that you don't talk about those things. I don't think she ever read another word of mine, out of fear of what she might find. Now she's dead; so it enabled me to talk about her and talk about things around that.

WDB: One of my students, after reading *The Sacred Journey,* was struck by the influence of Naya, your grandmother, and the absence of much mention of your mother's influence.

FB: He was dead right. That's terribly perceptive. Of all the people, she was my true parent, the way grandparents are apt to be, because they don't become involved with you in the complicated, emotional ways that parents do.

WDB: Reading *The Sacred Journey* or *Now and Then,* one cannot help but be struck by the personal revelation going on there, and I've heard you comment on how eerie it is to meet strangers who know so much about you. At the same time, however, I've always sensed a kind of detachment as well — certain blank spots in other areas. Maybe your mother has been one.

FB: She certainly has. Absolutely. I've been very conscious about that. I've never touched on her, except for one key moment of my life, which at the time I didn't know was a key moment — the scene I describe in *The Sacred Journey* — where a friend called up in great distress and she encouraged me not to go help him but to stay with her. I wrote about that because I was very confident she wouldn't read it. I am sure she never did, which is incredible if you think about it. If your child grew up and wrote his or her life, I should think you'd devour it, be fascinated by it. What could be more interesting than that? But she was so afraid of the past, so many complicated, shattered feelings, feelings of guilt and the rest.

WDB: And beyond the autobiographical update, there's another collection of pieces in the offing?

FB: Yes, that's right — that's what I'm working on now. It's a matter mainly of just retyping them, making a few changes. I'll include some recent sermons and a couple of articles I've written for books that are supposed to come out soon. One of them is a book edited by an American poet, Alfred Corn. He got a lot of literary people — John Hersey is one of them, John Updike is one — to write an article each on a book of the Bible, and he asked if I'd write one on 1 Corinthians, which I love. So I did that, and there's another book edited by Leland Ryken, a member of the Wheaton College English Department, which is supposed to be a sort of literary guide to the Bible. He asked me if

I'd write a novelist's view of the Bible. I did that for him, so these will be part of the collection, as well.

WDB: Now in addition to all this, you're also thinking about something in the *Godric* and *Brendan* strain. Only this time, it's to be a woman saint?

FB: Yes, that's the next thing. The next book to write will be that one. This business of collections is just a matter of sitting down, typing them out, and shipping them off. But there are a lot of things I've wanted to write about for years and years and things I've tried to get at again and again. I wanted to write about Bermuda; it was the most magic time in my life. I was a child of ten or twelve. You can no longer see the Bermuda I saw, because it is not there anymore. It was a place of such enchantment; I can't describe it — no cars. Can you imagine no cars? I wanted to write about that. But really saints are the only people that interest me right now. I've been unable to find an historical woman saint that I could write about, so I've decided to try to concoct one. I tremble inside with the thought of that. I don't know if it will work at all. You never can tell. I've written two or three novels that remain unfinished because they didn't work. One was about the biblical Jacob that got up to about sixty pages before I ran out of gas [eventually published as *Son of Laughter*]. It was too hard to try to bring to life a period so ancient. I began to think it was sounding the way illustrations in gift Bibles look — people dressed up in what you know isn't what they wore.

WDB: Apart from the writing, you expect to do more speaking?

FB: Yes, that's right. I go to New York and San Francisco for the Trinity lectures with Maya Angelou and James Carroll. Then two weeks in Texas next summer and Los Angeles and Seattle next fall; I'm doing more than I ever did before. The Texas thing will be much like this Iowa tour, except that I will stay at one place — a retreat center — and various groups will come to see me.

WDB: You have said that you were pleased by John Irving's mentioning you in his *Prayer for Owen Meany*. He was your student at Exeter?

FB: Yes. He was a very shy kid; his stepfather was a member of the History Department. That's a hard role in a boarding school — to be a faculty brat, as they say. I had him in Religion rather than English

39

courses, and I think I was the only person he knew at that point who had ever written a novel. He was writing stories in those days, and he would come trudging up the path with one of them and we would talk about it.

WDB: Were you startled that he expressed such gratitude to you in *Owen Meany*?

FB: Yes, it was startling, although we have been in occasional communication over the years. I remember about ten years ago, out of the blue, he called me up and asked if he could come to see me. Because of my doom-ridden self, I thought that something terrible must have happened to him and he didn't have any other minister. It wasn't that at all. He just wanted to say hello. So we have kept in touch. I was still very surprised by what he said. I wasn't aware of doing anything much for him.

WDB: Are there other contemporary writers that you either read a good bit or stay in touch with?

FB: Well, of course my oldest friend is James Merrill — Jimmy. He has won every prize there is to win — he won a Pulitzer Prize, he won the National Book Award, he won the Bollingen Prize — and yet he remains relatively unread because many of his poems are very difficult. He's my one really good old friend who's a writer, but it's as friends rather than as writers that we stay in touch. I have never really lived in close proximity to writers and publishers and all that.

WDB: Did you ever run across Annie Dillard or Walker Percy?

FB: I would love to run across Annie Dillard; there is nobody writing in the English language that I admire more.

WDB: So you have been reading her.

FB: Oh, just about everything. The only one I haven't read, oddly enough, is *Pilgrim at Tinker Creek*, because I had a feeling it was sort of a *Walden*, which has never been one of my favorites. Actually, I'm told that's not the case at all.

WDB: She talks as you do about paying attention to one's life.

FB: I know. And she pays attention herself. In her last book there was an odd reference to me. She alluded to something I had said, which, on the printed page, seemed perfectly bland. I couldn't think why anybody would remember anybody who said anything as bland as that. Nor do I remember having said it. But no, I would walk ten miles to talk to her. Walker Percy I have read a little, and I must say he just leaves me literally cold. That's just the right word for it. I don't feel any excitement, any passion. It seems very cerebral and planned out and cold. I always feel that the characters sound like what I imagine Walker Percy would sound like. I have a hard time believing in them as real human beings.

WDB: You've introduced me to many writers through interviews like this. Once, for example you mentioned that you were reading Anthony Trollope so I went out and read Trollope. You mentioned Robertson Davies, so I went out and read Robertson Davies.

FB: Oh really! Yes, I like him a lot.

WDB: So who are you reading now?

FB: Well, I greatly admire Gabriel García Márquez. *Love in the Time of Cholera* has a richness of detail that makes it wonderful. He evokes this sort of steaming, decadent, colorful, fascinating South American city. I'm reading now, of all things, Shirley Temple's autobiography. There was a terribly good review of it in the *Time's Literary Supplement*. She's an almost exact contemporary of mine, so I'm interested. It is a fascinating book to people of my generation.

WDB: Do you enjoy biographies as a rule?

FB: I read a good many biographies, that's right. I get a kick on somebody; Mark Twain is an example. I spent two or three years reading everything I could find about him.

WDB: What gratifies you most at this stage of your career?

FB: You can't help but be gratified when people pay attention to you. This group of people here in Iowa, for instance, who are willing to put this whole thing together to bring me here, or when I'm given some honor, it's gratifying. What robs me of real gratification is what I think I inherit from my past, the feeling of "if they only knew."

WDB: The impostor syndrome?

FB: Yes. Nonetheless, I am gratified. I'm terribly gratified too, if that's the right word, by Harper and Row. They have brought back into print so many books of mine that would have long ago died. That's a tremendous service. And they're publishing this children's book in spite of two children's publishers who turned it down as too grown-up. My friend Clayton Carlson at Harper's said, "I like to think of myself as publishing not just books but authors." It's a wonderful feeling to know that somebody has enough interest in you to publish virtually anything you write.

WDB: *The Wizard's Tide* was turned down because they felt it was inappropriate for children?

FB: Two unrelated publishers said the same thing. They both thought it was too old for children.

WDB: After your success with *A Long Day's Dying*, you said strangers wrote you letters, which made me feel appalled because that's exactly what I did almost thirty years later. Besides the fact that strangers write you letters, what's the most bothersome and galling thing for you at this point?

FB: Oh, strangers writing me letters isn't galling. It's one of my greatest gratifications. I don't know how many letters I get a year; I've never counted them, but my guess is around five hundred or so a year. I can't help but be moved by some of them, even if they may be giving me more credit than I deserve. People say extraordinary things: you saved my life or you helped me do this or that. How could I not be gratified by that?

WDB: I think many people are very taken by this idea of being actively present in one's own life that you so underscore in your work. How do you do it? Are there active disciplines that you cultivate? Do you meditate? Do you go out and watch for the opportunity to put things together? Can you talk about that?

FB: I don't do any of those things. It's appalling how much I don't notice. We live on a road two miles up the hill, and every once in a while I'll be driving up that hill and say, "My God, I never saw that house before." I've been driving up that hill for thirty years. I notice some things though, and I don't know why. I have no technique for it.

WDB: I hear this echo throughout your books, this "Whatever you have done for the least of these, you have done for me." The man in the pickup truck or the woman on the next seat in the theater. I guess in my own life I'm constantly wondering how to do that. How do I learn to pay attention to things like that; is it just a matter of attitude? Is it a matter of just shaping myself that way?

FB: It certainly wasn't for me. I don't remember any conscious decision to pay attention or any technique for paying attention. When I was a boy I thought what I wanted to be was a painter, and I did a certain amount of that. I had a cousin, also a good friend; he and I used to trudge off to the Metropolitan Museum in New York City (my grandparents had an apartment nearby), and we would copy pictures in our sketchbooks. I always did portraits, and if I'd been a painter, that's what I would have been, a portrait painter. I've always doodled faces; I don't know why that should be. But I do notice faces for some reason, not that I try to or think it's a good idea to, but just because I do. I can't understand, or explain it.

WDB: I was at a conference recently where some people were reading papers about Walter Wangerin, and he was in the audience. I thought that was a bit awkward. How do you feel about being an object of discussion?

FB: The only time that has happened to me was at Berkeley.

WDB: In Marjorie McCoy's class?

FB: Yes. And it was really like that scene in *The Adventures of Tom Sawyer*, I guess, where Tom and Huck attend their own funeral. I think the McCoys recognized me, but I don't think anyone else did. The room was filled with people who had read my books. They were dealing that day with the autobiographies, and to hear strangers talk about my childhood and discuss people I had known and loved was an eerie experience.

WDB: How often do you preach?

FB: I don't know; my guess would be a dozen times a year. That doesn't mean a dozen new sermons; I usually have a traveling sermon that I can adopt to any occasion — weddings, circumcisions, bar mitzvahs, funerals. That's about what I do I guess.

WDB: Where do you stand with the contemporary church? What do you think we should do?

FB: Be more like Alcoholics Anonymous. I was at a huge church in Minneapolis last year. I said to them that the best thing for people like them might be for the building to burn down. If they lost all their money and had nothing left except each other and God, then they might come much closer to being what the church originally was and that I think Jesus intended it to be. I think that much of what goes on in most churches doesn't feed people, doesn't give them what they're starving to death for. At least it doesn't feed me.

WDB: If the church is not helpful for you, and, as you've said, your family situation has changed, are you being driven more and more into a kind of aloneness? I mean, what do you do for community, for artistic and spiritual support?

FB: I'm trying to learn how to be quiet, be still. I've never been any good at meditation, partly because I've never seriously tried. But I try to stop the internal dialogue. You try not to think of anything. The way you do it, one way at least, is to watch, to relax and say, "I'm going to watch the thoughts that come to my mind." If they come, I dismiss them, let them go. I'm finding that if you start watching the thoughts come into your mind, your mind stops producing thoughts. If you watch a child playing, the child stops playing. To a degree, what happens is something like that. I mean your mind just stops, and when that happens you seem to become something other, something deeper than the thinker, the internal chatterer. I believe there is within us this image of God, which is perhaps another way of saying it. Inner light is another. There is something deep within us, in everybody, that gets buried and distorted and confused and corrupted by what happens to us. But it is there as a source of insight and healing and strength. I think it's where art comes from. For instance, partly out of that inner place I've written things which were a tremendous help to me. *Godric* was one. At a time when I was in desperate need, out of that deep place came this holy old man about whom I knew nothing, and he became really for me a kind of saint. I can't explain it. The words were mine; I put every word he says into his mouth. It was my pen, but I was drawing on this deep source. Does this make any sense at all?

WDB: Do you like the word *mystic,* or do you like the word *listener* better?

FB: *Listener.* I've been reading Matthew Fox's *The Coming of the Cosmic Christ* for instance. He's saying we have neglected the whole mystic dimension of religious faith. We tend to think mysticism is irrelevant to the problems of the real world and associate it with monasticism or something, as divorced from real life. But Fox makes a great deal of it. He talks about how Christianity has developed a patriarchal god who is judgmental above all things and has overemphasized original sin. One of his books is called *Original Blessing*, and that's the other part of the picture. Original sin, yes, but blessing too. We were created by God, given this wonderful world, and now, in Fox's terms, our great sin is that we are destroying our mother, the earth. There are all sorts of ways in which we have lost touch with this inner sense of belonging to the earth and belonging to the power who has created us. Fox is giving words to so much for me; it's the most exciting book I've read for a long time. He's not really kooky. Some people have said he's New Age; he divorces himself from that. He says New Age is too narcissistic; it doesn't go out and do anything much. He says you've got to keep on doing things. He's worked it out awfully well in some interesting ways and traces the development of Christianity in the rationalistic, patriarchal, judgmental, guilt-ridden, stream as opposed to the creative, life-affirming, mystical stream. I commend him to you.

WDB: You obviously view yourself in some ways as a critic of the church. What about social critic? Do you ever feel yourself at odds? Are you comfortable in a shopping mall or an amusement park? Do you feel yourself at odds with society like Mark Twain, who said it's all based on a national lie or Robert Frost, who talks about his "lover's quarrel"?

FB: Well, I love shopping malls. No problem there. The supermarket we use is like a club, so I don't feel at odds there. But, I do get terribly tired of popular culture. When I see the movies, and the paperbacks, and the television things that are big time, it makes me sick. So does most of what goes on in national politics.

WDB: You are obviously drawing from values in your writing that are at odds with what is popular. I went into a bookstore here in Cedar Rapids yesterday — part of a chain known as the Zondervan Family Bookstores.

FB: I know the Zondervan publishers.

WDB: I do this wherever I go; I test out three or four names, one of which is yours. Sometimes they have Buechner on the shelves, but this store didn't even have Buechner in their computer, not even in their "We can order this for you" category. I wonder. The mall book-shops and all of that, what do you feel when you walk in there?

FB: I feel sad to think of all of the unread books and depressed by the ones that are read, yes I do. I hate to find a book store that doesn't have any of mine in it. I always have a jolt of pleasure when I find one that has mine.

WDB: You mentioned J. D. Salinger yesterday, one writer who is, of course, still widely read. I don't think he has ever appeared before in any of the lists of names like Agnes Sanford, James Muilenburg, and Paul Tillich, influences that have appeared here and there. So I was surprised to hear you speak of Salinger as an important influence.

FB: Yes. I'm not sure I've ever said that before, but I do think it's true. He was the first writer I ever encountered who really did have X-ray eyes, eyes that see beneath the surface of things to the tears of things. Do you remember in *The Catcher in the Rye* those touching, wonderful passages where Holden Caulfield sees the deep human need within even the most unpleasant people who wander through his life? They are human beings and he misses them, as he says at the end of his story.

WDB: And, of course, Salinger is looking back to Nick Carraway in *The Great Gatsby*, isn't he? Nick, too, sees beneath the surface of Gatsby to "romantic readiness" and all that. Is that a book for you?

FB: I love *The Great Gatsby*. I've not put all this together, and it is strange because you're telling me something about myself I didn't recognize. I think Antonio Parr [*Bebb* novels] as a narrator was a little bit like Nick Carraway as a narrator. Both are detached and yet involved, and both have an elegiac tone to their voices.

WDB: I think often of your short story "The Tiger," which seems very Salinger-like.

FB: Oh, God, you even read that. Yes. It is like Salinger.

WDB: But it is Fitzgeraldian too, isn't it? Doesn't it evoke an age in the same way Fitzgerald goes about it?

FB: That's very shrewd of you; that's excellent.

WDB: The story is particularly interesting partially because it is the only short story you've done, but I've wondered about the Fitzgerald connections. I know your father attended Princeton at the time Fitzgerald was there.

FB: Yes, and they knew each other, though I don't think terribly well. But they were friends; they were there about the same time, and they belonged to the same club at Princeton.

WDB: Why no more short stories?

FB: It's a terribly hard form. With novels you can take all the time in the world to do what you want, but with short stories, your time is so short that any mistake is magnified. I think, too, a lot of it is that I love books so much as objects. If you write a short story, you may eventually have a collection that will become a book; otherwise it appears in a magazine and gets thrown out. I love to write things that end up on a shelf somewhere. I'm a book person, and more than just being a writer or reader, I like to have books around. Playing with them. Collecting them. Sticking them on the shelf.

WDB: You mentioned *The Return of Ansel Gibbs* a moment ago, and I've talked to you before about *A Long Day's Dying* and *The Seasons' Difference,* and "The Tiger." Do you look on this early work of yours as embarrassing? You say very dismissive things about them. Is that because you regard the writing there as not as fresh and good as your later work? Or are you thinking about changes in your vision as a writer, or what?

FB: Well, I don't know.

WDB: My own sense of "The Tiger," for example, is that there's a wonderful evocation of scene there, a golden setting that works to frame the poignant longing of the central character, and *Ansel Gibbs* has always been one of my favorite books. I think there is fine humor there and a god-hauntedness. I've always thought it's a mistake to try to divide your career into pre-Christian and post-Christian and use those kinds of phrases. Do you feel ambiguity about your early writing years or feel disdainful toward the early books?

FB: Maybe it's like coming across a letter that you wrote when you were twenty-two years old; I feel a sort of revulsion. How could I have been so naive, or so dumb, or so inarticulate, or so something or other? Some of it is just that. I would draw a distinction between the very earliest novels like *A Long Day's Dying,* and *The Seasons' Difference* on the one hand and *The Return of Ansel Gibbs* on the other.

WDB: There's a wonderful portrait of Muilenburg in *Ansel Gibbs.*

FB: Yes, yes, that's good. That was a true portrait of him because he was a marvelous man, and I think I've done some justice to him.

WDB: During the six-year gap between *A Seasons' Difference* and *Ansel Gibbs*, you were working in the inner city of New York?

FB: That's right. That's when I was in seminary. *Ansel Gibbs* was the first book drawing directly on my fledgling Christian experience. But those earlier ones, I don't know. I think it's the way I feel about myself in those days as I look back. I kept journals when I was in college for a while, and I remember coming across some of them years later. I don't even remember now what I found in them, but I was so put off by the person they revealed that I destroyed them. And that is more or less the person who wrote those first books.

WDB: You've sometimes referred to the first two books as being written for a teacher, self-consciously aiming at an audience. Yet I find unforgettable that searching Peter Cowley of *The Season's Difference* and that business of fishing in the sky with a kite — fishing for God. The first time I read that you didn't like that book, I kept thinking. "Well, why doesn't he like that book?"

FB: One reason I didn't like that book was because, of all the books I've written, it took the worst beating. The first book had been so successful, and that's apt to happen to a second book. Norman Mailer's second book I recall, *Deer Park*, took exactly the same kind of terrible beating after the success of his first book, *The Naked and the Dead*. I think that's part of my reaction, remembering those reviews. That wouldn't be true of *A Long Day's Dying* because it was received well. Also, *The Final Beast* is another book I wrote which took a beating. I think it was because I had just been ordained, and people knew it. So many reviewers, I think, focused on the ordination, saying, "He's been ordained so you can imagine now what he's going to write about. Now he will sound like a priest and all that sort of thing." Luckily I was teaching at Exeter at the time, so I had a lot of other things to think about. There were some awful, embarrassing reviews. I remember one in *Time*. I can't remember what it said. I cringed with horror.

WDB: It's funny that there were so many good ones too. Amos Wilder wrote a fine review. The *New York Times* reviewer talked about your "justifying the ways of God to contemporary humans." Many spoke of the daring mix of the sacred and the profane.

FB: I don't remember those. Really?

WDB: Even John Davenport, in his own kind of way by saying you had "stepped in it," was saying that you had done a good thing.

FB: Yes, I do remember that one; that was a good one. I liked that.

WDB: I read, in a recent interview, where you dropped a cryptic observation that nobody picked up on. You said that you "cannot live in the world without getting involved." Do you remember talking about that?

FB: Well, I was probably referring to a realization that came at some point in my life, probably later than it comes for most people, that the world really was in danger of being blown up. Certainly, what's going on in the newspapers seems to me to have a great deal to do with who I am. Somehow, most of the big news when I was young didn't seem to have much to do with me and my life. Whether this happened or that happened, I simply went on with my business. But when you realize that things happen, the whole show could blow up, then you can't help but be involved.

WDB: Are you more aware of global issues and social issues?

FB: I suppose I've become involved in those issues as those issues involve me. We are involved. We can't help it. Even the Grateful Dead. My daughter Dinah put together a series of filmstrips showing the destruction of the rain forest in South America. She did this for a Grateful Dead show, and my wife and I were, of course, invited. We had never been to such a thing before, and we didn't know what to expect. We had been to rock concerts but never the Grateful Dead. I mean, it's a special crowd. The first thing that amazed me was that the Grateful Dead are all old men. I thought they'd look like what the Beatles looked like in the sixties, but they don't. Jerry Garcia looks older than I do. That was number one. And then of course it's a real cult, and they all get up and sway and swing. The amusing, touching, funny thing was that the average age of the audience was between twenty-five and thirty, and they were dressed the way the deadheads dress, in special tie-dyed shirts, and here are my wife and I dressed very much the way I am now, the way people my age dress, and we stood out like sore thumbs. And these young people come up and they're all smoking pot and swaying, very gently, and they tap us on the shoulder and say, are you enjoying yourself? It was as if we had green feelers coming out of our heads and came from some other planet. They wanted to make sure we were having a good time. And we did have a good time.

WDB: I've asked you before about your stint as a visiting lecturer at Wheaton College. Given the fact that you often talk about faith as not ultimately logical and the evangelical's tendency to base faith on logic, I wonder if you ever felt uncomfortable there.

FB: No. I never, never did. Some of the preachers they had in chapel weren't my dish. I felt their sermons were too explained, too full of answers. But overall, I felt nourished and comforted at Wheaton by the presence of people who were true believers. I loved being there, and some of those people got to be really very good friends of mine. And I found a wonderful church. St. Barnabas Episcopal Church. High Episcopal in the sense that they chant and use incense, and so forth. But also evangelical; I don't know quite in what sense they are evangelical, but that's what they call themselves.

WDB: I remember an interview in 1982 or so where you mentioned *The Brother's Karamazov, King Lear,* and the poetry of Gerard Manley Hopkins as recurring sources for you. Do you still go back to these?

FB: Yes, they were tremendous influences. Absolutely. And Graham Greene, of course, was the most important. Just that one book.

WDB: Just *The Power and the Glory.*

FB: Just *The Power and the Glory.* That's right. I have read a few of his books since then, one or two of the recent ones. They depress me in the same way that late Hemingway depressed me. It is as if the old machine is still working because it is such a wonderful machine, but the real power that was operative in *The Power and the Glory* is no longer there.

WDB: Have you read *The Captain and the Enemy* or *Monsignor Quixote?*

FB: I read a little bit of *Quixote* and it seemed to be a parody of *The Power and the Glory.* A pathetic parody.

WDB: *The Final Beast* is the first of your books where I really see the influence of *The Power and the Glory.* Nicolet, the clownish clergyman, and the strikingly haunted whiskey priest seem to be brothers of sorts.

FB: Yes. Absolutely.

WDB: *The Final Beast* also seems to be a book where you do considerable remembering: your father, Agnes Sanford, your days as a minister. You talk so much about this remembering business. In our attempt to open up the old rooms, what about the pain? What about the not-so-innocent past? The Saul past? The Augustine past? The painful, painful past? In *The Sacred Journey* you talk about "mooning" over the past. Is there a point where that conscious remembering becomes unhealthy, destructive?

FB: It has caused me tears sometimes. A lot of what went into *The Sacred Journey* I went through first with a therapist. And then I shed tears about it, but they were as tears usually are, wonderfully healing. I've never shed tears that I wasn't glad of it. But remembering has never caused me pain in any destructive or anguishing sense. The only thing I can imagine as dangerous is that you might take refuge in the past like old people who can't stop talking about what it was like sixty-five years ago. It is also true that as you grow older, your long-term memory becomes a bit more vivid and your short-term memory fades. It's true for me in the way that I can remember Bermuda, for instance. I can remember Bermuda, if I set my mind to it, with such totality that I'm almost sucked back into it. I mean, I can almost imagine that with one tiny little turning of a screw I wouldn't be here anymore. I'd be in 1939. But that would be a very pleasant kind of madness. I don't see it as a real threat.

WDB: It can be releasing rather than painful to remember?

FB: Yes. Releasing. Also, it is a powerhouse of creativity when it is tapped. I feel that whole Bermuda episode of my life is an artesian well, a volcanic thing. It's so full of magic, so full of power and beauty. If ever I could tap into it somehow, it would blow my roof off.

WDB: Of course, *The Final Beast* was the first book to appear after your ordination, and we have talked before about how you made your choice of a denomination. You wrote me once about how your choosing the Presbyterians was almost like tossing a coin. I think that was the phrase you used.

FB: I chose the Presbyterian church because George Buttrick, a minister who much helped me, was a Presbyterian, and if it was good enough for George Buttrick, then it was good enough for me.

WDB: Do you work at home now mostly?

FB: Yes, I have for years. Ever since way, way back when I used to go to a church building and write in a Sunday school classroom. I did that because it helped to convince me I was doing legitimate work.

WDB: Do you have many editors? Does your wife, for example, read through your drafts?

FB: No, nobody does. I used to put my wife through those terrible exercises when I was new to being a full-time writer and sort of uptight about it. I would work a whole day and maybe I'd write a page if I was lucky or a paragraph if I wasn't lucky. And at the end of the day I'd make my poor wife sit down, and I'd read it to her to get her reaction. And I'd always say, before I read it to her, "No matter what you think you've got to tell me you think this is good because that's the only thing that will see me through the next day." I shudder even to think of the position I put her in. I haven't done that for a long time.

WDB: Do you miss teaching?

FB: Whenever I do it, I remember what fun it was. But I don't really miss it.

WDB: I heard once of an exchange between William Gass and John Gardner. Gardner said he wanted everyone to love his books, and Gass said that would be like wanting everybody to love his daughter. What side of that do you come down on?

FB: I wish more people read them. I couldn't resist having everybody read my books.

WDB: The final section of *The Sacred Journey* is entitled "Beyond Time." Do we any longer have a vocabulary to talk about such ideas? Is there a sense in which we leave nonbelievers behind at that point?

FB: What I meant by "beyond time" was that there are times in your life when you feel you are getting whispers from something eternal.

WDB: Does that require faith?

FB: That's a good question.

WDB: I sometimes wonder about a book like *The Power and the Glory*.

Does it require faith, finally, to get to the affirmation that goes on in your books?

FB: You mean, can a person without faith read a book like *The Power and the Glory*?

WDB: Yes, in what way does a person without faith dismiss Greene as he is often dismissed? Oh, that's the Catholic novelist writing to a thesis. Or for Buechner. Well, he's a minister; he's got a message. You can't read him.

FB: I wonder if anybody has ever been converted by a book? Or, at least, given a push in that direction? I can believe it might be so.

WDB: I'm preparing, just now, to teach a course devoted to your work. What books would you recommend for a class of undergraduates, books of your own.

FB: The *Bebb* books, I suppose. They're accessible and have a good bit of entertainment going on. And *Godric*.

WDB: When people ask, Which of your own books do you recommend that I start with, what do you tell them?

FB: I was just asked that question recently by a friend of my daughter. I told him to start with *The Alphabet of Grace*. I think that will introduce me to him. I don't know. It's sort of a toss-up. I would stay with the fiction except for those who already have a religious sense.

WDB: You have important things to say, I think, about the writer who is also Christian. You have been forced to deal with a readership often suspicious of religious answers and an age that may well be post-Christian. Do you try to stay in touch with your own cynicism when you write?

FB: If you're not being honest, what are you doing?

WDB: Walker Percy says the function of fiction is to tell us something about ourselves that we already know but don't know we know. That sounds consonant with you somehow.

FB: That's very good. I think the basic sickness is homesickness, and I think that is true of everybody. At some level they know it, but they've never had any way to say it.

WDB: So as a writer, you try to give us ways of articulating what we already dimly know about ourselves?

FB: We're all so hungry, so hungry for each other and for lots of things, but it does seem to me that the basic hunger really is for the Word of God. And a lot of people don't know that. So the job is to try to make it understandable, make it real.

ROBERT OLEN BUTLER

ROBERT OLEN BUTLER

On Madness and Longing

"The books are gifts and whatever is to become of them will be best for me in a way that is beyond mere earthly success. So I want to keep writing books, and whether people like them or not, or even publish them or not, is unimportant to me."

Robert Olen Butler has been around. From the steel mills of southern Illinois to high school teaching, from taxi driving to magazine editing, from freelancing to newswriting, from the intelligence corps in Vietnam to college teaching in Louisiana, Butler has written his way through it all. Now enjoying the prestige and success that came with the Pulitzer Prize for Fiction in 1993, Butler looks back on a writing career that began on the subway commute to his position as editor of the *Energy User News* in New York City in the late 1970s. Writing on legal pads, Butler produced *The Alleys of Eden,* which was rejected by more than twenty publishers before Horizon Press published it in 1981. The novel draws on Butler's experiences in Vietnam, a subject recurring in many of his other novels. But the book's sensitive portrayal of the Vietnamese refugee demonstrated Butler's difference from the other writers of the

Vietnam story. His gift for empathetic rendering of the Vietnamese people was to flower in his volume of fifteen short stories, *A Good Scent from a Strange Mountain,* for which he won the Pulitzer Prize.

Other novels of the 1980s bring to the fore Butler's preoccupation with spiritual longing and the desire for human connection as expressed in sexuality, along with the return to issues spinning out of the Vietnam years. Butler's 1994 novel, *They Whisper,* is something of a departure in its up-close depiction of madness and obsession. Ira Holloway, haunted by past lovers and nearly undone by his wife's fanatic Catholicism, struggles to maintain a relationship with his son as he tries to find his own way through to meaning.

Recently married to novelist Elizabeth Dewberry, Butler has expanded his career into screenwriting. But he returns again and again to characters from his stories who have insisted themselves upon him. Giving these characters their voices, Butler remains one of our most prolific and polished novelists. He spoke with me in a Louisville hotel lobby in February 1996.

▼   ▼

WDB: You wrote a piece in 1982 for *The Writer* in which you talk about allowing your characters to assert their own personalities. Is that the key to your success in fiction?

RB: Fiction is an art form. You cannot defy the essential qualities of the art form you're working in unless that defiance fits organically into the larger vision of the work, and that's rare. Fiction has several qualities. First, it's about human beings and it's about human emotion. Nobody really would debate those things. But the other thing about fiction is that it's a temporal art form. It exists inescapably in time. You ask any Buddhist how difficult it is to exist for even thirty seconds without desiring something, without wanting something. My favorite word in this connection is *yearning.* Fiction is the art form of human yearning. And so for me the work of art begins when there is some very strong sense of a human being in my unconscious. Although these people come from the deepest concerns of my own personal self, they nevertheless exist as others. Before I can begin to write from them or about them, I must have a deep intuition about their yearning. And once that's there, then it's a matter of listening to them and letting them speak. Most of my novels are in the first person, and I much prefer that mode now. The right organic decision again and again has been to let my characters speak for themselves. So it's a matter of listening to the voices of the characters.

WDB: Hearing those voices is a gift?

RB: Yes. It feels very much outside myself. And what you're listening for in the voice is the subtext, the yearning beating in the subtext beneath everything spoken.

WDB: You say somewhere that the writing of fiction is fundamentally sensual.

RB: Absolutely. Fiction is unlike other forms of discourse because it does not deal in the matters of the intellect: analysis, abstraction, summary, and generalization, the modes of discourse for nonfiction writing. The focus of the reader is not on an intellectual grasp of the abstractions of what the character is saying, but rather the moment-to-moment revelation of the personality of the speaker. And that is a sensual matter. There is a certain response to the ideas or the analysis, but there is a deeper response to the revelation of personality. That's the only legitimate way in which abstraction finds a place in fiction. The primary experience is moment-to-moment through the senses.

WDB: You've said that your influences are Daniel, Jeremiah, Isaiah, and Luke. Was that a fanciful observation?

RB: No, I think the King James Bible has palpably influenced my voice.

WDB: You have a Catholic background?

RB: No. But my second wife, the mother of my son, was intensely Catholic, and I learned to speak in those terms. The particular kind of fanaticism that was dominant in our household at that time certainly wasn't the terms in which I was seeing the universe, but the King James Bible, a wonderful document of storytelling and voice, certainly had a profound influence.

WDB: When I first read your comment about Jeremiah and the others, I wondered if you were thinking of the writer as prophet.

RB: Well, you know E. M. Forster's *The Art of the Novel*. He refers to artistic vision as prophecy. I do believe the artist and the preacher are basically in the same business. We respond to the moment-by-moment sensual flow of existence on planet earth, and we are subject to that deeply embedded personal fear that we are utterly alone here in spite of the surface appearance of other preachers of similar sorts floating around us. And we observe the ways in which disaster befalls us in this world and notice that things seem to be in utter chaos in the universe. And artists and prophets look at that experience and have some deep intuition that the appearance of chaos is false. They suspect that somewhere behind that chaos is order. The prophet — and we can throw in others too, by the way: scientists, philosophers, psychiatrists, or whoever. They have their scientific laws and philosophical principles and psychoanalytic insights, and the theologian or the prophet has a moral insight or a dogma. The artist has the work of art. And all of us are trying to say that there's order behind the chaos. Those theologians and the others are comfortable expressing their vision in abstract terms. They work in terms that can be communicated as laws or principles to be grasped by the intellect and applied to life. The artist is terribly uncomfortable with that kind of expression. The artist goes back to the chaos and the ways in which it is experienced, moment to moment through our senses, and pulls out bits and pieces of that sensual experience. The artist gives it back to the reader reshaped. In selecting and shaping and structuring the sensual experience, the artist creates a vision of order for the reader, not as an idea, not as a set of principles, but as a kind of harmonic that's set up in the reader, a resonance. You thrum to a work of art; you don't understand it intellectually.

WDB: But the prophet also tells us things that do not resonate.

RB: Yes. William Gass says, "We do not judge a work of art; a work of art judges us." Art illuminates the limitations of the individual reader's soul to some extent. And there's a good precedent for this approach. The works in which his activities are recorded make very clear that Jesus of Nazareth never taught except in stories, in parables. You want to know about the kingdom of heaven? Well, there's this guy who owned a vineyard and he had a son. In fact, Jesus gets really

60

pissed off with Peter out in the boat on the Sea of Galilee after Jesus had just taught in this way to a bunch of people. Peter was the first academic, the first literary critic. He wants to know the meaning of the stories. And Jesus reacts angrily to Peter.

WDB: "Let those who have ears. . . ."

RB: It's the ears. He didn't say let those who have a mind, think about this. He said, "He that hath ears, let him hear." That's sensual. Miles Davis, the great jazz trumpeter, says, "You don't play what you know; you play what you hear."

WDB: I suspect your more recent novel, *They Whisper,* may be somewhat controversial in the way it connects spirituality and sexuality. Ira, your central character, finally decides that sex may be grace.

RB: Well, it's a kind of secular sacrament.

WDB: Is that a just reading of that book?

RB: Yes, I think that's certainly how he sees it. It doesn't leave him a place where he's whole. Even in the end, Ira is not whole. And he knows it. The book moves to that understanding. But he does see sex as a kind of secular sacrament. Sometimes things physical resonate into the cosmic sphere. I found it particularly irritating when critics took Ira to be a womanizer. He's capable of finding any woman beautiful. And the absolutely individual personal shape of their bodies is, for him, connected to the deeper mystery of personality. And that's why, indeed, as an expression of love and attention to a woman, he imagines himself even speaking in her voice, and he does. For Ira, it is a way into a larger connection.

WDB: Many critics talk of Fiona's madness, but there's also Ira's madness. There are two madnesses there. She is obsessed with Catholicism, and he is obsessed with the past. And you do get a sense of some kind of lostness in Ira as well.

RB: Right, and he finally gets a sense of it.

WDB: So you think that's finally the power of the book?

RB: Even the man who is richly responsive to the other is still alone. Karen Granger is his holy grail. That first image which he comes back to at the very end of the book is that image that is at once absolutely intimate and yet absolutely innocent as well. That combination. He just can't get them together. He can't pull those things together.

WDB: I suspect *They Whisper* will be misread in the same way that John Updike's *Rabbit, Run* was misunderstood. Both novels reach toward this connectedness. But this preoccupation with the other runs through all of your work, even the Vietnam material. Your understanding of refugees and the children of dust makes me wonder what you make of our contemporary preoccupation with multiculturalism? In *The Alleys of Eden* and in *A Good Scent from a Strange Mountain* you explore the human growth that occurs through human encounter with otherness. How do you respond to the multicultural conversation that we continue to have?

RB: The multicultural conversations in our culture seem to be moving dreadfully towards separatism instead of true connection. I'm not comfortable making sociological or political observations in the abstract, but that's certainly a very dangerous kind of attitude to be taking.

WDB: At least part of the power of *A Good Scent from a Strange Mountain* is that a lot of those stories could be about anybody.

RB: Absolutely. All of them can be. They are all really about the nature of love and kinship and human connection and the shaping of identity. And, indeed, responses to the book have been in those terms. On book tours I have had people from Italy, France, Germany, even a white woman from South Africa, come to me and say, "I love this book, and I hope you understand it's not about the Vietnamese: it's about me." It's not even just immigrants either. We're all immigrants of a sort. We've all left something. We've all been exiled from somewhere, even if it's just from our childhood. The book that really inspired *A Good Scent from a Strange Mountain* was called *The Glory of Their Times*, an oral history of baseball players, by Lawrence Ritter. I was reading it during the year before I wrote *A Good Scent from a Strange Mountain*. It's twenty or so voices speaking in first person straight off a tape recorder about pre–World War I baseball. So I read all these first person narratives in voices of men who were speaking from a place of exile. They were speaking with great regret, remorse, wistfulness, love, and nostalgia, and still seeking to understand their present identity in relationship to the identity they once had in this foreign country they were exiled from — the country of baseball and of youth. How do I shape my own sense of identity in the present in relationship to what I've left behind? It's an absolutely universal human issue. It has nothing to do with the Vietnam War or any one culture or another.

WDB: In *Alleys of Eden*, you say, "Every art cuts away whole areas of human experience to focus your attention on a selected few elements. Then you can see those elements as you never have before. Painting cuts away sound and words so you can see better, music cuts away words and vision so you can hear better." You offer a definition of art as that which pares down, gives us the essences, calls our attention. Can you elaborate on that?

RB: It comes back to human yearning. And you have to deal with it in terms of the senses.

WDB: Because I began with your most recent novel and worked my way back, I was aware of this sensual business in all of your books. I remember a character in *Sun Dogs* who talks about "a madness of great purity." There's something about this madness that is admirable, even attractive. But it is madness, nonetheless. And many of the stories are preoccupied with the potential pathology of religious fanaticism.

RB: Yes, the yearning for faith leads to madness sometimes. It's not the faith itself. One yearns to believe in something beyond one's self. In *They Whisper*, Ira makes the case for Fiona's absolute logic. For her to be that desperate is a kind of logical corollary to the faith that she's pinning her sense of the world on. We all must claim faith in something. Even those who somehow order the world in a way that excludes faith ultimately end up having faith in that. Once you place an idea about the universe at the center of your identity, it sits there and forms decisions about the world and reactions to the world in a way that is a kind of faith. How do you make any decision, how do you react in any way, without some premise? Faith is a kind of premise to the universe that each of us carries around. We don't know how to walk across a room without some sort of premise. Faith itself is not the culprit here. We must have faith, just as we must worship something. Ultimately the most important decisions and the most important reactions you have are in service to that, or based on that.

WDB: So the deepest, most powerful emotions we have can somehow get warped so that we wind up obsessed?

63

RB: Your desire for faith is so intense that you panic and put your faith in things that really are not natural to the way you, in fact, see the world.

WDB: So it is a matter of dishonesty or delusion?

RB: I guess it's ultimately a matter of dishonesty. Certainly. Dishonest in that there's a disparity between what you're shaping all your decisions on and how your deepest self, your own unconscious, is really responding to the world. When there's a disparity between those two things, terrible things can happen.

WDB: Yet *Sun Dogs* ends with Wilson Hand's amazing joy?

RB: Yes, *Sun Dogs* is my most openly Christian book in the sense that Wilson Hand enacts the central Christian ritual.

WDB: The Eucharist?

RB: Exactly. He's looking for some ultimate. He's in search of faith. He's in search of the ultimate meaning of things. And everything is a blind alley — sex, and his work, and this mystery that he's in the midst of. Ultimately there is only this act of sacrifice. In his week of captivity in Vietnam, he experienced a kind of stripping away of all the surface things of life, all the material things. And he had a glimpse of the abyss or the infinite, whichever it is. Figuring out which drives him through the book. And then his joy comes in this bizarre, isolated place in which the only act is an act of self-sacrifice. And that's the source of his joy.

WDB: He's able, finally, to clear away all the clutter, including even his clothes.

RB: That's it. And his own attachment to his own life. He thinks, "For the sake of this other person, I will die. So that person can live."

WDB: It's a powerful, surprising book. It's not a novel you finish and go to sleep on.

RB: It was wildly misunderstood by critics. They wanted to read it as a badly written detective story.

WDB: You rather broadly satirize the oil crisis of the 1970s in *Sun Dogs*, and you seem to move more and more to a general sarcasm toward many of our cultural values. I'm thinking of "Relic" in *A Good Scent from a Strange Mountain* and that wonderful story, "The American Couple," where you give us a hotel full of game show winners. Do you aim to make us laugh at ourselves a bit?

RB: I've been moving more in that direction. I've just finished a story called "Titanic Victim Speaks through Waterbed." I think it may be the most profound story I've ever written about absolute, essential things. And yet there's a funny angle to it. A funny surface. And "Jealous Husband" is a very funny story, but it's a very serious thing. In the checkout lane at the grocery store, you see that people are drawn to the notion that there might well have been UFO's that kidnapped nuns, or that children can be born with Elvis tattooed on them, or that men come back to be with their wives in a reincarnated state as parrots. Somehow those things seem to me to be the wonderfully rich ways in which to explore the very serious issues that confront us at the end of the twentieth century.

WDB: You are developing your gifts as a humorist?

RB: Yes, but humor has to be organic to the vision. If you sit down to write a story that's going to be funny, that is as much writing from your head as when you sit down to write a story about some political point.

WDB: You can't try to be funny?

RB: No. The true work of art is not a known thing before its creation. You do not as an artist decide what the novel is going to say and then construct something to say it. I try to explain this point to my own students. What is the difference between literature and non-literature? Why is it that John Updike is an artist and Stephen King is not? Or why is Jean-Paul Sartre not an artist? Because the nonartist knows before he begins to write what effect he wishes to give to the reader. Then he constructs something to do that. Stephen King wants to scare the shit out of you, you know. Jean-Paul Sartre? I guess he wants to scare the shit out of you too. The artist does not know. The artist does not understand what it is exactly, what that vision of order is, until the art object is constructed. And that's the difference. To have any preconceived effect, even if that means to be funny, is the antithesis of the artistic impulse.

WDB: And that's also why you resist talk of themes and are suspicious of critics? I mustn't take one of your books, say *Countrymen of Bones*, and try to summarize it?

RB: No. The only true answer to the aboutness of *Countrymen of*

Bones is to sit down and read those eighty-six thousand words again. That's what it's about. It's irreducible. The process of analyzing literature in a classroom situation is useful only if the last assignment is to forget everything that we've said. Because you go through a process that's artificial, especially for the purpose of adding a string in the upper or lower register of the instrument within the reader that thrums. We want our students to read a work of literature and resonate in that harmonic way, to thrum with the work. But it's not about this or that; it's about what it is. And having said that, *Countrymen of Bones* has to do with what people are capable of; it has to do with the varieties and the inevitability of violence in the human spirit.

WDB: The good man, the archaeologist, discovers that he has within himself the capacity to do what's being done on a global scale?

RB: He's the one who kills.

WDB: How much research has been involved in books like *Countrymen of Bones?*

RB: Well, I grew up near the Cahokia Mounds in Illinois. And I've spent time in the desert near where the bomb was tested. I did have to do some research about the making of the bomb. But I focused on the sensual things, like the cloud chamber and the shape of the lens, which becomes a kind of sensual metaphor for the way in which Lloyd's psychology works. He's constrained to the point where he implodes. In thinking about the process of the bomb, he talks about the plutonium waiting in the center like a bride. For me the work of art resonates together through the senses at every level, in all its elements. So plutonium waiting like a bride is a very sensual thing, something concrete, and yet the pattern of the sensual thing echoes into the larger patterns of the book. And that's the way art creates its meaning without being didactic, analytical, or interpretative.

WDB: *On Distant Ground* was somehow the most difficult of your books for me, and I don't know why exactly. It's like this huge joke has been played on David Fleming and in some way on the reader. Fleming imagines this connection with the Vietnamese prisoner, bases everything on the connection, and turns out to be dead wrong.

RB: The intuitive connection that he saw was a bogus connection because it wasn't really a connection to the other. He was seeking his own face in the other. That's the ultimate spiritual lesson of that book. If all that we're doing is just seeing ourselves in the other, then we have not left ourselves in order to really join the other. You can, I suppose, extend the metaphor to the Vietnamese experience. We never really understood the Vietnamese. We went into Vietnam looking for ourselves. We had an image of American democracy that had to be delivered to others.

WDB: And an image of rightness: we're right and they're wrong?

RB: Yes. If we understood the other, we never would have been involved in that. We never knew who the Vietnamese were. We had no clue. The proof of that is manifest today. We thought the Vietnamese were about to open themselves up to Chinese hegemony in Southeast Asia. That was the last thing they were going to do. They had two thousand years of animosity toward the Chinese. And we never knew that. Or we saw the rise of Stalinist Communism. The Vietnamese are pragmatists first and foremost. Look at what's happened to Vietnamese society today under that Communist regime. It's a thriving marketplace over there. As soon as they saw the impracticalities of the Communist system, they let it go. And that's the way they always were. Ho Chi Minh really did go to Versailles in 1918 in his borrowed suit thinking Woodrow Wilson would surely understand his aspirations. He based his own declaration to the French government on Wilson's Fourteen Points. As late as the end of World War II, Ho Chi Minh expected Franklin Roosevelt to understand his aspirations. This was a pragmatist.

WDB: I wonder if others have spoken to you about the powerful understanding of grief and parenting in *Wabash*? That book resonates with fatherhood issues that sound in all the stories from *The Deuce* to *They Whisper*.

RB: My deeper concern is human connection and identity, and certainly fatherhood is an important one. I have a very close relationship with my father, and I am in a very intense and demanding relationship with my own son. Because those were ongoing aspects of my personal life, they opened up as subjects for my imagination as well.

WDB: And fiction is not rearranged autobiography?

RB: Quite the contrary. Graham Greene says all good novelists have bad memories. He said what you remember comes out as journalism. What you forget goes into the compost of the imagination. And writers who rearrange autobiography, meaning that they are working from literal memory of their own life, are going to fail as artists because the artist must be free. In the work of art, everything is organic. Everything resonates into everything else. No life is as neat as that. Everything is negotiable, everything is pliable, in the process of creation.

WDB: Reviewers of *The Deuce* couldn't resist comparisons to Salinger. Did that surprise you?

RB: No. Any cynical, sixteen-year-old male narrator is going to prompt that sort of comparison. It didn't surprise me. My editor even embraced that on the jacket. But it was not written with any influence of Salinger in mind or with any preconceived effect. Actually, that book began as often happens for me, through wondering about a secondary character in another novel. *The Deuce* was initially conceived as a book about the sixteen-year-old son of David Fleming. I wondered what that child was going to turn out like. And so that's where that book began.

WDB: The stories that make up the larger story of *A Good Scent from a Strange Mountain* question the dangers for the refugees in embracing this new culture, the place where there are no fire crickets. There is much here about the new mythology being forced on these refugees. Is mourning part of what's going on there?

RB: Sure, but the Vietnamese are very pragmatic, and in all those stories they are adapting the old and the new. Somehow they blend things together. They are responding with their own sense of loss and exile and also with their own sense of personal mythology, their own folklore, and they combine it with what they find around them. I think it's the melting pot at its best.

WDB: So they are less likely to be victimized than we are?

RB: Absolutely. In fact, I've had Vietnamese readers who were deeply appreciative of the book as a kind of vision of how they might become American without losing all that they have been.

WDB: So, among these letters you get, some are from Vietnamese people?

RB: Oh, many. And they say I got it right. I've had appreciative letters from people who are half Vietnamese and half American. They've thanked me for giving them the Vietnamese half of themselves.

WDB: And now the Pulitzer Prize. The impact on your career is obvious. All the other books were out of print?

RB: Everything came back into print afterwards, yes. The fundamental thing that the Pulitzer did was bring me into the consciousness of the general public. And once that happened, the combination in the books of seriousness and attention to strong storytelling, I think, has opened up a pretty sizable group of readers for me.

WDB: And now comes Hollywood?

RB: Well, *They Whisper* is under option. My son just started writing a screenplay of *Countrymen of Bones*. My movie agent is going to try to find a director for that. And I wrote the screenplay for *A Good Scent from a Strange Mountain*, which is very much alive out there. I was hired by Mirage Enterprises, Sydney Pollack's production company, and they hooked up with Warner Brothers. I wrote a screenplay for them called *Dark Grace*, a film about a Brazilian faith healer, of all things. On the strength of that, they hired me to write a movie from a biography, *The American Gothic*, about the Booth family, Edwin, John Wilkes, and Junuis Brutus Booth particularly. I enjoy the form. My M.A. is actually in playwriting.

WDB: Someplace you say that it was your drama training at Northwestern that taught you to be a writer.

RB: It was actually oral interpretation, a really good discipline for a writer, because it's a critical approach to literature through performance. Oral interpretation is based on the premise that every piece of writing, even your cereal box, has an implicit narrative persona. You can look at the text and induce an emotion, a personality. And then as a performer you embody that personality and perform the text. That's what oral interpretation is about. It's a wonderful discipline for a writer.

WDB: You've clearly reached a time of great pleasure in your life.

RB: Yes, and I am greatly thankful. It has truly been a remarkable time.

WDB: And despite the film work, you continue with the fiction?

RB: Absolutely. And I write to understand myself to start with. Those flashes of insight for the reader are first discoveries of the writer. Everything that you understand about the deepest issues of the universe is unearthed in the process of creating the work of art. And so there are those moments of surprise and recognition when I learn something deeply true about myself that I never knew until this moment. That's the experience of the artist at work as well as of the reader.

WDB: And you're at this every day?

RB: To be a fiction writer, you have to write every day. You cannot write weekends or next week. You cannot just take some time off to write a book. The link you have to forge to your unconscious is so demanding and frightening. The great Japanese film director, Akira Kurosawa, says to be an artist means never to avert your eyes. And that's the unflinching courage that you have to maintain. You plunge into your unconscious to face down whatever demons are there. To do that is terrible. If you've not been doing it for a while, you go there and discover you want to do anything else but write. My fingernails need clipping. The toilets need cleaning. I should really organize my receipts for my taxes next year. Anything but this. If you go back every day, it's still painful and difficult, but not nearly so much as if you don't go there every day. And if you stop for even four or five days, when you go back, it's like you've never written a word in your life. That opening just seizes shut and erases itself. So you must write every day as a fiction writer in order to create anything of worth. There's no excuse. There's just no excuse.

WDB: What's the next novel going to be?

RB: Well, the next book will be *Tabloid Dreams*. The next novel is a book called *Cleave*. And it's about Benjamin Cole, the now-grown-up little boy from *Wabash*. I was probably eight weeks of work away from finishing it when Home Box Office commissioned *Tabloid Dreams,* and it became important to finish that first. We want that book to come out in conjunction with the premiere. I'm still writing the stories, but my editor is editing as I send him the stories. So that volume of short stories will be out with the HBO movie.

WDB: And finally, there's the pleasure you have as the primary editor of Betsy's work and your marriage.

RB: Yes. She's an amazing writer. We were both at bad places when we met, artistically and otherwise. And we've helped one another enormously.

WILL CAMPBELL

1962 — *Race and the Renewal of the Church*
1972 — *The Failure and the Hope: Essays of Southern Churchmen*
(edited with James Y. Holloway)
1977 — *Brother to a Dragonfly*
1982 — *The Glad River*
1983 — *The Lord's Prayer for Our Time: God on Earth* (with Will
McBride and Bonnie Campbell)
1986 — *Forty Acres and a Goat*
1988 — *The Convention: A Parable*
1989 — *Chester and Chun Ling* (with Jim Hsieh)
1989 — *Covenant* (with Al Clayton)
1992 — *Providence*
1997 — *Bluebirds Always Come on Sunday*
1997 — *Shugah and Doops*

WILL CAMPBELL

By the Fire

"Being miserable seems to hold folks together. But when they're easy and everything is going right, they drift apart. Everybody goes home for a funeral."

I talked with Will Campbell beside the open stove in his log cabin study on December 28, 1990. Nashville was gearing down from Christmas, and the country was gearing up for the Persian Gulf War. We continued the conversation at Gass's Grocery Store. Subject of books, articles, and comic strips, Will Davis Campbell has been a maverick Baptist preacher and writer probably ever since his baptism at age seven in the Glory Hole of the east fork of the Amite River in southwest Mississippi in 1931. Friend to the country music set, the civil rights rousers, and the Ku Klux Klan, Campbell has become known for his eccentricities — outspokenness, corn whiskey, a chaw of tobacco, and a cherry wood cane.

A Yale graduate with a drawl and a righteous anger, Will Campbell should be better known for his books, *Forty Acres and a Goat*, *Brother to a Dragonfly*, *The Glad River*, and others. *Brother to a Dragonfly* is a remarkable view of the civil rights struggle as well as a portrait of the schizophrenic South. There's a touch of Faulkner here, and Twain, too. And a glimpse of ourselves. Campbell expects to be eulogized in death as a "good ole boy" who "just had some crazy ideas." And the crazy ideas of the memoirs and the novels glimmered now and again as he responded both to the questions I asked and to the ones I ought to have asked.

▼   ▼

WDB: Let me ask you first about audience. To whom do you write? Or do you think in those terms?

WC: I really don't. I guess *The Convention* is the only book I ever wrote with an audience in mind, but it was a lesson in humility because that audience totally ignored me.

WDB: Southern Baptists?

WC: Both factions. I didn't expect the so-called fundamentalists — that's a misnomer by the way; they're really not fundamentalists in the historical sense, only in a theological-historical sense, but that's what they call them — anyway, I didn't expect them to pay attention to it. I must say I thought the moderate faction would take to it, but then, when that didn't happen, it made sense. In the book they don't come off much better than the other side, really.

I've never thought much in terms of a reading audience. Writing is a disease — you catch it and you don't ever get cured, and you don't really think about where you got the virus or what the antidote might be. Obviously, poverty is not the antidote.

WDB: You don't ever feel sort of awkwardly between a Christian audience and a secular audience?

WC: Not really. I guess I never thought about that until quite recently. There was a piece about me in the current issue of *Rolling Stone.* I just assumed from what I knew of *Rolling Stone* that this should be a very hostile bunch. My friend Jessi Colter is a very religious woman, and her position was that this article would give me a hearing with the "secular audience." She says millions of people will read about me. I think she overestimates. I haven't seen an issue of *Rolling Stone* in twenty years, but

I doubt if millions read it. They probably look at the ads — some of the rock articles and stuff. But her point was a lot of people would get an exposure to the gospel who never would have got it, if I wouldn't talk the way I do. If my mouth wasn't so foul. Anyway, I didn't read it. Probably more from arrogance than humility, although there is a very thin line between those two. If the guy said neat things about me, that's bad for my humility, and if he said bad things about me, then that's good for my hostility. So I just won't read it.

WDB: So for you the whole writing act is fairly private; you don't worry too much about what people buy the books?

WC: No. I never have. In fact when *Brother to a Dragonfly* came out, I was amazed; I guess I had never thought in terms of people back home reading it. You know, it just didn't occur to me that this thing would show up in middle Mississippi. All of a sudden I started getting kidding from some of my friendly cousins, and a woman from Chattanooga told me that her mother wanted to read the book but wanted her to bring it in a paper bag. Then it sort of started getting around; it hadn't dawned on me who might read it. The language for example — I mean the language in that book is in the vernacular. It's in dialogue, and most of my foul words are in the vernacular. You know, we didn't say heck or darn when I was growing up — we just didn't do that. My father finally cooled it locally. One of his nieces asked, "Why does Will put all those bad words in his books?" My father said, "Well, hon, we all talk one way in the living room and we talk another way if we're way back in the north pasture and the mule's run over a hornet's nest and took off tearing up the harness." He said, "My boy was writing about hornet's nests." That pretty much stopped it. Then my sister-in-law sued me — well, that's pretty conclusive evidence that people do read what you write. It hadn't dawned on me till that point that there'd be any controversy. You need to distance yourself. If you don't, it's propaganda.

WDB: Do you get letters from people, say about *Convention*, critical letters accusing you of attacking the institution?

WC: No, I don't think I got a single letter like that about that book. I would get reports from people who would say, "It sounds like he's making fun of us" — which I was. They make fun of themselves; I was just reporting it. I do get lots of letters. I answered one last night from a boy who said, "I'm not part of your world; I'm part of the motorcycle world. And I'm not a good person, but I'm trying to be because I lost my lady six months ago and she was my rock. I know that she's with the angels and I want to join her." Very sad letter. So I wrote, of course. He said, "You said God loves us all anyway, and I want to know if that's true."

WDB: Had he heard you speak, or had he read one of your books?

WC: Never heard of me. He saw that *Rolling Stone* piece. He never heard of me or read anything by me.

WDB: But I take it you don't spend a lot of time worrying about whether or not people like you out there? Is that fair to say?

WC: Well, I really don't. We all want social acceptance; that's a very strong temptation. I learned pretty early that that wasn't always possible. The race thing, for example. I don't revel in controversy; I really don't. I like folks to think I'm a pretty good old boy. But I had to conclude that there were folks who didn't. But strangely enough, that comes around in its time. There were a number of years when I couldn't go back home to Mississippi; I did — but it was rather judicious choice of the time of day that I showed up and left. But now, no problem at all. In fact, I'm amazed by one old boy who was my best buddy when I was growing up. We had a secret handshake and all that. He would send me little messages through my brother, Paul. "Tell Dave I still love him but I don't like his program." I stopped by the little trailer where he lives down on the river when my father died back in August; he didn't know about my father. I had been with him when we were about thirteen when his father died, and he was very apologetic that he hadn't been with me because he remembered that. And he said, "You know, I was with you all the way when you went through that civil rights stuff." I wanted to say, "Well, you kind of kept it a secret."

My family has a reunion every fourth Sunday of May at a state park. I guess it was for about ten or twelve years there, no one ever mentioned it to me. I talked to my father about once a week. It never came up. But then, maybe it was eight or ten years ago, I came home and we chatted as usual, and then he said, "Well, I guess you'll be with us fourth Sunday." It kind of surprised me, and I said, "Well, I don't know Dad, what's the temperature down there?"

"No," he said, "that's all over now." The very ones who used to want to string me up were the first ones to come up and hug my neck and call me cousin. They may still say "nigger" after five o'clock on Friday, but Monday morning comes, it's Mr. Robinson. They're all working in one federal program or another.

WDB: Do you ever go into religious bookstores and look around, or do you have a sense of the kind of books that are being read in religious circles?

WC: I don't guess I do. And I haven't been in a religious bookstore in a while. Eerdmans has done a couple of my things, but there was quite a controversy when *Convention* came out, a controversy with the Baptist bookstores. The fella who's a friend of mine who acts as my agent took the manuscript to the Baptist bookstore people and asked if they were going to handle the book. And they said they just couldn't do it. And then the press started embarrassing them a little bit, so they came out with an apology saying that if anybody wanted to buy it they would order it. Of course, they could order *Penthouse* too, I guess.

WDB: So you couldn't buy *Convention* in Baptist bookstores?

WC: You could order it, but you couldn't go in and buy one. It wasn't stocked. The Baptists were having their annual convention in New Orleans, so they said they would take forty copies. I don't know if they sold the forty copies or not.

Well, I don't know how you account for what goes in these bookstores. A writer friend and I were talking about that yesterday. I read an article in the *Tennessean* about some guy whose first novel sold five hundred thousand copies — I never heard of him. I said, "John, who in the hell is this guy?" And he said, "Oh, he writes these romance mysteries." I said, "Well, who buys them? Where do they find them?" He said, "They're buying them in the supermarket, newsstands, truck stops."

WDB: Well, it does seem a strange state of affairs sometimes. Does it bother you as you think about your own work?

WC: Well, I guess it has always been the case that most of us tend to buy the things that we are already in agreement with. Not just Christians; I suppose no one likes to be challenged. I suspect they're not going to pay money to be insulted.

WDB: How often do you preach these days?

WC: Never on Sunday. Except this Sunday — I'm speaking at a Baptist Church in Charlotte. I think it's somewhere between Unitarianism and the Druids theologically. The minister there called, said he was going on sabbatical and was having different preachers come up. He said he wouldn't let just anybody in his pulpit, and he couldn't get anybody for the last Sunday of the year. Some folks wanted to have nobody, and I was as close as they could get to nobody. So they'd settled on me. I don't know why I said I would do it. I really end up doing more than I'd like to do. I've been trying to cut back on it now, because I'm trying to get in gear to do this book that I've been wanting to do for a long time and never seem to get started on.

WDB: What are the projects you're working on now?

WC: Well, I'm trying to write a social history of one section of land down in Mississippi, section 13 [*Providence*]. It is a section of township 23, North Range. And this was a cooperative farm back in the late 30s and 40s and interracial. It was something of a parallel to the tenant farmer's union, an attempt to be a showplace of cooperative farming. They never really pulled it off, but I wouldn't say they were a failure, because they had a very successful medical clinic there and some educational programs and other things. Then the war came along and a lot of them became old-line socialists and liberal democrats, Roosevelt democrats, and then after the war, in 1955, the white citizen council ran them off. And I've been on the board of that land ever since. Providence Farm it's called, a strange name. Providence Plantation was on that same land. I wanted to give the land back to the Choctaws, but I wasn't able to pull that off.

So I want to write about the first removal of the Choctaws. I'm not going to go back in the prehistory of the Mississippian period and all that, but I'll begin with the Choctaw removal and what Andrew Jackson did and try to humanize that God-awful period of American history. It is as if someone came here and said you got to move out of this hollow; we want your land.

They were a nation. They were civilized, had schools, the majority of them Christian by then. They would have these meetings, brush arbor meetings, and the preacher would come to Vicksburg and Natchez, whites sitting on one side, Choctaws on the other. I'm trying to write a book without once using the word Indian.

WDB: Using specific tribes?

WC: Yes, nations. Some people like the phrase *Native American*. It seems to me that's more demeaning. They weren't Americans. We called them that. What do you mean Native Americans?

Then I plan to write about the plantation period and the second removal, when the Providence Farm people were run off, and close it out with that. It's going to be a hard book to write without being self-serving and saying I was the hero in the thing because I insisted to the end to return it to the Choctaws. It's the same old story, you know. The white folks skim off the top and give the Redskins the bluffs.

WDB: Thomas Connelly in *Will Campbell and the Soul of the South* talks about your involvement in Providence Farm. And he cites all these descriptions people use for you: "guerrilla minister," "social activist," "boot-leg minister," "Jeremiah" or "Hosea," the "conscience of the South," or the "soul of the South." My favorite is "socratic southern gadfly." I'm wondering if any of that fits, or is it just "failed country singer?"

WC: That would probably be closer. I don't know. I don't take any of that too seriously. Not even Amos would claim to be a prophet. So I'd be a fool to go around and say that. I ran into somebody the other day who is an associate dean in a law school, and I asked him where he went to law school because we have a boy who is a lawyer. He said, "I didn't go to law school. I'm not a lawyer; I'm an ethicist." I have never heard anyone claim to be an ethicist. It's almost like saying, "I'm a prophet." You know, I've heard all those words at one time or another. But part of it is folks need that kind of person that they're describing. They need somebody to oppose or a folk hero, and if one doesn't appear they just go out and create one. They say, "Hey, this is our boy." And I just refuse to take that too seriously. I guess it troubles me sometimes. No one wants to wind up as some comic strip character. In the comic strip *Kudzu,* I am Will B. Dunn, who's very funny most of the time. But it got in my way because I had to quit wearing my big black hat, which I dearly loved.

WDB: I was thinking back to *Brother to a Dragonfly* particularly, and *Forty Acres and a Goat.* There's obvious biographical content in those books. Is that true to a lesser extent in *The Convention* and *The Glad River?* For example, is Doops Member's war experience in *Glad River* something of your own war experience?

WC: No, not at all. In fact, I didn't think about that when I was writing it. Percy and I talked about it a lot. He didn't like the novel at first.

WDB: Walker Percy?

WC: Yes. And then the novel came out and he called me one night and said it was a great novel. And I said, "I thought you didn't like it." And he said, "Well, you fixed it." I had changed one line after we talked. He was saying that Doops should have gone on and let that no-good preacher baptize him. Then he quoted that passage about the efficacy of the sacrament not being dependent upon the morality of the priest. And I said, "I'm not trying to write a Catholic novel. I'm trying to write a Baptist novel." He said, "There's no such thing." I said, "Well, you've been called a Catholic novelist." He said, "I know, but there's no such thing as that either."

Anyway, Percy said I was Doops. And I said I wasn't Doops. And I accused him of being that doctor in *Second Coming.* And he said, "Yeah, sure I was." Okay, but I wasn't Doops. He wouldn't let it go. He told me I was Doops whether I knew it or not.

WDB: I wondered that too when I read the book.

WC: I wasn't aware of it. Of course everything is autobiographical; everything you write is autobiographical. You come in here and say, "Good morning." That tells me something. It is an autobiographical statement. It's saying, I speak English for one thing. I'm an American.

WDB: Were you pleased with *Glad River?*

WC: Well, I think one shouldn't try to grade his own works, but I think it's the best thing I've ever written. The critics didn't agree, but what do they know?

WDB: They were more taken probably with the civil rights emphasis in *Dragonfly.*

WC: Probably. And people, the book critics I've noticed, not just about myself but about others, they resent what I call genre hopping. If you start out writing biography or autobiography, they don't want you jumping in and writing novels. Plus, I think my other interests and activities have gotten in my way some. But I wouldn't change that. I don't think of myself as a writer. Someone asks me what I do. I usually just say, "About what?" or "When?" I don't do the same thing twice very often. But I don't know that anyone has ever written about me as a writer.

WDB: It's usually Reverend Campbell?

WC: Yes, right. Or as an eccentric character or whatever. I'm not the writer that Walker Percy was and never will be, but they would have no problem when they write about him. They are writing about a writer and his writings. But I don't know anyone who has written a piece about Campbell's writings. They get into the civil rights stuff or my language or my whiskey.

WDB: Yes, I remember the last line of the review in the *Tennessean* about *Glad River* said, "Whatever you think of Campbell's politics, this is still a good book." The reviewer had to justify it on those grounds.

WC: Yes. That's the sort of thing I mean.

WDB: Are there ways in which the novels like *Glad River* or *The Convention* become vehicles to talk about issues that are particularly important to you? For example, in the end of *Glad River* you get into capital punishment. And in *The Convention* there is a strong sense of anti-institutionalism when Dorcas resigns and refuses to accept the presidency. Lots of stuff about the awful cuts stained glass can cause. Do you think of stories in that way as you begin them, or do you just sort of let them write themselves with the issues emerging where they will?

WC: Yeah, I do. Again, everything is autobiographical, so these things that are important to me are going to pop up. Just as in Walker's work; he was trained as a physician, and it always came up one way or another, but I didn't start out to just make a statement about the death penalty.

WDB: That would be propaganda?

WC: Yes! If I really got into that, I could be the lawyer, the judge, the prosecutor, and everything. Sometimes I think I'm a frustrated lawyer anyway.

WDB: Now Webb, your son, is a lawyer, right? Is he still in Nashville?

WC: Yeah. He's doing quite well.

WDB: How is the aging, the kids growing up, leaving home? Does that change your perspective? The empty-nest syndrome and all that kind of stuff?

WC: Well, I miss them. I like having little children around the house. When our first one went away, I just thought I was going to die.

WDB: Was that Penny?

WC: Yeah. She went to Southwest in Memphis. Brenda, my wife, said, "She's not going to Hong Kong. She'll be home this weekend." "No," I said, "she'll never be home again. She's gone." Which is true. When they graduate from high school, you just might as well tell them good-bye. Then the second one did it her own way. And she moved out a little bit at a time.

WDB: That's Bonnie, right?

WC: Yes. Then, when we took Webb to Wake Forest, Brenda was the one who collapsed.

WDB: Well, with the years, as you look back on the civil rights movement, do you find your perspective has changed? Do you find yourself circling back? Going back to where you started?

WC: Not consciously, I don't. I have questions about how much we accomplished and how much we didn't accomplish. But then I never really considered myself part of the civil rights movement.

WDB: It was sort of dumped right in your lap.

WC: I've known since I was a child that the gospel couldn't be proclaimed in a vacuum, and that we could go paddling around Patmos with Paul from now until doomsday in the first century. In our churches, we kept it back in the first century. You can read 2 Corinthians, the fifth chapter, every Sunday morning in any Baptist or Church of Christ steeple in Mississippi or Tennessee and people will say "Amen." But if you start saying, "Brothers and sisters, what this means is that worldly standards no longer count in our estimate of anything.

What that means is there's no such thing as race. Race is a category that is wiped out. What this means is there's no such thing as communism and capitalism and North Vietnam and South Vietnam. These are human categories, human standards, and Paul says these are no longer of any account. You don't consider these things anymore." That's when you start getting into trouble. I didn't realize how strange some people found it until it was pretty much over. When I began visiting and befriending people who were active in the Klan, that's when I started getting a perspective. There never was any dramatic turning point like Paul saying I must see Rome and go to my people or whatever. It never dawned on me that it wasn't a very elementary thing. People go to visit captives because they are captives, because they are sick.

WDB: So you were surprised by the criticism?

WC: I was very surprised. There is nothing, nothing about ideology, that I can find in the New Testament. It's just not there.

WDB: Well, when you read about the Persian Gulf buildup or the retrial of Byron de la Beckwith for shooting Medgar Evers, are there wistful echoes in all of that for you?

WC: Sure. The Byron de la Beckwith thing. I don't think there is much question that the guy did shoot Evers. But it seems to me to be a touch of self-righteousness now that Mississippi is going to try this seventy-year-old man. They milked him for all he was worth when he killed Evers. Now they are going to milk him for all he's worth by convicting him even though they turned him loose twice before with the cooperation of the state administration and the White Sovereignty Commission, which was an agency of government. But now they are going to prove to the world that they're not really like that, and they're going to lock him up this time.

Most of my friends are saying "Hurrah," and I suppose Evers's wife is saying "Hurrah," and I can understand that. But it's just Caesar existing for the sake of Caesar. Now there's something in it for the state to convict him. Just as there was something in it to acquit him earlier. It all makes you want to ask, "Where were you when I needed you?" Now I know that there was a conspiracy in Mississippi to do me in, too.

WDB: But it's only been lately when you found all this out.

WC: Yes, I wrote about it, but I didn't really believe it.

WDB: I remember the incident with the Ping-Pong balls at the University of Mississippi when you began to get death threats.

WC: Yes, that sort of thing. Joe, my brother, called me when I was on my way down to Mississippi. He called me in Huntsville, Alabama. He said, "Daddy says you shouldn't come home." But I really didn't believe it. You know, we all think we're born to live forever and other people get killed in swamps. But it did happen, and I expect pretty much the way my old buddy relates it now. They wanted me dead.

But six or seven years ago they invited me back as the annual speaker for the Pike County Arts Council. And they built that thing up, you know, the Pike County Arts Council, where twelve or thirteen people get together once a year to hear somebody speak. They started out with a little ad in the local paper, "Will Campbell's Coming Home." That's all it said. Then the next week there was a cartoon with a dragonfly and "Will Campbell's Coming Home." And they kept building this up. A sweatshirt was made with a dragonfly and "Will Campbell's Coming Home." And I didn't know what was going on. And then the banker, who held a pretty big mortgage on the paper, went down and asked the editor, "What's the biggest picture you've ever had on the front page of the *Pike County Journal?*" They searched the morgue and found that when Franklin Roosevelt died, they had a quarter of a page. So they had this half-page picture for "Will Campbell's Coming Home." Well, I got down there and there were all these police cars that met me, and I thought, "What the hell is going on here?" All these buses by the State Street Theatre, and streets roped off, and high school kids out. "Stratford has its William Shakespeare. Oxford has its William Faulkner. We have our Will." What a guy that publicist was. That was just the preliminary.

I was going to speak the next night, so I stopped to see my old buddy — first time in many years. I stopped at his house. He invited me in, and I said, "No, I'm in kind of a hurry; let's just sit right here under the tree." He said, "No, I do my heavy entertaining in the kitchen." I wasn't too sure why he wanted me to come in. So he went in and opened a beer from the icebox and put it down at his place.

Then he got another one and put it in the middle of the table and didn't open it. He said, "That's if you want it." He remembered that scene in *Brother to a Dragonfly* when Joe is having a bachelor party and he had his two bottles of Four Roses, and I offended him by not drinking with him. That was what my old friend had thought about. Well, this was four o'clock in the afternoon, and I don't really like beer, and I don't drink anything at four o'clock in the afternoon, but I drank that one. He leaned back and said, "What might I do for you?" So I said, "Tomorrow night they're either going to make a fool out of me or a hero."

"Well," he said, "You're going to be all right." I told him I thought I might need a little support, but he thought I meant protection. And he said, "You're going to be all right. About 80 percent of the people love you. But," he said, "there's always those others. And if those old wheels out there and this emphysema will let me, I'll be there."

So the old State Street Theatre was packed, with people standing in the aisles. It had nothing to do with me. But with that kind of buildup I could have filled that theater with that little beagle hound out there doing the speaking. People who never heard of Will Campbell saying, "What's he done? We knew little worm-eating Dave Campbell, but what's he done for all this? Why are we having this celebration?"

And just as the house lights were dimming, I saw an apparition, a woodsman; you know, you don't hear leaves crunching or anything, but he suddenly appears. My old friend. I saw him slink in and hunker down in his bib overalls. And like an eagle, he didn't miss a movement that was made. If anybody had tried to get at me, he'd have blown them away. And then when it was over, I never saw him. He was gone.

WDB: Well, it sounds like your perspective on your calling has stayed pretty much the same over the years. It seems like you respond to just whatever comes to the door.

WC: Yeah, I think so.

WDB: And your theology, despite Yale University and all of that, is it still, "We're all bastards, but God loves us anyway?"

WC: Right.

WDB: So you don't think of yourself as a southern writer or a Christian writer or a minister or any of those kinds of phrases?

WC: I think anybody is a fool who tries to think of themselves as anything. That's something for other people. I live in the South. I was raised in the South. That makes me a southern writer, or a southern breather, you know. Then when I wrote *Glad River*, I chose the South Pacific because I was there and I knew something about it.

WDB: So faith has something to do with the writing simply because faith has everything to do with you, I guess.

WC: I guess. You know, I don't think about it.

WDB: Well, I want to talk a little bit about this anti-institutionalism, for want of a better phrase. Do you have much involvement with the contemporary church?

WC: No.

WDB: Where do you get your support?

WC: That's very difficult for me to talk about. But I don't have any problem finding support or finding community. I have a friend, and we go down to Gass's Tavern because it's here and we're here. We knew everybody in there and everybody knew us. No big deal. The noon drinking crowd — coke, beer, hamburgers. Once when we left, my friend said, "Will, I'm not criticizing you. I know you kind of like to think you run with all kinds of folks, but as for running buddies couldn't you pair off with a little better class of people? You know these are trash."

I said, "How many people do you know that you can call at three o'clock in the morning and tell them you need them and they'd be there as soon as they could get their britches on?"

"I guess I don't know anybody," he said. "Everybody in there would. And I would for them, and they know it," I told him. Now, to jump from there, to say that Gass's Tavern is the church, I think would be a mistake. It would just be to replay the drama and say to the world, "Build a tavern and everybody go there twice a week. Go on Friday night and Saturday night because they got music, and they'll let you sit in with the band and fulfill that need that you have to be a country music star." That's not it either. So you don't ever name it, or I don't, because if I name it and put it on my bumper sticker that I found it, I'm going to run it. You can bet your life on that. I'll run it, and I can run it. Just as I can run any big steeple if anybody's fool enough to offer me that job. On seventeen hours a week, I can run it. I don't know how I arrived at that figure. Some ecclesiastical actuary I guess helped me on it. I can do it all in a seventeen-hour week, but I would never again see that as my vocation; that's the way I make my living, running that institution. There's a way to do it. I was trained to do it, and I can do it. Including the sermons. Most of it in my judgment is totally irrelevant to what goes on in the world. The "big preachers," the "good preachers." It doesn't mean anything, you know. That guy's a powerful preacher. What does he do outside of the pulpit? Or what do the people do when they hear this great sermon? I forgot what your question was, but that's the answer.

WDB: Of course, a steady stream of people are going out the back door of our institutions, and you've had a good bit to say about the tendency of systems toward corruption. Do you feel outside and alienated? Is there a risk that your voice will just be ignored? Has this happened?

WC: Oh, I think it has happened.

WDB: But you don't feel damaged by it?

WC: No, I really don't. I guess in all fairness and candor, I was a little disappointed when *The Convention* didn't get a hearing. It got some attention, but it stayed pretty much in the closet.

WDB: There's still something in you that would like to call those institutions to their senses?

WC: Yeah, I guess. My boy read *The Convention*. He said, "Aren't you afraid someone is going to sue you?" He thought he knew the real life models for the characters in the book. But who wants to go into open court and claim to be an ass? I wouldn't want to say, "Hey that's me he's writing about there."

WDB: And you called it a parable after all.

WC: Yeah.

WDB: What do you read these days? I've been struck by the names that show up from Martin Luther King to Studs Terkel to Robert Coles. And there's Percy, whom we've talked about. Which are the ongoing voices for you now?

WC: Oh, I don't know. I don't read a lot. I'm not proud of that. I'm a very slow reader. I have a friend down at Mercer who went to school with me. He says, "Campbell has written more books than he's read." People used to call me a scholar. He says, "Campbell can't be a scholar; he's never read forty pages of anything." But I'm a very slow reader and I am involved in a lot of different things, and I just don't take the time to read. I have friends who write, and I read what they write. I read a lot of manuscripts people send me, requesting blurbs, and try to help them get published and that kind of thing. Walker and I always read everything one another wrote before it came out.

WDB: Was his death marked very much in this area? I was disappointed to see little mention beyond the obligatory paragraph in *Time*.

WC: I didn't go to the service, but I had an interesting experience around that time. My father spent a lot of time with my kid brother and his wife in Covington, Louisiana. He never closed his home in Mississippi, but he commuted back and forth. So when he was really ill, I was down there staying with him in Covington. Sitting up with him, early one morning, about two o'clock, I was struck by the irony that here two hundred yards up the bayou was Walker Percy fighting the same pale horseman. And two Mississippians, one of the yeoman class and one of the aristocracy, one internationally known writer, the other one no one knew, but both noble men, both good men. Both fighting the same battle and losing, both having won at some time earlier.

And I thought about writing a paper. About that time Joe Wright, who was another friend of mine and was one of the Wilmington Ten, died. And I thought about writing a piece. Joe Wright, Walker Percy, and my father. But I never did it.

My daughter, who works for the North Carolina Press, said there was quite an imposing gathering in Chapel Hill. And there was one in New York. And of course, Walker wasn't a popular writer. I don't know as he ever had a book on the *New York Times* best-seller list. I don't believe he did.

WDB: Not even *Moviegoer?*

WC: I doubt it. That book was a sleeper. It won the National Book Award by accident. It was all pretty much sewed up, and a woman who was one of the judges was in a book store in New Orleans and ran across *The Moviegoer*. She had never heard of Walker Percy. She got them to consider it, and it won.

I don't think it was the best book he ever wrote. I liked *Love in the Ruins*. But he thought *Moviegoer* was his best book. But what does he know?

WDB: What about others of the so called religious writers? Do you read Flannery O'Connor or Frederick Buechner?

WC: Well, I like O'Connor very much. I wish I could have met her. I never did. I didn't like her at first. When I first read her I thought she was making fun of my people, the poor — an annihilation of the hillbillies, down-on-the-redneck approach. But it wasn't. God knows what she'd be turning out now if she had lived. She died very young. Buechner, you know, I never really read; I don't know why. You know, sometimes you shy away from books because you think they might influence you.

WDB: Buechner says exactly the same thing. He shied away from O'Connor, in fact, for that reason.

WC: Well, I didn't shy away from her.

WDB: Well, what about that hillbilly stereotype? Is that still the one legitimate joke you can tell without being labeled racist, sexist, or homophobic?

WC: It seems to be. That's the one that hasn't made it into the PC lectionary. Walker used to tell me I was too sensitive about that. "It's easy for you to say," I told him. "You were to the manor born and you're not a redneck and I am." But, I'm astounded at how sophisticated and urbane people use *redneck* as a synonym for prejudice. Redneck and bigot used synonymously. That's not what the word means. It never has been what it means.

WDB: It's one who toils in fields, right?

WC: Yes. I've written several pieces about that in small journals and checked all the dictionaries I could find, and they are all very consistent with the definitions: "One of the poor, white, rural, working class of the South" — period! Except, it usually says, "used disparagingly." And I think it is an evasion to say "redneck." It allows us to think we're not the racists; the rednecks are the racists. We are the racists. Every white person in America is a racist. That doesn't mean he or she is a bigot. It just means we had an advantage from the day we were born. I figure I overdo the subject for emphasis.

WDB: How do you feel about being a subject at academic conferences? People come to your door and ring you on the phone wanting to come see you. You obviously resist becoming a folk hero. But your stuff is starting to come up at academic conferences.

WC: Oh well. They gotta have something to talk about.

WDB: What about the children's book you did last year? How has that done?

WC: Well, it hasn't been any big seller, but I enjoyed doing it.

WDB: Will you do any of that sort of thing again?

WC: I don't know. Probably not. Abingdon came out here and asked me to write a children's book. Shocked me. I'm scared of three-year-olds. They tell the truth. "Do you like me?" we ask them. "No!" they'll say. Now when they get about eight, you know, the phone rings, and we put a hand over the phone and say, "Now this is Aunt Lara; you come here and you tell her that that purple muffler that she sent you for your birthday is your favorite and that purple is your favorite color." And the kid will come do it. We call it manners, but it's just lying.

But after they left, I recalled that I have this friend, Jim Hsieh, a Chinese fellow. I had done their wedding, and then they had a little boy who got sick, had a brain tumor, and I baptized him. They asked me to do it, so I did it. And when he died I did the service, so we got very close. So I told them if he could be the artist I would do it, and we would dedicate it to their boy. They looked at his work and sent it to New York and did all the stuff that art departments have to do, and so we did it together. That's why I did that.

I'll never forget that boy's operation. I got down to the hospital and they were waiting by the elevator. And the surgeon came in and didn't give them any hope at all. They fought it as much as they could until the end. Then they asked me to baptize the baby; by then it was about daylight. So I went racing down to a friend who runs a lending library. I told her I needed a prayer book. Jim had grown up in an Episcopal school in the Philippines. His father was a Chinese diplomat of some kind. And she got me a prayer book, and I went into the intensive care unit and told the surgeon I'd been asked to baptize the boy.

He said it was out of the question. Then it dawned on me somehow that he knew who I was and knew I was a deep-water Baptist. He thought I was going to submerge this child in a tub. I said, "I'm not arguing with you, Doctor, but I will simply touch my finger in the water and touch his forehead." And he said, "Oh well, that's okay. I didn't understand that." So I went to his bed. He was a little fella. Half his head was covered with all these tubes and everything. The nurses were changing shifts; you know how the nurse going off reads all the orders and everything. The nurse coming on kept saying, "This child is jaundiced. We better call the doctor." Finally I said, "He's supposed to be that color." She looked around at me and went on protesting that they better page the doctor. Finally I said, "Ma'am, this child is Chinese. He's always this color."

WDB: So you went ahead and did the baptism then?

WC: Yeah. More important than kids' books, I suspect.

WDB: Which book of your books would you recommend to people coming to you for the first time?

WC: Well, I wouldn't name one. That's like picking one of your children.

WDB: I gave a copy of *Glad River* to a friend a few months ago. I thought she should know about you. She's seventy or so years and from these parts. She's gone to the Church of Christ all her life. She was shocked at all the bad words. But she stayed with it to the end, and now she has gone out and gathered up all the other books. But we had to talk about all those bad words.

WC: Yeah, I remember once going on one of those talk shows. You've got to be a fool to go on one of those. You get all the kooks. So I knew as soon as I was introduced as being a preacher from Mount Juliet and a friend of Charlie Daniels, they were going to start calling in. And sure enough, the switchboard lit up.

This one woman, I could tell she wasn't gonna waste no time. She said, "Well what do you think, Reverend Campbell, about Charlie Daniels using bad words on the television?"

"I don't know ma'am; what did he say?"

"Well, I couldn't repeat that," she answered. So I offered to call off some bad words and let her just indicate the bad ones with a yes or no. "You don't have to say them," I told her. "Did he say prejudice?" "No." "War?" "Nuclear bomb?" "Why, no."

WILL CAMPBELL

"If I don't know what he said and you can't tell me, I can't very well express what I think about it," I finally told her. "Those are the worst words I can think of." She could see we had a problem.

WDB: Your books have a Faulknerian or Twainian storytelling feel to them. Full of tales. I remember them by the tales. Skippy with his ice cream in *Forty Acres*. The baptistry story in *Glad River*. The military funeral in *Glad River*. Do you have a stock of stories back somewhere from which these anecdotes show up?

WC: Well, I went to a military funeral once — one similar to the one in *Glad River*. The soldiers fired the salute, and a very obese grandmother was scared and fell back. One of the grandchildren shouted, "My God, they've shot Granny!" And there it was.

WDB: You've sometimes talked about your "era of pseudo-sophistication." I don't know exactly what years you had in mind when you used that phrase, but what did you mean by that? How are you different now?

WC: Well, you know I went to Yale Divinity School, and it's hard to get over that. There is something about the Ivy League. I don't know. You know, I'm proud I went there. Teachers, people I met and so on, but I guess I'm talking about the calabash pipe, listening to a Bach fugue, and so many things. All the posing.

WDB: Connelly also talks about your calling us to a sort of primitive Christianity. How is that different from what the Baptist and Church of Christ folks around here mean when they talk about being "the New Testament church?"

WC: I am amused at the current controversy among Southern Baptists. They want to say they're going back to the true church. They are not; they are a modernist movement. If they want to go back to the sixteenth century and talk about the Anabaptists and the primitive band who did not serve on juries, did not go to war, and the rest, I'll be glad to talk with them.

WDB: Do the Baptists talk about tracing their origins back to Christ? You know Church of Christ buildings often have markers saying "Founded in A.D. 33."

WC: Right. There is some of that. I don't think there is as much as there once was. I remember once when I was a student in college. Some kid came into a history class. He had heard a discussion on

92

Baptists as Protestants. "Did you know the Baptists aren't Christian?" he asked the professor. "Yes, son, most of them I know aren't," the professor said.

When I was a kid, the clergy weren't as sophisticated or educated as they are now. And most of these folks now know in their heart of hearts that no one believes the Bible literally. They won't kill for that claim. They know that fighting over a text when we don't have the original is absurd. So what if it is in error? It doesn't exist and we don't know what's in it. That's a crazy fight. It's insane to fight about something that no human being has ever seen.

WDB: Do you think the religious leaders, the ones that you talked about particularly in *The Convention*, are as cynical and clear-headed about it all as the ones you parody there? Or are they, and this may be worse, are they honestly misguided?

WC: Oh, I think the majority of them are honestly misguided. I think some of them don't give a damn who the president of the Southern Baptist convention is. But they care a great deal about who is president of the United States. But I think that was a very cold and calculated cynical plan to take over the convention. And it worked. They worked on it for ten years and got it all.

WDB: You refer to the whole televangelism industry as "electronic soul molesters." Is it hard for you to extend mercy there?

WC: It is. I don't watch it very much. I used to watch Ernest Aingly. Get someone who hasn't heard a human sound all his life and make him a faith healer.

WDB: Is it a bad time to be a writer?

WC: Oh yeah. But there's no finding a cure for the virus.

WDB: What galls you these days?

WC: President Bush and this Persian Gulf thing. He never should have sent all those children over there.

WDB: What do you find most satisfying at this stage of things?

WC: Being alive, I guess.

WDB: Do you get satisfaction out of the responses you receive from audiences when you go around and speak?

WC: I guess so. Unless they're hostile, which sometimes happens. I don't really like to make speeches. I like to have made them.

WDB: I've already said how much I like *Glad River;* it reminds me of *Catch 22*, a war novel on one level, but much more than that, too. There's fecal imagery right at the heart of it. Christ as sludge. God as sludge. Is that something you would say is our call today? To somehow fertilize the earth?

WC: I think our call, our vocation is to be free. That's what Jesus is about; that is what we should be about. I learned a long time ago that I am less free than my father was. My children are less free than I am. My father was less free than his father was. It's very difficult. I remember when the Social Security Act was being passed. I think I wrote about that somewhere maybe. William Randolph Hearst took out full-page ads in all his own papers. He said if we do this, then big brother is going to know how many times you've been married, how much money you have in the bank, and all the rest. People know everything about me today cause it's all there.

A part of the thing that happened to Gary Hart deserves sympathy. Mr. Hart, I think, was flaunting his loins, but that wouldn't have happened forty or fifty years ago. So we are becoming something of a technological concentration camp.

WDB: Do you still feel the failure of the church as much in the context of all of this? I was reading your essays in *The Failure and the Hope*. They reminded me some of Martin Luther King's "Letters from the Birmingham Jail," where he talks about the failure of the church to be the church. He said the church is a thermometer instead of a thermostat, registering change rather than creating change. Do you still feel that failure of the church?

WC: Of the institutional church, the structured church, yes. And I think that this has been going on for years, really. There's a book of Edith Hamilton's that I have made such a part of me. It's a little book called *Search for the Truth*. There's one brief chapter about the church, in which she said the great church of Christ was founded by a group of young zealots often willing to die for Christ. But they did not trust him; they could not trust him to build the church in his way. So we get dogma, doctrines, and theologies. Confessions of faith. None of which Jesus talked about. He talked about a cup of cold water. But right off, we have to be about installing a global sprinkler system. And

94

her point is that once you start formulating dogma to contain and systematize Jesus, the real message of Jesus, the essence of Jesus, is pretty much out the window.

And that's what's happening among Southern Baptists today who have always boasted of being noncreedal. Now they're more creedal than Rome. But the fight is about the creed. Again, what difference does it make to believe that some nonexistent, never-seen, document is in error? The fight became a defense of dogma long ago.

WDB: And you grieve over this?

WC: Yes.

WDB: What does a mourner look like these days? Is our call to just be whoever we are and respond to the needs that come our way?

WC: That's all I know.

WDB: Tom T. Hall calls you a "Jesus-loving agnostic."

WC: He says he didn't say that.

WDB: Is that close?

WC: I doubt it. I remember something Waylon Jennings said. Waylon had some sort of problem, and Jessi Colter, his wife, wanted me to talk to him. I always have trouble with that, with being an ecclesiastical peeping Tom prying into the state of someone's soul. One night we were in Greensboro County. We'd shot all the ducks and ships in the video games and played all the gin rummy we could stand riding on the bus from Greensboro to Tampa. I said, "Waylon, do you really believe?"

He said, "Yeah." Conversation was sparse that night.

I said, "What's that supposed to mean?" He said, "Uh-huh." I think that about gets it.

ELIZABETH DEWBERRY

1990 — *Many Things Have Happened Since He Died*
1994 — *Break the Heart of Me*
1997 — *How to Get to the Magic Kingdom*

ELIZABETH DEWBERRY

500 Words a Day

"I don't know how to write in a guarded way. You have to go to what is raw in yourself."

While finishing up her doctoral dissertation on Hemingway at Emory University in 1988, Elizabeth Dewberry found herself a part-time pursuit, a novel that she never intended to publish. *Many Things Have Happened Since He Died* appeared in 1990 to reviews that recognized the power of the narrator's struggle to come to terms with an abusive husband and a legacy of fundamentalist faith. By age twenty-one, Dewberry's narrator has lost a husband, a child, her faith, and nearly herself. Now wondering what it has all meant, she offers us a sort of unedited journal that tells the story directly and leaves readers with a sure sense of her escape, however narrow.

Break the Heart of Me appeared in 1994 with another female narrator, Sylvia Mullins, who is trying to "pull herself together" in a parade of memories that bring pain. Images of her abuse at the hands of her grandfather haunt the text, along with the shrill oratory of her high school boyfriend, a true believer in the second coming, who converts young Sylvia to his own fiery literalism. His suicide in the wake of

99

failed predictions is another weight on her. And Sylvia would like to believe in God, but in the end she is "shy around God" — uncertain about religious faith.

In our conversation in February 1996 Elizabeth Dewberry traces her own growth as an artist as she talks about the church of her youth, the surprise of her first book, new directions in the career, her recent marriage to novelist Robert Olen Butler, and manuscripts that have to be thrown away.

▼   ▼

WDB: When you talk about writing, you speak of finding that place beyond experience, the deepest wells of true imagination. What are the resources that get you there?

ED: Well, I read voraciously, just constantly. In fact, I started writing my first book, *Many Things Have Happened Since He Died*, when I was studying for my Ph.D. orals. And that very intense reading sparked something. So the reading and writing were definitely connected. Lately, however, it's harder and harder for me to read. I still don't fully understand this, but too much reading interferes with some part of my creative process. I guess I've just moved to a different place. When I find a book that I enjoy, it is still one of the great pleasures. But there are fewer and fewer books.

WDB: Readers must suggest books to you all the time. Don't people say, "You remind me of Edgerton," or Lee Smith, or Kaye Gibbons, or Dorothy Allison?

ED: Yes, and I've read and enjoyed all of them. People have said to me for years, "You have to read *Bastard out of Carolina*." And finally I did, though not all of it. It was distracting to me. Maybe the similarities made me uncomfortable. There are some similarities, but Allison is doing a very different thing. That's the kind of thing that I used to be able to read and really learn from. Now I've reached a point where it doesn't work that way.

WDB: Frederick Buechner says that he avoided Flannery O'Connor's work for years for fear that they were plowing the same field.

ED: Yes. I can't read Faulkner anymore. I used to love Faulkner. I wanted to do my dissertation on him. But now there's something that takes me a little bit out of my work when I read him. I do love Flannery O'Connor. But, I still think of myself more or less in the beginning of my career as a writer. Since I'm coming to my own sense of my voice as a fiction writer, I find myself less able to give other fiction writers the attention that you must give when you read a novel. I cannot give myself over to their voices.

WDB: What about the role of research in your books? Did you research the country music world for *Break the Heart of Me?*

ED: That was from living in Nashville. At Vanderbilt I did an internship at what was then called Priority Records, the gospel label of CBS. So I learned something about the music business that way. We had Johnny Cash, and a guy named Carmen, and David and the Giants. And we had an old-fashioned gospel quartet, the Cathedrals. When I was doing the book, I called my former boss and told him what I needed. He set me up for a couple of hours with a performer who was just about to have his first album come out. He was in exactly the position my fictional character was in, so that was really helpful. And I read some books on what agents control the business, that sort of groundwork.

WDB: You're not a drummer?

ED: No, but I talked to a couple of drummers. I just made a few phone calls. I find the best way to do things like that is not to ask specific questions, but just ask them to tell me about it, and then you pick up their vocabulary.

WDB: Have you been criticized for treating your southern characters too stereotypically — rednecks, hicks, and grotesques?

ED: No, the thing that I've been criticized for is being really critical of fundamentalists. But not southerners. I don't think that I'm attracted to the same kind of people that Flannery O'Connor was. I don't think that my characters are freakish in any sense. I think they are very normal people. Maybe that says something about my view of normal. And I just don't think of it in those terms when I'm writing. I write from the point of view of the character, and so I'm trying to understand that character. So if a critic sees it as stereotyping, if I'm truly understanding the character, then there's not really anything I can do.

WDB: Whatever your treatment of fundamentalism in your books, you clearly understand the fundamentalist ethic — the attempt to be in the world but not of it. And there's the powerful consideration in *Many Things Have Happened Since He Died* of the notion that God will not give me more than I can bear. The book finally says, "Yes, He will." I wonder if the novel is at least partly about coming to terms with the failure of a certain kind of religious faith. Could it be said that both of your novels are loss-of-faith books, or would it be closer to say they are about rearrangements of faith?

ED: I think they are about a loss of faith in the church. I don't think they are about a loss of faith in God. Organized religion is not a bad thing, but faith in it is. I've had some Christians criticize me for writing what I do, but others have said "This is what needed to be said."

WDB: What do the fundamentalist Christians say to you?

ED: I grew up in a very conservative, fundamentalist situation. My parents call it evangelical; I call it fundamentalist. Our church fought battles over things like whether it was sin for women to wear pants, because there's one verse in Exodus that says women should not wear men's clothing. Well, what if they're women's pants? And that was a very big issue. And wine drinking was an issue. I remember one day thinking, if God is as concerned about these things as we are, then he's very picky, petty even. I remember one time going to Colorado and looking at the mountains and saying, if I lived here I could believe in a God who wasn't petty. But for people who are caught up in that world of literalism about the Bible, a Christian narrator who cusses pretty well ends the book for them. Cussing is sin. So I've had criticism from people who felt I was criticizing holy things.

WDB: That must be difficult for you when in fact you are trying to explore biblical ideas like "Wives submit yourselves to your husbands." And the literalist says, "That means what it says." *Many Things Have Happened Since He Died* is a dramatic rendering of how that verse is a real problem. So here she is in an abusive, crazy relationship, trying to do what the Bible says.

ED: Yes, it was a very painful thing for me. And I would not have been so honest in that book if I'd planned on publishing it. I was really trying to work through those issues privately, and I think I did it in a work of fiction because I was so located in my religious training that I wouldn't allow myself to question it all directly. But I could question it through someone else.

WDB: It was almost a trick you were playing on yourself? And writing the first book was writing yourself out of fundamentalism in a way?

ED: That's what happened, yes. When the book came out, reading the reviews was like going into counseling. Everybody was saying, "Why does she stay so long?" And it helped me see my own life issues more objectively. It was a very strange process.

WDB: What about your family and people that knew you well? Were they shocked by *Many Things Have Happened Since He Died*?

ED: Everybody was very surprised. Nobody who knew me from my childhood or even from graduate school expected that book to come out of me. Most of my childhood friends just didn't understand it, because they are still in that fundamentalist mind set. It was a difficult thing for my family. My parents, at that point, really didn't think that things like that happened. They didn't think that church-going men abused their wives. But right around the time the book came out, a woman in their church was being severely abused by her husband. And my father helped her get away to Michigan where she had family and would be safe. So they had this long plane ride together. Finally my parents realized that I was speaking for women that needed a voice, and it changed all of our lives. It really did. And *Break the Heart of Me* opened their eyes to something about molestation. Well, I won't say that. I won't say my book opened their eyes. I think that a personal experience did and helped them understand the book, and then the book, I hope, contributed something too. It changed us all, because we had to come to terms with agonies that I've had for a long time. I was finally able to face it through someone else's voice, and then we all had to face it. I don't know how long it would have taken us to be honest with each other about where we were without the book.

WDB: You still speak with obvious warmth about the passionate faith of these people you went to church with. Do you feel some indebtedness for having grown up in that kind of world?

ED: Oh, it was a rich world. It really was. Despite all the problems of that kind of church, at the center of it was God. It often turned into a petty manifestation — your consciousness of your soul is manifested in whether or not is it wrong to wear pants. But what I feel like has lasted out of it for me is a deeper, greater consciousness and a sense of a trying to wrestle with spiritual things. It's interesting, though, because I think we were taught to believe the Bible literally and not wrestle with it.

WDB: God said it. I believe it. That settles it.

ED: Yes. But when it's real to you, and you're trying to be honest about it, I think you have to wrestle with it. So I'm grateful for all that. Despite all their problems, the vast majority of those people are truly sincere. They wanted to do the right thing. So they wanted to know whether it was a sin to wear pants. And I have compassion for that. They wanted to please God, so they wanted to know which he wanted them to wear.

WDB: And the literalists teach us a veneration, a respect for words?

ED: Oh, absolutely. Remember those sermons that trace back every word in a verse to its origin? I love that verse in John "In the beginning was the Word and the Word was God." Words are holy. Even their strong reaction to cursing shows the belief that words are powerful, words shape lives and souls. And, of course, through words you can actually communicate with God. That's powerful stuff for a writer.

WDB: I can see why your friends and teachers were surprised when your first novel appeared. I've read your scholarly work on Hemingway, and I'm amazed that the voice there came out of the same imagination that produced the novels. Is there some bridge between those two things?

ED: I wrote my dissertation as I was writing *Many Things Have Happened Since He Died*. I tended to do one month on one and one month on the other. And I found that each was a nice escape from the other. Each gave part of my mind a rest. At that point in my life, they were complementary. I haven't written anything on Hemingway for a while now.

WDB: Now you are mixing in playwriting?

ED: Yes, I need something other than fiction.

WDB: Do you see yourself going back to a classroom soon?

ED: Not anytime soon. I really had a bad experience at Ohio State. I am really happy to be out of academia for a while. Not that I think all schools are like Ohio State, but I still feel sort of scarred by it all. Scholars devalue creative work, feeling like a book about a novel is more valuable than a novel. It was demoralizing. I don't want to do that again for a while.

WDB: There is something startling in the style of your fiction. The dramatically personal style is so far from academic prose. In *Many Things Have Happened Since He Died*, you say, "If anyone reads this you will know why I did what I did. It's all true. It is the truth, the whole truth, and nothing but the truth." The prose is so unguarded. Where does that come from?

ED: It is the only way I know how to do it. I've written two unpublished novels, *The Last Southern Gentleman* and *Touch Me, Touch Only Me*, as attempts to try something else. But it doesn't work for me. I don't really even understand why. I really do hope that as I grow as an artist I can have access to other ways of expressing things. And playwriting has helped that because obviously you cannot be so internal with your characters. So I feel like I'm growing to where I have access to other kinds of voices.

WDB: You have to go from what is torn and troubled in yourself? You write from that place where dreams come from, as your husband says it?

ED: Yes, the place where dreams come from and the place where yearning comes from. I have to go to places in my soul that I want to understand better, and the only way I can understand them is to tell their story. If I can understand it a different way, then I think it would be better to write an essay about it.

WDB: Do you write for yourself, or do you write for some audience out there? It sounds like you're driven to write because it's something that you have to do.

ED: It's partly that. I don't think of myself as one of those people who is so driven that I couldn't do something else. Although when I go for a long time without writing, I do start feeling anxious. I do have a need to write, but I'm uncomfortable with a picture of myself as driven by voices. It's not that. It takes some discipline, and there are times when I feel stuck and when I can't figure out what I'm doing.

WDB: So there's craft, skill, and hard work involved to try to get those one thousand words a day?

ED: I'm happy with four hundred. A good day for me is one single-spaced page. Maybe five hundred words. But often there's less than that. Then I'm irritated with myself, and I say, "Okay, they were valuable words." And then occasionally I'll do more than that in a day, but that's actually really pretty rare. I have to be flexible because of how we travel and everything. Ideally, I write in the morning and a little bit again in the afternoon.

WDB: So you'll get that page in four hours of work?

ED: Yes. And it varies. Sometimes a page will come really fast, and then I sit there for another three hours and finally say, "Well I guess all I'm going to get is a page today." And then other times it will be four hours of constant work for one page.

WDB: I wonder if there's something of the satirist in you. You get in nice punches at things like marriage encounter weekends, and Oprah and pop culture stuff. Do you have the instinct to put a needle in there a little bit?

ED: Yes, I guess I do. The other day, as we were driving up to Kentucky, we passed a sign that said "Tattoos while you wait." Now, I think of tattoos as Flannery O'Connor territory, but I might have to use that. I do enjoy those absurd things and I play with them. But I don't intend it as a spoof. It just comes out that way. It's not ever my intention to poke fun at someone through my fiction. It comes out that way while I'm trying to accomplish something else, while I'm just trying to reveal the world through this character's eyes.

WDB: Your first novel reminded me of *Huckleberry Finn*, in a way. The narrator is limited, doesn't always get the joke. She tells us things and apparently doesn't see the irony. And so the reader has a little sense of watching the world through the eyes of the character who is not seeing everything the reader is seeing.

ED: I do like to work with an ironic gap. I like that space that irony gives you. It's like looking at things from two points of view at once. I like that. It's a fun place to be in. But for me it has to do with trying to reveal perceptions and the differences between perception and reality rather than trying to get a jab in at Oprah or whatever. Although when it comes out that way, I don't mind it at all.

WDB: But when you have a narrator who's living in a culture that gets its wisdom from Oprah, and that wisdom clearly has not given her the substance to live well, that does become part of the point of the book.

ED: Yes. But it's too easy to decide to take a jab at Oprah.

WDB: The publishing history of *Many Things Have Happened Since He Died* is amazing in itself. The publisher just snapped it up. No rejection letter. Was there any reticence at all? Did they ask you to rewrite anything?

ED: The only suggestion they had was to put the other voices in italics. And I think it needed that clarification. I didn't fully understand the suggestion at first. I wish now that I had understood more fully what my editor was saying. I do think that the ending is the weakest part of that book. I'm not going to ever rewrite it, but I learned a lot from that book.

WDB: The ending is weak because the reader doesn't quite understand the motivation, doesn't see why the narrator decides to keep going?

ED: Somehow what's really happening in her loses focus at the end. She doesn't want to think about herself. She wants to rewrite the book. But somehow I think the novel should also get at what's really happening in her. We need to see where this emotional journey has taken her. I think it cheats just a little bit at the end.

WDB: I get the sense that the narrator narrowly escapes. She's escaped suicide. She's escaped various kinds of disaster. And she's going to be okay, barely okay, but she's sort of sneaked through. By keeping in the edits, you suggest that the past is important. That seems to me to be a pretty dramatic theme in this book. You even have one chapter that's just a blank page. What did the editors think about that?

ED: Oh, they loved that. I think if you like the book, you like that. If you get the book, you get it. That didn't seem to any of us to be an option to rewrite that because it is intrinsically part of the book. I was lucky in my editor.

WDB: Is it fair to say you merge memoir and novel? Some critics label you as a writer of autobiographical fiction.

ED: No. It is a fictionalization of a lot of issues that were very personal to me, but I'm not her and those things didn't happen to me. I don't see it as a memoir at all.

WDB: Why do you think people thought that?

ED: I guess the narrator's insistence that this is a memoir was convincing.

WDB: You take your title for *Break the Heart of Me* from Langston Hughes, who was writing of his love-hate relationship with the South. You have a character in the novel, Miller, the RCA vice president, who according to Sylvia "doesn't belong in the South." Then she hates herself for having that attitude. Do you feel some of that ambivalence about the South? Do you think of yourself as a southerner?

ED: Yes. I was born in Birmingham in 1962. The riots happened when I was a year old. I think it's impossible to be born there at that time in history and not be ambivalent about your home. What is this place where you spent your childhood completely oblivious to the terrible things that were happening? But they weren't happening in my consciousness, and I found out about them much later. I was in graduate school before I read Martin Luther King's "Letter from a Birmingham Jail." And then on a more individual level, my childhood was a time of innocence and everything, but there were other things about it that were all very painful. So I have the same feelings about my personal history as about my geographical history. I will always think of myself as a southerner. When I lived in Ohio, I never felt like I was home there. And as soon as I moved to Louisiana, I did.

WDB: Did you think about what it meant to be southern for the first time when you were living in Ohio? Or had you clarified that at Emory or Vanderbilt?

ED: Well, I guess I'd thought about it but had not come up with very much. It was hard to get a perspective on that. I still get asked about the qualities in my work that other people perceive as southern. I'm just trying to write about human beings as I understand them.

And I guess the human beings I understand best are southerners, but I don't think they are uniquely southern. The things that I came to understand about the South while living in Ohio were the things that I love about it. I think almost all southerners feel this sense of guilt for the South's past and a resentment of that guilt because I didn't do it. It's hard to try to look at the South from a non-southerner's eyes and see beyond the history of racism and the poverty. There's a lot more to the South, and those things exist elsewhere in the country. I think the South becomes a scapegoat in a lot of ways.

WDB: Many contemporary novels strike me as issue novels. I sense this a bit in Dorothy Allison or Barbara Kingsolver. I talked about this with Doris Betts, whose novel *Souls Raised from the Dead* centers on an issue of medical ethics. I always wonder what comes first, the issue or the story. You seem to be saying that you just let characters live, and whatever comes in comes in.

ED: Yes. I wrote eighty pages of *Break the Heart of Me* from the twelve-year-old girl's point of view. Then I didn't know where to go with that book. Later, in another kind of rush, I wrote two molestation scenes which are in a very different voice because they are retrospective. And then twenty-three-year-old Sylvia is another voice. So for a long time I had all these voices telling the same story, but I couldn't figure out the structure of the book. I was reading about molestation and its effects, and in that reading you end up reading *Sybil* and the *Three Faces of Eve*. I thought, "What if I have a narrator with multiple personality disorder?" Finally, I figured out the structure. Sometimes it's when she's twelve and sometimes it's when she's twenty-three. But it was a very organic process. It definitely had nothing to do with me searching out the issues.

WDB: Did it come as easily as the first book? It sounds like there were lots of stops and starts in the second book.

ED: This is complicated, because I was writing *The Last Southern Gentleman* at the same time. And it would not work. In writing *Break the Heart of Me*, I would slip back into that place where dreams come from. So the one book was working and the other wasn't. I could feel the difference.

WDB: How long did *Break the Heart of Me* take?

109

ED: I think it took a couple of years. Four, if you count *The Last Southern Gentleman*, which I think was part of the process of writing the book. And the book I'm writing now is the same thing. I wrote another book for two years; now this book [*How to Get to the Magic Kingdom*] is going to take me probably one year to write.

WDB: So you write two for every one that appears? I hope you don't do this through your entire career! Talk about this new one.

ED: I've got a little over a hundred pages. I just started in October. It's another southern female narrator, and it has the same interior quality as my first two novels. My agent says it's another Betsy Dewberry character, but it's not the same. This narrator has been in a bad marriage for a number of years and is on her own for the first time. She's struggling to come to terms with her identity and with God because she has grown up believing that divorce is wrong, and finally she says, "I doubt God thinks too much of me, but I don't think too much of Him either, because if He wants me to be in this marriage for the rest of my life He doesn't give a damn about me." I think it's going to come around to a kind of spiritual and sexual awakening book. And this is a kind of journey that I guess I'm interested in because it happens a lot in my fiction, but she is having to move from one understanding of God to another and from one understanding of sexuality to another. So it sounds similar to what I've done before, but it feels different to me. She's a different person.

WDB: Was *Break the Heart of Me* angrier in some way than *Many Things Have Happened Since He Died?*

ED: Probably. I was angrier.

WDB: In the first book, it seems as if you restrained yourself a bit, especially on the religious side. There was a sense of, "Well, maybe they're right." But in the second book it was, "No, they're wrong." I remember Sylvia saying, "Those TV preachers. I wish I was as rich as they are." There's more anger, more cynicism. Do you think that's a fair reading?

ED: Yes, probably so. And I think this book that I'm writing now is less angry. I'm certain of that. I think this new book is going to be a book of redemption. I don't see *Break the Heart of Me* as being a spiritually redemptive book. But it does have that "Amazing Grace" passage at the end.

WDB: There's a spiritual longing in the book. There's Bible verses and hymns. The role hymns have played in Sylvia's life keeps floating in. And there's the clear difference between rejecting institutional Christianity and God.

ED: Yes. But I think for Sylvia, it's a matter of trying to salvage what she can out of the religion that has ultimately left her very angry. And finally she does salvage a few good things: hymns, the consciousness of grace, and the possibility of healing. But I think this new book is moving from salvage to a fuller kind of redemption.

WDB: Yes. *Break the Heart of Me* is a movement toward something. Sylvia emerges toward grace, toward forgiveness, for everyone except the grandfather. There's some catharsis there. As with the first novel, we sense that she's going to be okay.

ED: This new book doesn't even start with doubt. It starts with a need for redemption instead of a need to figure it out. She's kind of moved all the way through her doubts until she's to the point where she just barely believes. It feels to me like she's moving toward an understanding of the consequences of the absence of God in her life; the other two characters didn't get that far.

WDB: She's further along on the journey?

ED: Maybe so. But who knows? By the time I finish the book, it might be a completely different thing.

WDB: I know you spoke at the Milton Center last year on the same program with Annie Dillard. What did you talk about there?

ED: Well, we were just talking about the relationship between words and God. When I was writing *Break the Heart of Me*, I had to come to terms with the fact that I was molested as a child. So I didn't know how to talk about that book honestly without talking about that and what that did to my faith. It rocked my faith pretty severely, of course. I grew up believing in a God who would never give me more than I could bear. Then I realized that all the time I had been believing that, I was being molested. It reshaped the way I understood the world. So I just talked about that process, which for me is ongoing. At that point, it was still a pretty raw wound.

WDB: Talk a little bit about the playwriting thing. I know almost nothing about that. You did an adaptation of *Many Things Have Happened Since He Died* for the stage?

ED: Somebody in Atlanta did it. I wanted to be more involved in that process and felt shoved out. I really wanted the ending rewritten for the play and was not given the opportunity. I saw the play, and it was a good production, but I felt I was losing artistic control of my work. The last contract they asked me to sign gave them permission to turn it into a musical without even telling me, much less consulting me. A musical! And even though only three sentences were added by the adaptor, he was to own half the movie rights to the book after twenty-one performances. Literally every piece of dialogue was straight from the book. I never signed anything for them to have permission beyond that. For me it was not about credit; it was about control. My agent didn't know what to do. I didn't know what to do, but I decided to give it a try on my own. The Humana Festival people gave me a chance. They commissioned a ten-minute play for last year's festival. On the basis of that, they commissioned *Flesh and Blood* for this year. I feel so grateful to be here now.

WDB: So *Flesh and Blood* has been how long in the writing?

ED: Well, at that point I was writing another play out of my head. It was called *Baggage* and it was about five people whose luggage is lost at LaGuardia Airport. My cast included a snake-handling preacher whose snake didn't arrive. A taxidermist is there for a competition, and his entry doesn't arrive. And I had a suicidal divorcee, and more. I think that was a necessary process because what I was trying to do was to learn how to tell a story through dialogue without access to internal consciousness. I had to learn how to move people around on the stage. It's a very different process, with one set and a limited number of characters. So that was a learning process for me, but I sent it to Actor's Theater and the director called me and said, "This isn't working." He gave me a crash course in playwriting. He told me some other things that I needed to know. By that point I was working toward a deadline. I had another month. I was really discouraged because I had worked hard on that play. And I began to think, "Maybe I should just tear this thing apart and rethink it." But the problems with the play were organic, too. Part of the problem was that the characters didn't know or care about each other, so there wasn't conflict between characters. Each one had his or her own kind of emotional arc through the play, but they each had to do it separately. That doesn't work very well on the stage, because they become five unrelated monologues almost.

WDB: So you started over with *Flesh and Blood* and your characters are members of a family?

ED: Yes. And they have a stake in one another's lives. So I wrote a draft in two weeks. And the whole thing took twenty-seven days.

WDB: So you continue the two-for-one habit? Do you literally discard the manuscripts, or do you just file them away?

ED: Well, I haven't actually thrown them away, but I'll have to throw them away before I die, so somebody won't try to dig them out. But I think I am learning more about the artistic process, so I can become a little more efficient. Also, I understand that if I have to write some work and throw it out before I get to where I'm trying to get to, then that just might be part of my process. I hope I can get better at knowing when it's not working.

WDB: But you see yourself going on in playwriting?

ED: Yes. But unlike Bob, who can keep two projects going at once, I'll go back and forth for extended periods.

WDB: As you did with your dissertation and *Many Things Have Happened Since He Died*?

ED: Yes. Bob can write his fiction in the morning, work on his movie in the afternoon, and then read over his fiction again before bed so it will be in his mind as he sleeps. I can't do it that way.

WDB: The Pulitzer has clearly made a remarkable difference for Bob in terms of his career. You've had your own successes — prizes, honors, good reviews, and all that. What has that done?

ED: I don't have that much success, that many people pulling on me. My success has freed me up to be able to write full-time.

WDB: And given you confidence?

ED: Yes. If I hadn't had the two well-received novels, I wouldn't have had the courage to write a play. I wouldn't have believed that I could do it. I was afraid I couldn't do it, but I had enough confidence that I was willing to give it a shot. And I don't think I would have done that without the previous success. But really, in every novel you start over, in the actual writing process. Having been well reviewed for the last novel doesn't make a whole lot of difference.

WDB: Do you ever feel overwhelmed by the sense of how important a book can be?

ED: Well, I don't feel overwhelmed, but I do feel that there are moments in the writing process when you feel you are being given gifts. If the words are gifts, then write them down gratefully. In that sense, some of the insights the books have into the world are things that I wasn't able to articulate outside of the books. There is something about the process that feels beyond me as an individual.

WDB: What role can books play in our kind of culture? Do you think of somebody out there picking up this book and having his or her life changed by it?

ED: I don't think of it as a goal. But people do come up to me and tell me that is true of my books. "You have told my story for me" is the highest compliment that I can get. "You have spoken for me something that I wasn't able to speak for myself." So, yes, I really do believe that books do that. People complain about MTV and everything, but there is something in the human soul that yearns for story, for quiet, for a deeper understanding of the human condition. Books provide those things more than any other medium.

WDB: When someone says you have spoken their story, you feel humbled and surprised?

ED: I can't say that anymore I feel surprised, because I've heard it so often, but in every case I feel grateful. Those are moments of real grace from God, because where else would it be from?

CLYDE EDGERTON

1985 — *Raney*
1987 — *Walking Across Egypt*
1988 — *Floatplane Notebooks*
1991 — *Killer Diller*
1992 — *In Memory of Junior*
1995 — *Redeye*
1997 — *Where Trouble Sleeps*

CLYDE EDGERTON

Dusty's Flying Taxi

"Raney, if what you grew up with was all right for everyone,
the world would be quite different."
"I'll say. And for the better."

Beside the couch where he writes his stories, Clyde Edgerton has taped
up a sentence from Paul West: "Anyone who is a pilot is never only
a pilot, but navigator, geographer, engineer, hermit, mystic, beloved
explorer of God." The sentence fits.

Edgerton takes chances in his stories. *Raney* chronicles the first
months of the marriage of an unsophisticated country girl and her
big-city, liberal husband. By the end, we've laughed at and with both
of them. *Walking Across Egypt* offers a Bible-reading literalist who is
bent on doing good. And she does. The chances taken in *Floatplane
Notebooks* include a talking wisteria vine and a reaction to the 1960s,
complete with a journey to and through the Vietnam experience. *Killer
Diller* reprises characters from *Walking Across Egypt* but centers on a
caustic look at the power and hypocrisy of certain religious institutions.
In Memory of Junior, labeled "a larky, down-home chronicle" and "a
sunny, funny anthology" by the *New York Times* reviewer, circles on the

117

aphorism "You're history longer than you're fact." And *Redeye* is a western, of all things. Edgerton has paid close attention to his own history, and his readers have been the beneficiaries.

I spoke with Clyde Edgerton in his office on ninth street in Durham, North Carolina, in August 1992. His office is advertised merely as "Dusty's Flying Taxi," and the guys at the eatery next door have heard that "he's around here somewhere." His wit, his dubiousness about neat categories, and his sense of what a writer is called to do all found their ways into our talk.

▼   ▼

WDB: I see pictures of Eudora Welty, William Faulkner, and Mark Twain here on your walls. Good company. And you've been compared to at least one of them. How does it feel to find yourself in the same paragraph with Mark Twain?

CE: I can't complain. I wouldn't complain about that for a minute. He was one of the first people I really enjoyed. I enjoyed reading fiction before I started writing it. I think I probably had some secret wish to eventually become a writer, but I was thirty-three or thirty-four before I started seriously. Reading Twain was a delight, and it seemed that my most important experiences were reading fiction. I think that's how I ended up writing it — because the books I read were so important.

WDB: There's a lot of Mark Twain in your books. Meredith and Mark in *Floatplane Notebooks*. And there's sort of Huck and Jim stuff going on with Wesley and Vernon in *Killer Diller* when Vernon turns out to be superior to Wesley. I love the joke there about using the car for the can opener.

CE: I like that one, too. Originally, Vernon was not in *Killer Diller*. In the early drafts of that book, I had an evangelist. I'd met him once when I was in the mountains by myself. I had started to leave this little breakfast cafe, and in walks this guy wearing a blue suit and a red tie and carrying a red Bible under his arm. I stopped and watched him go to a booth, take out a pack of cigarettes, light one up, order a cup of coffee, and put his Bible down on the table. I couldn't get over this character. He had a kind of a flat red face and looked mean, but he had this Bible, and he was smoking cigarettes, and he was so dressed up. So I hung around for a bit to hear him talk. I didn't get anything out of him, but as I drove away I could see that I had to write about him. First I wrote a short story which was no good. But as I started writing about Wesley and Phoebe in *Killer Diller,* I put him in because I wanted to write about him. He was kind of a confidant or advisor to Wesley, but he never did work because I never knew what his theology was. I couldn't figure it out. I think he was so much the fundamentalist that I had trouble with it, almost personally. So I just decided to get rid of him. So then this Vernon character came along. I didn't know exactly how it was going to fit, but I just started the book with Vernon. It was much better having him than this other guy; I don't know what will become of this other guy.

WDB: The evangelist is still floating around out there?

CE: He wants to be written about, but he didn't cooperate the first time. I just couldn't get him right.

WDB: I know bits and pieces about your background: you were born around here, your flying, the well incident, the Eudora Welty stuff. All the business that reviewers and interviews get into with you. What else can you say about your background that brought you to writing?

CE: I once saw an article in *Southern Magazine* about being born late. I feel connected, more so than a lot of people I think, to the stories of my grandfather and great-grandfather. These go way back, of course. It's almost like I'm in the wrong generation; I'm spanning these two generations. My mother is really as old as a grandmother, and her father was as old as a grandfather, and I'm close to that grandfather, although I never met him. Somehow the years 1904-1920 are interesting to me simply because of my mother's stories about my aunts and uncles growing up. As I hear them talking about growing up, I can visualize those times and places better than later times.

WDB: What about the religious background and how it shows up in your books?

CE: Well, there is that, but I need to say at the outset, I am not an essayist or a preacher. So I'm not about the task of purposefully, consciously trying to persuade in any direction. My joy comes from describing in fiction. I believe it's true that people write novels out of different reasons, and some have a kind of mission in mind. Maybe it is related to a specific idea about God or maybe vaguely connected to justice in some way. I don't have a clear mission in terms of communicating ideas or themes. That doesn't mean it doesn't happen. I'm aware that the novelist becomes a part of the novel in ways he or she is not aware of. I'm interested in telling stories that entertain. Beyond that, what I want the reader to do is to keep reading. I'm interested personally in my characters. In general I want my plots to be a consequence of character rather than the other way around. There are those God-backing novels, but I don't think one of my purposes as a novelist is to write those sort of novels. My purpose is to write stories that do to readers what Mark Twain, Eudora Welty, Flannery O'Connor, and those people have done to me. I wanted to have that duplicated in other people, so I took it upon myself selfishly to enjoy putting onto others what had been put onto me. That meant letting my characters do the work.

Now, of course it's true and I understand that whatever made me up will in one way or another get into the novels, and what made me up is certainly connected in many ways to religion. I grew up in a Southern Baptist church and in a family which was regular in church attendance; that's the best way to put it. We were not fanatical about religion. There were people in our church who were a little more fanatical and some a little less. We were kind of on and off when it came to prayer meetings and the like. Once in a while we went. I haven't talked much anywhere about the early stages of my life, say from the time I was six to the time I was fourteen. I remember I had a recurring physical problem where I would find myself unable to urinate and would be rushed to the hospital. It was scary, and as I think about that I realize that that had more of an impact than I had remembered. I had just kind of forgotten all about that. Those were scary events. And when I was seven, I joined the church, or accepted Jesus, or was saved, or whatever the term was. In the Baptist church it was "saved." I was seven. It was an emotional experience and I cried.

And I can remember what I said; my mother wrote down what I said to the preacher, and I did a little testimony afterwards. That was the big experience of my religious life.

WDB: Were you drawing on that some with Mark in *Floatplane Notebooks* where he rededicates his life?

CE: Yes. I don't think I ever did that, but I remember being very conscious of ages. For example, my mother and father had each been saved and joined the church at twelve, so I headed that off by five years. And then I remember keeping an eye on all my friends to be sure they did it by the time they were twelve or fourteen, and most of them did. I remember being conscious of that. I remember Sunday school and the ritual and emotion at the end of the service when the call to come forward came. I remember being aware of what was going on, but what I am most aware of now is the presence and the continued friendship of the elderly people in the church. When I go back to that community to read and do some music, I am struck that some of those people have read all my books and may have philosophical reasons to shun me. But they choose not to. It seems to me the strength of those kind of people is that the concrete person stands to them solid and full of value, and whatever ideas or abstract thinking that person may be doing or may have done seems to be refreshingly unimportant.

WDB: You go back on the day they decorate the graves?

CE: I go back to visit my mother quite often, and also for funerals. When someone in my family dies, I get a reunion with a lot of people I haven't seen for several years. When I was small I saw these people every week. Some of them have died now, a good many, and some are dying as we speak. It is interesting from my perspective because I've been away, first to school and then the Air Force. Now I go back and experience these people and see how valuable they are and how valuable they were. When I left home to go to school in Chapel Hill, I'd be at home occasionally and I'd go to church. But then when I went into the Air Force, I was pretty much on my own. I began to move away from some of the political stances of my church. I remember the racism which was evident in the church and some of the intolerances which I believed I didn't have. I was judgmental about that and other things. Finally I began attending an Episcopal church. That's what I do now.

121

WDB: Was there a time when you were angry about the Baptist background and all that?

CE: Oh, yeah, and I still am. So many people in the national eye claim to be speaking for the Jesus of the New Testament. Given what I read that Jesus said, what these people are saying and claim in his name seems to be ludicrous. I see an acceptance of that by people of my religious background. I have no doubt that most of the people in that church that I grew up in are not uncomfortable with what I am uncomfortable with. It is up to me to decide how to think about that, and I am slowly coming to a kind of intellectual rejection. But I hope to continue to be comfortable with these same people on the basis of all the rest we have in common or may have in common. And I do admire in these people a certain kind of loyalty to ideas. That we do share.

WDB: So there's much that you do still appreciate?

CE: Yes. That background, that upbringing, those people.

WDB: My own sense is that the satire of pious fundamentalism in the worst sense is somehow sharper in *Killer Diller* than in *Raney*. Was this because of the turmoil at Campbell University after *Raney* was published? Are you trying to expose the mentality that you were victimized by at Campbell?

CE: Oh, yes — the Campbell experience. The Campbell experience certainly had a lot to do with *Killer Diller*. That's one reason I feel less comfortable as an artist with that book, because I was scratching my own itch. The source of that book was different from the source of the other books. I had firsthand knowledge when I wrote that book that I didn't have when I wrote *Raney* about how organizations can operate through fear. Although I had studied that in education and administration, was in the military for five years, and had worked at four or five colleges, I was nonetheless somewhat surprised. Power can really be misused.

WDB: Things were better at Saint Andrew's Presbyterian College?

CE: Yes. Much better. They had a tradition of writing dirty books and not worrying about it. They had a tradition of tolerance of written ideas in fiction and nonfiction among their own faculty, so that was never a problem.

WDB: So-called popular Christian fiction is an interesting phenomenon just now. I don't know if you've heard of Janet Oke or Frank Peretti — the sort of books one gets at the religious bookstore. There is, apparently, a good bit of writing aimed at the Christian audience. I am uncomfortable somehow with the notion of Christian fiction; I don't like Christian as an adjective there. But others — and dare I number you among them? — seem to write out of the context of the fabric of faith without being propagandistic, or doctrinaire, or simplistic.

CE: I would hope that what you feel, what draws you, is a consequence of how I've written characters or how my characters have behaved. The whole question of how the behavior of fictional characters reflects either the moral beliefs or the values of the writer is a fascinating question. I don't mind talking about that. I can't deny that I wrote the work, of course, but I'm working to make characters real, and I'm working to respond to human beings in a story rather than fashioning some kind of hopeful way for people to live. I know that justice and injustice and racism and fairness and the use of power are matters of concern to me. One reason I got involved in the controversy over my book was that I found myself a victim. I was stuck with a two-year-old child, and my wife had just finished her job, and Campbell holds my contract behind its back and says, "We had some problems with your book." It was a pretty clear reason to fight. So I got involved in that because I thought I was being unjustly treated. It's difficult for a white male who's not poor to find himself in a situation where he's mistreated. And this shows up in *Killer Diller*, but it's not the aim of the book.

WDB: I guess most of your readers started with *Raney*. It's difficult to understand what the fuss was about at Campbell. I like Raney's naturalness as opposed to Charles's artificiality. She's supper and he's dinner. He's books and she's common sense.

CE: Yeah, I was just thinking about Raney as I left to come here. I saw a neighbor who was going on vacation, and he was taking scuba diving stuff. I said, "You taking your frog feet?" and he didn't know what I was talking about. He said, "What's frog feet? Oh, you mean fins?"

WDB: Didn't the folks understand that the satire goes both ways in the novel? Or did they think you were just blasting the Baptists?

CE: I'm not sure that they understood the satire at all. There were certain things that hit some of them, and those talked to the others. They were unable to read it as fiction, because I don't think they read fiction very much. The word satire is uncomfortable for them. I don't think they've had much experience with satire. And there was drinking going on and sexual activity, even though it was between Raney and her husband. The people at Campbell mentioned three problems they had with the book: it was, they said, "a caricature of the body of Christ, it featured a clash between old and new with the old being replaced by the new, and it featured the use of alcohol." So they clearly did not see how I'd tried to be honest about both sides. That shows you right there that they didn't get both sides of it. I had worked so hard to get the balance right between Raney and Charles. I've looked at some of the early letters that my publishers sent, and I see the work I did to make Charles more likable. I think the book might have been more to the university's liking early on, before I built Charles up a little more. Deep down I wanted to let Raney tell the story, and I was having a good time using my native dialect for the first time — seeing the power in that. It started as a bunch of short stories and then developed into a novel. What I wanted people to say is "I really didn't like Raney's ideas, but I liked her." That goes back to what I was talking about before but didn't realize it until this interview — to the best in these people that I grew up with. Those people, even if they've read *Raney*, and some of them have and have every reason to wonder why I said this or that. But those people respond to me as a person rather than as someone who has ideas. That's good and bad. That's probably what some people thought about Hitler, for example. Think of him as a person, rather than his ideas, and you're in trouble. In another way I like the notion, and it was my aim in the book to get people to say "I liked her but couldn't stand her ideas."

WDB: I had dinner the other night with a woman who had read the book and didn't have much use for Raney. My own sense was that Raney was changing dramatically. Obviously, both Charles and Raney change; they wind up going to an Episcopal church. But, I know, Johnny

Dobbs, the black man, ends up staying at the Ramada Inn. Some things change. Some don't.

CE: Yes, Johnny Dobbs — a black godfather — that was a big move. In one draft I spent more time on that, but I changed my mind.

WDB: These people that you talk about going back to see at your mother's, I suspect they would not be movers and shakers in the Baptist Convention. Did you get mail from people objecting, say, to the feed bag scene in *Raney*, specific things like that? I guess I'm asking about audience. From whom do you get mail?

CE: With *Raney*, I received only a few negative letters about the language or whatever. And I still get a few on the various books now and then. One elderly woman wrote and said I didn't have to use that sort of language. I had one from a fanatic, funny stamps all over the envelope. There was a review that said that *Raney* was trash. But I've heard from Baptist ministers who say they've used part of *Raney*. *Raney* and *Walking Across Egypt* are being used in Methodist and Baptist churches, I understand.

WDB: A *Los Angeles Times* reviewer called you an "idiosyncratic writer." What does that mean? Do you have any sense that you are out of the mainstream in some way? If so, does that bother you?

CE: I guess I may be out of the mainstream. But I've had letters from people about *Raney*, people from Canada and Brazil, even New Jersey, all sorts of people, saying that Raney's family is like their own. That's refreshing to hear because it gets us beyond the southern business to something that might have to do with hope and fear. Many people have said this is a true book.

WDB: So you don't really think of yourself as a southern writer any more than you do a Christian writer?

CE: I think of myself as a southern writer more than I do as a Christian writer. I just have a problem with Christian as an adjective. It throws me. But an article that's recently out in a book on the University of North Carolina Press discusses me in those terms.

WDB: What is there about this area of the country? Peggy Payne, Fred Chappell, Reynolds Price, Doris Betts, Ferrol Sams, Kaye Gibbons, Lee Smith. Why so many writers around here?

CE: My theory is that this area was predominantly agricultural and now it's academic — all these universities. People with agricultural backgrounds ended up getting ideas. Tension was produced, and one of the easiest ways to get rid of the tension is through writing stories. And then there's people like Doris Betts, a good teacher. And Tim McLaurin and Randall Kenan. Have you read any of Randall Kenan's stuff? He's a black writer who grew up in North Carolina. He's got a book called *Let the Dead Bury Their Dead*. There's a lot of religious influence there.

WDB: You've done a good bit of teaching too. Besides Campbell, you've taught at St. Andrew's Presbyterian College and Duke University. Do you teach creative writing? How do you go about that? Walker Percy says teaching writing is like the mysterious process of entrail reading or chicken fighting or something like that. You say Doris Betts is a good creative writing teacher; what do you admire in the way she works? How do you go about that process?

CE: I never took a course from Doris, but I went to a workshop once. The things she said about writing struck me. I remember someone asked her why she was a writer. She said there were "stories she didn't want to die with." I thought that was pretty interesting. Talking about fiction, she said it could indeed be moral, but you had to give the bad guy or the bad woman all the advantages you could to avoid the white hats and the black hats. She talked about getting two characters into the story very quickly, commonsense kind of hints like that. Be careful of flashbacks, be careful of the verb "to be," and I find myself right now writing along and remembering her words. I'll have something like "He was there," rather than "He stood there." I'll go back and change it because of these little things that she said. She also had a form for analyzing short stories which I used last time I taught fiction. I've taught fiction maybe four or five times — creative writing. Each time has been quite different. I have moved away from having students read the stories aloud, which is a common practice. I think peer response is good; however, I think that the last person for a writer to listen to about his or her writing is another writer. Editors and teachers are usually more objective because of their experience with stories. What I try to do now is talk about image as the beginning of a story, not an idea or a plot but an image that either involves or is immediately followed by a character. So I send them out to try to become conscious of anything, whether it's a word or a phrase which someone utters, which can be an image in a way, or just a kind of snapshot that strikes them. I tell them not to worry about why it strikes them but to write it down and take those images and slowly find out what's inside them. This is why I try to stay away from ideas. You must not try to be too fine as to why the image strikes you. Why the image strikes me has already been set up by some mystery, which has to do with things that you're probably interested in as an interviewer, but as a writer all I'm interested in is that it struck me. So I write it down, and often it's an image. I try to get them thinking in that way, and I didn't know what would happen by talking to these people that way. I didn't know whether they'd be completely open-mouthed and confused the entire semester, but enough of them told me that it was helpful to them that I would do it this way again.

I also have them adapt stories that they like by authors they like. Sometimes I use a reader's theater format, because that's one way I got introduced to Eudora Welty. Doing "Why I Live at the P.O." helped me hear the language over and over. I got an appreciation of the story by being a character in the story. Adapting the story to an oral format was meaningful, so I ask my students to do that. So we work from image, and read aloud. In the last part of the course, they analyze a published short story to see if they can find out who they like. It's difficult because they're reading polished, finished stories by very good writers. I try to make them understand that when they analyze a published story, they're beginning to see how to revise. So as they talk about dialogue and scene and do summaries, I tell them to go over the text the way they would go over a first draft. What it's all about is rewriting. Most writers revise, revise, revise, so I try to teach revision through analyzing finished stories, working with images, and the reader's theater.

WDB: You have degrees in English and education. I know you've taught a good bit. There's even a gentle satire on American education that runs through a lot of your books. For example, I remember the debate that Charles has with somebody at dinner about how important it is to know the state capitals. Mattie in *Walking Across Egypt*, a character tremendously endearing to the reader, is pretty suspicious of what goes on in the schools. They don't teach people what to do with their hats anymore, she says. I assume you're sort of spoofing what you've picked up along the way?

CE: Well I know my characters well enough to know what they will or will not say, but I have to choose this or that. I'm very much a disciple of John Dewey even though he gets a bad rap from just about everybody nowadays. He had a lot of common sense about how to educate children. It is based on an approach that demands structure and hard work from teachers. These days it often gets translated into relational groups and all that. I wanted to be a teacher before I wanted to be a writer. I think I was interested in the mental part of it a lot. I never thought of college as teaching; I thought of the demands of high school as what teaching really is. For me, teaching students who are curious about a subject is not teaching. The tough job is teaching those who definitely don't want to be there; that's when you start teaching. My intellectual thought and learning and talking and reading had to do with getting high school people interested in English. So I had my heroes like James Moffett, who wrote a lot about teaching reading. I used his book a good bit. I used Dorothy Heathcote's ideas about teaching drama through improvisation. She'd put children into various situations, say, in a wheelchair, and get kids interested that way. A very excited kind of learning would come out of it. I suppose I was liberal in terms of my educational views; I had crazy ideas, you know. I was always interested in the methods; I was fanatical about getting students interested. So I had an opportunity to confront in all kinds of ways some of the stubbornness of the institution. We don't like to change. It saves institutions, but it is often a kind of stupidity and doesn't help. It's kind of fun to run up against it.

WDB: It might be argued that *Raney* and *Killer Diller* are both in some way about how to read the Bible. I remember when Charles first introduces into Raney's life the cultural boundness of the biblical text. And obviously Wesley figures out that there's two different creation stories in Genesis, and everything gets complicated from there on. Wesley is also the one that keeps holding to the general principle in Matthew 25, which he's learned from Mattie. Wesley insists that "God is love." But one of the college administrators tells him that's not enough to say. Is your own view close to Wesley's?

CE: When I started writing *Killer Diller*, I had to go back and read the Bible. I had never read the Bible all the way through, and here I was confronted by a character who needed to read the Bible. I couldn't have him read the Bible if I didn't read it. And it was a dual task; I was reading it for me and for Wesley. It was as though as I went along with Wesley. When he wanted to run off at the mouth about what he was reading in the Bible, I let him do it. It was a lot of fun because Wesley was a little more confident than I would have been; I would've been a little more intellectual, a little more constrained, a little more whatever, but he could just go on and on. So I got to Leviticus and got bogged down, just like everyone else, so I didn't read anymore. But I did jump over to the Gospels and read those straight through. So I had Genesis, Exodus, and the Gospels. By the time I finished those, I had far more than Wesley needed. I'll need a reason, another book maybe, to make me go back and read other parts, but I do want to. I am interested in Samuel, Psalms, and other things. But I have watched people use the Bible to back up their own beliefs, and I have had those moments of amazement and inspiration at certain passages, so I end up more like Wesley.

I think most of us have a period of enlightenment that lasts from the time we are about thirteen to nineteen and again from somewhere between thirty-five and fifty. Most people go through these enlightened periods where they know everything about everything. During my period of enlightened enlightenment, I was cold to the Bible, because I was cold to the way people handled the Bible. Then when I was able to start reading it like I did with Wesley, which wasn't that long ago, I was perhaps coming out of my period of enlightened enlightenment. I discovered an amazing document. So many exciting stories. It's like Wesley says: it's funny what they teach in these little conservative Sunday school classes.

WDB: Your novels, by talking about Noah and Lot and David and those flawed Old Testament superstars, imply a criticism of our current talk about family values and piety. Our religious culture talks about getting it right when those Bible stories are all about getting it wrong. But things somehow turn out okay in the end.

CE: Yes. And what you can do with those stories is so much fun. I'm thinking about the story of Tamar and her father-in-law, Judah, for example. Remember how he had slept with her without recognizing who she was? And he'd given her his staff and belt as a kind of pledge. Later, she turns up pregnant, and Judah is righteously indignant and ready to burn her for her immorality. That is, until Tamar shows him the staff and belt of the one who made her pregnant. Suddenly it's "Wait a minute boys; let's not burn her!" Those stories are so dramatic. But I never heard that story mentioned. The sex part just had to be left out, I guess.

WDB: Well, the sex stuff is part of the irony in *Raney*. There's so much openness there; I mean they talk about anything at the dinner table. There's that sort of southern openness and frankness and directness on everything except sexuality. That's just a closed shop. Charles does his duty and you just aren't supposed to talk about it. Is that because of the influence of the church in Raney's life? Is that what she's been taught about sex?

CE: Since this is an interview for public consumption, I have no comment.

WDB: Well, for Raney it's such a joyless business. Have we just got it all wrong over the years?

CE: That subject has been pretty well tracked by historians and others who have written volumes about the Victorian period and all that. The subject of sex got to be like the subject of war in many families. When I think about Raney's family or the family in *Floatplane Notebooks*, I see that no one would talk. In *Floatplane*, Meredith is going to Vietnam and nobody talks about it. I've heard of so-called New England families where folks would sit at the supper table and talk politics every night. I admire that and wistfully think about it. But I don't think that's very true in southern families. War was certainly something never talked about in my family, one way or the other. And sex. When my mother was growing up, she thought babies were found under collard leaves. She had actually looked for a baby there. I talk about some of that at the end of *Floatplane Notebooks*, some of these misconceptions created by silence. But I guess it was best that she did shut up and not talk to me about sex. Now I try to talk to my daughter, but when you look at it over a relatively short period of time, you stop complaining about your upbringing.

Just a few days ago my daughter found a jock strap in my truck. She couldn't figure it out, but she saw immediately that I was embarrassed. Of course one of her friends was with her, so she tried holding it out the window and wanted to know all about it. So when her friend got out, I explained to her exactly what a jock strap is and how it works. So we're picking up on all that. We go from a collard patch to nothing to "Let's talk about it when your friend leaves."

WDB: What about the tradition of stories that tie families together. I like the Decoration Day business in *Floatplane* as a reminder of family history. Are we losing some of that?

CE: I have an innate optimism about the need for people to tell stories or hear stories. Recently I heard someone say that our need for narrative is stronger than our need for love or shelter. I can't go that far. Without love people have no reason to tell the story. Love is to be there for you when you want to tell your story. It's a concern that someone has, a pleasure in hearing you. Without that there's no love, and without that you die. Now we all have a machine to do what people used to do — talk. I'm not just yearning for yesteryear, but people have no choice today. To whom would they talk?

WDB: The landscape has changed; even the South has changed. You've got your share of Hardee's, Wal-Marts, and all that. Do you lament that?

CE: Yes. Recently I was driving to the coast to see Tim McLaurin. He's written two books you'd like — *Keeper of the Moon* and *Woodrow's Trumpet*. He's kind of a new writer. And you should read Larry Brown, that book *Facing the Music*.

Anyway, I enjoy driving to the East. You can drive to the coast and find places like they were thirty years ago. I usually go the back way and take my camera. I just visited Larry Brown in Oxford, Mississippi. He lives outside Oxford in a rural area that reminds me of what it used to be like here twenty or thirty years ago. It's changed a whole lot — starting to be like Atlanta.

WDB: One other question that gets back to the Episcopal versus Baptist business in *Raney* and to your own experience of moving from the latter to the former. Do you have any admiration, however grudg-ing, for those folks out there in the literalist crowd? I mean, as you look around you at so-called liberal Christianity do you ever lament the lack of what Raney calls "spunk"? (I remember that as her summary of the Episcopalians: they have "no spunk.") Sometimes I look over my shoulder at the pulpit-pounders of my youth and feel some ad-miration for their passion and energy.

CE: I agree 100 percent. I'm passionate about certain things, but I'm not publicly passionate the way fundamentalists preachers are. I could wish that more Episcopal priests would go out and scream about stuff. I just read a book, *Your Blues Ain't like Mine*, by Bebe Moore Campbell, an African American woman who lives in Los Angeles. She wrote a book about a murder in Mississippi in the 1950s. She shows a surprising empathy with the white wife of the white murderer. One of the great lines in the book comes when the white woman finally loses it and starts screaming and they put her away; she says, "I should have started screaming a long time ago." That is a good line. The impulse not to scream is a problem. There is a refreshing element in a show of passion, and Raney notices when the passion is missing.

WDB: Another central virtue in your books seems to be honesty. I remember Mattie, for example, teaching Wesley to look people in the eyes. Mattie is straightforward. Is trust why we admire her?

CE: I don't typically worry about my fictional characters being real people, but in some ways Mattie is like my mother. My mother is a person, like many older, southern women that I meet at readings, who will come right out and ask you whatever they want to. There's a kind of directness. It's also covering up vulnerabilities, covering up other things, but it's refreshing and I was taught that. I was not taught how to put on a condom, but I was taught how to look people in the eyes and shake their hands.

WDB: What about that title for Mattie's book, *Walking Across Egypt*? Does it simply mean doing the impossible?

CE: It was sort of unconscious. I didn't have a title for the book. I had two titles, *Slowing Down* and *Shall We Gather Together at the River*, and they were bad titles. I was looking through *The Golden Bough*, just for a reference, and came across a sentence about someone walking across Egypt for some reason. What I had in mind for a title was something like *To Kill a Mockingbird,* a title that has always struck me as being slightly offset. So I had a title without any reason to use it, and then I rewrote the book to make the title fit.

WDB: Mattie says she doesn't have any more business taking in a dog than she has walking across Egypt. That, of course, becomes the big issue of the book: Will she take in the dog, and will she take in Wesley?

CE: Yes. I had to go back and write that in. I figured that if I had her thinking about a song through the whole book and using that phrase, "walking across Egypt," it would be enough. By the time I finished the book, I had written the song "Walking across Egypt," so I put it in there at the end where they all gather around and sing it. It was one of those cases where not having a title improved the book.

WDB: There's a kind of strange violence around the edges of the book, and it's not where you'd expect it to be. The shady characters, Wesley and Lamar, are not the villains. It's the people next door who sleep with guns under their pillows.

CE: Unfortunately, the play version of the book overdid that. I didn't mean to underscore the violence so much as the humor. I was driving once with my mother, when we passed one of her neighbors walking along the road. She had on a walking outfit. I slowed up and leaned out the window and said "How you doing?" She said "Fine." She had a Kleenex in her hand; she pulled up the Kleenex, and there was a pistol. She said, "Ain't nobody gonna jump out of the woods and get me." It just blew me away. I went home and decided to play that up a bit for humor and let one of the characters sleep with a pistol.

WDB: Have you heard from Hollywood?

CE: Most of my books have been optioned at one time or still are. For every hundred books on option, maybe one gets made into a movie. *Walking Across Egypt* was on option but isn't now. *Floatplane Notebooks* was on option once and isn't now. *Raney* has been on option twice, and now a group in Atlanta has it. *Killer Diller* is now on option for the first time.

WDB: As with *Raney,* the satire in *Egypt* strikes me as two-sided. Mattie thinks the whole problem is that the world has forgotten God.

She marks the end of courtesy with the moonshot and integration; at the same time, however, she turns out to be the moral center in the story. There's something there that reminds me of *Huckleberry Finn*. Huck, clearly outside of all the institutions, turns out to be the moral center. And you have Mattie, who takes Matthew 25 literally and seriously, setting up her own ragtag feast and feeding everybody. She turns out to be the superior person in the book. You poke gentle fun at her, but she wins through somehow.

CE: She's just naive enough to practice Matthew 25. Naive in a good way. She has a lack of pretense and doesn't focus on herself and what's in it for her. Of course, there's not much in it for her. Taking in Wesley is going to mean real problems. I don't know how far readers go in figuring this out, but her own kids haven't turned out so well, and now she's trying again. If we judge Mattie, we have to say she did right; she lived what she preached. Maybe she's overly enthusiastic in seeking attention through cooking or love or whatever. But that's probably what a lot of us do. I'm sure I write books to get a kind of attention. It's part of giving and getting; it gets very complicated. And I don't know to what extent she's responsible for how those kids turned out. It's an interesting question for me.

WDB: Yes. Robert gets his ideas from *Parade* magazine, and Elaine is sort of Flannery O'Connor grotesque. She reminds me of Joy-Hulga in O'Connor's "Good Country People."

CE: Joy-Hulga is one of the best characters in modern fiction. That's one of my favorite stories too. I thought about that character a bit as I wrote *Egypt*. I remember that my idea for Elaine to be a teacher was a last-minute thing. I was so happy I thought of it.

WDB: In some ways everybody in the book is kind of a cripple. Even Mattie has weaknesses. Everybody is a cripple, but it turns out okay, somehow. And you do that in *Floatplane Notebooks*, too. Michael Pearson quotes you as saying that *Floatplane* is not an antiwar novel. I assume that's along the same lines that you've been talking here, that you didn't sit down and say "Okay I'm going to write an antiwar novel" any more than with *Killer Diller* you said "I'm going to write an anti-religious-institution novel." But you are obviously drawing on your Vietnam experience?

CE: I guess if it has to be called something, if it has to have an adjective, it wouldn't bother me to call it an antiwar novel. I would hope it would have that effect. I had written maybe ninety pages of dialogue and a little action about the war. It was a very polemic discussion among the pilots about the war which directly reflected some of my own experience over there. I threw all that out. As I worked through it, I realized that what was most true about the war was what happened at home after the war. I've always been very much impressed with Hemingway's "Soldier's Home." I was impressed with it because, the first time I read it, I didn't have any idea what it was about. I read it long before *Floatplane*, of course, but I finally realized it was about the aftermath. I realized that my book had to be about what happened at home after the war. I didn't know as I was writing it who was going to be hurt or who was going to be killed or what was going to happen. So I went through a lot of stuff before it ended up being what it was.

WDB: How do you feel now when you hear the news about war and rumors of war?

CE: When the Persian Gulf War started, I heard interviews with the pilots. That made me remember my own flight training and experience. I entered ROTC in 1962. I just wanted to fly airplanes, so I didn't look twice. In 1966 I was in Texas flying, and then I was in Japan. I never looked at the war movement except over my shoulder while I was flying this airplane, which was great fun. So by the time my thinking caught up with me, I was flying combat missions over Vietnam. I began to realize it was about much more than democracy, and I lost some friends. I was bitter. I was angry, not so much about what was happening, as about why nobody had bothered to explain it to me and help me make up my mind. Of course, that's the last thing a government is going to do when they have a war to fight. They're not likely to ask you if you want to go. They just say "go." They don't sit around at sunrise before you attack the hill and say, "Well, boys lets draw straws on who wants to attack the hill." But I was bitter about the whole thing and came back being bitter about it and couldn't even write about it. When I saw the Persian Gulf business start, and heard those fighter pilots talking, I knew what they were thinking. It was almost as if no time had passed, and they were my buddies. There they were, and I wanted to be part of it. Yet at the same time I deplored the whole idea of not continuing with the sanctions and other things to avoid the conflict.

WDB: You still fly some?

CE: Yes, but a year ago I flipped my plane on takeoff. So I haven't flown in over a year.

WDB: There's something about *Floatplane Notebooks* that makes it a different book from the other three. I'm not exactly sure what it is. The war business must be part of it, and also the Decoration Day chapters. I loved your response to the questions about your using the wisteria vine: "I didn't think Faulkner wouldn't have written about wisteria because I had. Conrad didn't not write about a ship's mast because Melville had." Did you write that?

CE: I guess I did. And you're right, it is a different book from the others. And that has to do with its history. For one thing, it took ten or eleven years to write. I wanted to write about the history of a family that resembles my own. I wanted to write about growing up; Meredith and Mark's adventures are based on some of my own. And I wanted to have something about the war in there. So I was tempted to break it down into three books. Finally, I wrote from all different points of view. After years of drafts, and after *Raney*, I finally finished it. The book is deeper; in almost physical ways, it is deeper.

WDB: And what about Decoration Day?

CE: I took my daughter when she was five or so. She just got worn out with all the stories. It just overwhelmed her. She wasn't ready for them. I remember when I was her age we'd go to the home place, and I needed to do that for her. It's a wonderful place. I'm lucky because nobody lives there and it's like the middle of a park. There's a big old wisteria vine. I guess I was pushing stories on her. There's a hill there called Sarah's hill, and there's all sorts of stories about the hill. My daughter fell off her bicycle there. So she had her dramatic experience, all right. She cut her leg, and I had to take her to the hospital; she's got that to remember. I'm sort of glad because that's exactly the one place on earth where I'd want her to take a scar from. That scar on her leg will always be with her, and it will always be from that one place. And that place is the core of my mother's family and has many other stories for me.

WDB: *Floatplane Notebooks* somehow worked more powerfully on the second reading. Was *As I Lay Dying* an influence there?

CE: *As I Lay Dying* is something I had read and did not understand the first time. So I went back and read it a character at a time. When I did it that way, I really understood it. But I knew the multiple narrator technique. *In Memory of Junior* also has multiple narrators. I never thought about making it like Faulkner. If I had, I would have made it much more confusing. I was trying to make it clear. But it just turned out that there was no other way to tell the story. It was a solving of a technical problem. How do you get those three stories in? In the first draft, I tried an omniscient narrator. It was horrible. I did it with Mark telling the whole book, and it was still horrible. I tried it with the vine telling the whole book. Horrible again. Then I had a student named Bliss in a class, and I liked the name so much I realized that I had to have a character with that name. I decided to let her marry into the family and tell the story. That finally worked. It's such an obvious way to tell about these people.

WDB: Because she's learning about it just as the reader is?

CE: Yes. And I didn't realize that for years and years. I had it so that all these people couldn't get clear views of one another. So I just accidently happened on Bliss, because I liked the name, and decided she could marry Thatcher. Then when she started talking, it really began to work. I appreciated her view of these people, and I like her way of talking. But I knew she didn't have the perspective to tell the whole book. She couldn't tell the history of the family, for example.

WDB: So you bring in the vine and Mark and the others?

CE: By that time I'd already come up with the idea of the vine, so I said, "Well, the vine can talk, and I'm going to have a bunch of people talking." Then it was just a matter of having them all talk and arranging their parts. Although I had decided early on never to let Meredith talk, because I wanted him to be the tent pole. That is, I wanted everybody to talk about him; I wanted to learn about people's responses to him. Then, as I was near the end of the book, I realized I'd spent ten years with this character and he had never spoken. I decided to see what would happen if he narrated. So the end of the book fell together; it needed hardly any revision. Meredith just worked really well for the last part.

WDB: I was confused a bit at the end. Does Meredith die in the floatplane, or are we supposed to assume that he dies later on?

CE: It's later. There used to be a last page, really, a newspaper clipping, and it was dated 2088. It was about a graveyard being discovered covered all over with vines. They had found a woman's grave with the date 1988. They had taken what they called a sonogram, a photograph from above, so they could see the bones and stuff, and they couldn't understand why her leg had been buried in another part of the graveyard. I took that last page out. It was just a little too much tagged on. My editor wanted some ambiguity at the end of the book and I agreed. So I was left with Meredith talking from the graveyard. The fact that it was italicized demonstrated that. But most people are confused by that.

WDB: Meredith's question is among the most moving things in Floatplane, I think, the question he asks when he returns from Vietnam: "What I'd like to know is what happened to God?" Is that sort of question, that sort of doubt part of the landscape for you?

CE: I wouldn't say active doubt. I would say an acceptance of mystery is more part of my personal landscape. I make a distinction between Meredith's view and my own. Meredith had experience with a culture which professed a knowledge of God and then, when he was put in a traumatic situation, he discovered that there was nothing to fall back on. The culture had not prepared him for war.

WDB: So the women in the Ladies Bible Class send him get-well cards and stuff just like they had brought in potato salad when somebody died, but when it got right down to it they hadn't provided him with the faith to deal with the trauma?

CE: I guess not. It is tough to go beyond what Meredith experienced. It is Meredith's question, and it's hard to go beyond it. In my own experience, when the church folks wrote me letters, I saw it as a kind and thoughtful thing. A couple of women from my church, without any reason other than that I was from the community, wrote me, and it was very meaningful. But one thing that fiction doesn't have to do that preachers are compelled to do is explain every question. In other words, if I were a preacher, I'd have to ask why this culture that professed a knowledge of God failed a soldier. And it may not be a good question. If I thought about it long enough, I would question the question.

WDB: You, of course, do have many characters who ask tough questions. There's Charles's response to Uncle Nate's suicide in *Raney*, for example, where Charles points out that "relying on the Lord" wasn't enough. You resist the urge to go beyond that insight?

CE: Absolutely. I'm reading *Ox-Bow Incident* for the first time now. I'm going to do some writing about the Southwest, so I thought it would be good to read even though it's dated. What I'm seeing happen there is that Wister has these characters getting ready to go out and lynch a man. And then the victim gives this eloquent speech about justice and judgment. To me it is poor writing. It's unrealistic. I can see the author and I can see that he believes what this guy is thinking. I don't want people to see the author, and that's one reason, I guess, that I hesitate in thinking too much about the answer to my characters' questions. My job is to describe as best I can. And for Meredith to be in a situation where there seems to be no God because things have no order and reason is, in many ways, interesting enough as it is.

WDB: There's a good bit of humor in the book — a lot of it dark humor. Meredith, after he's horribly wounded, likes to say, "What are they going to do, send me back to Nam?"

CE: Yeah, we used to say that when I was in Japan. I was flying the back seat, and that was not good.

WDB: Finally, it's a darker book for me, in part because Thatcher emerges at the end. He gets the last word. That reminds me of Jason Compson in *The Sound and the Fury*. The character I didn't like makes it and the others, especially Mark, plummet. Any comment on where that's coming from, or is it just kind of the way it wound up for you?

CE: Well, I didn't know what to do with Mark. After a certain point in writing a novel — and I think E. M. Forster has influenced me here — the beginning and ending of a novel are arbitrary. People have complained about the ending of *Walking Across Egypt*, too. In *Raney*, I was just waiting for her to make a decision. When she'd done that, the book was over; that's what the book was about. I figure it out as I go. That's important. Once I figure out what it's about, I know what is about to happen. And I know when I can stop. Between those times you've got to let the characters loose. Mark, like everybody else in *Floatplane*, was to lead to Meredith. Meredith was the core, the center of the book. I was always more interested in him than anybody else. Ironically, though, Mark's biography was closer to mine than Meredith's was. I put in some of my own story for Mark, probably unconsciously. I've never thought about this before, but my guess is that I was setting him as up against Meredith, and in some ways I wanted Meredith to come out on top. The most I can say about Meredith and the whole family is that for me they had a kind of lovely stubbornness.

WDB: The last scene in *Floatplane* reminds me of the controversial ending of *The Grapes of Wrath*. Isn't there some controversy going now over *Floatplane*?

CE: Yes, it's funny. It's not funny. It's funny. *Floatplane Notebooks* was being taught in eleventh grade in Hillsville, Virginia. A parent took the book, portions of the book, to an evangelist, J. B. Lineberry, and asked him for his opinion. He turned it into a cause. People could call a number and get six pages xeroxed from the text. Those pages, of course, included the scenes where Meredith first starts waking up after he is wounded, the scenes where he wonders about masturbating and about his sex life. Lineberry wanted the book out of the school, and he wanted the teacher fired. The usual rigamarole followed: letters to the editor and the rest. It's been mostly in the Roanoke area. The Greensboro paper did something on it, and AP picked it up. I don't know where it stands now. I think it's going to the school board. The evangelist formed a nonprofit organization. So it's a big deal. Some others whom I respect have objected to that scene, but it seemed to me that this was the way these characters would go. Most of the stuff from the time Meredith starts talking to the end of the book was written, more so than anything else I have ever written, in a trance. I wrote quickly and revised very little. And that is especially true of that last part, Meredith's part. By that time the characters were as solid as they had ever been in my head, and I felt very lucky in that this material almost wrote itself. I didn't have to plan what was going to happen. I just had to watch it and then tell what happened. Bliss was like Raney; she did change. Bliss was fun for me because she was an A student and she loved adverbs. She was just so much fun to write because she got so excited about everything in this family. I think she was the only one in the family that had any idea about what was coming, because they didn't talk about it. She was frustrated but she couldn't act. She was an admirer of Meredith all the way. You probably saw that more in the second reading than the first one.

WDB: Yes. And it is also marvelous how she becomes entwined in the family, the cooking and everything, as we get closer to her tenth decoration.

CE: Well, the controversy is unfortunate because it gets everything out of context. A local paper, an independent, left-wing paper, wrote about this Virginia business, and the reporter chose to take a couple of paragraphs from the book. He dropped in a couple of paragraphs verbatim. It bothered me because, for me, it's very private. I would never have read that part aloud. Most of the stuff which has any kind of profanity in it I do not read aloud, just out a sense of propriety. Just because I write someone thinking something, a reader should not easily assume that I might speak that way. People become offended because they see that kind of language as offensive. It's important for people to realize that a novel gets inside of a person just like a surgeon does. To see a heart being cut out or operated on is, in a certain way, offensive, but it's also fascinating. You only get at it if you are a surgeon; you only get at some kinds of things if you are a novelist.

WDB: So you had to be true to your characters?

CE: Yes, I had to let the characters be. Another example is the whole business of the word "nigger" in *Raney*. The word is offensive to me, even though I grew up with it, grew up saying it. I had to make some decisions about the use of language, and I've had to decide that in many ways I am like a painter. If I paint a tree and the leaves are green, it's my responsibility to paint them green. It's dangerous for me as a fiction writer to change the way people talk and think in a book. But I'm also sensitive about how people are offended, and I don't see anything wrong with that. I'm glad that I at least attempt to write what's true.

141

WDB: Is some of your ambivalence about *Killer Diller* related to how close it is to your experience?

CE: I'll probably always be a little more ambivalent about *Killer Diller* as a novel. There's stuff in that book that has to do with music which really works. Some of it I got right. But there were other things driving that book. It started from setting rather than a character. The setting was so rich, and it seemed like so much fun that I started out to have a good time before I realized that my resentment of organized power was emerging. I also had strong feelings about biblical interpretations, and all of this came together and may have caused me to force it a little bit. Some parts of the book I like a lot, but it didn't seem as spontaneous as the other books, as unplanned. I think the strength of the other books is in part a consequence of my just following some characters who were in my head. *Killer Diller* is more of an idea book than a character book. It's not my cup of tea.

WDB: You must have written *Killer Diller* during the time when the preacher scandals — Bakker and Swaggart and Falwell — were in the news. And your book shows a suspicion of religious institutions.

CE: Yes. In some ways, it's a kind of clichéd way to think about the church, but I do very much feel that way. I dedicated *Walking Across Egypt* to Lex Mathews, who died just before the book came out. He was an Episcopal priest, an amazing person. I had lunch with him one day after I first met him, and he said, "Let me just tell you something right off; I don't believe in any of that shit." I said, "What are you talking about?" He said, "All that stuff in the Bible." But he would die for the widows and the hungry and all that. I loved him. He would cuss like a southerner and he was just a crazy guy, but he had this religious passion. Even in *Walking Across Egypt* I tried to get the church people right, the way they were, those people who kicked Mattie out.

WDB: Yes. She had to go to a different church because she had befriended Wesley?

CE: Yes. She rebelled against the church. She said, "Okay, I'll go somewhere else." I find all that refreshing.

WDB: But *Killer Diller* is nastier somehow. In some ways the Sears brothers are so perverse; I wondered if you'd become carried away with your desire to blast the institution.

CE: My editor wondered about that too. He kept coming back and saying, "Look, who is this talking?"

WDB: It's a great spoof when Sears leads the prayer and tells God all the things he's been working on — I love that.

CE: And Vernon says, "Doesn't God already know that?"

WDB: Vernon is the perfect character there, of course. He is common sense and nothing else. But it seems to me finally really interesting that at the end Wesley is not some cynic out in the desert someplace pointing his finger at the church, but he is still in a church, just a different kind of church, a black church.

CE: That part is a dream, remember, but yes, Wesley would probably have become an evangelist if my editor had let it go that far. I trust my editor, and it didn't make much difference to me, so I said, "Okay." It was enough for me to have Wesley preach a sermon.

WDB: But the novel is not so much a rejection of religion. It's a rejection of a certain narrow world that Wesley's been exposed to. We see him grow out of that. He sees that literalism just isn't going to work.

CE: Yes. I think so. The new book I've started working on is narrated by Vernon. It's about the band from *Killer Diller*. They go to Key West. I've got about twenty pages. We'll see what happens. I don't know what's going to happen.

Photo by W. Dale Brown

DENISE GIARDINA

1984 — *Good King Harry*

1987 — *Storming Heaven*

1992 — *The Unquiet Earth*

Forthcoming — *Saints and Villains*

DENISE GIARDINA

True Stories

"Hit was you talked me into learning to read," he said. "I wanted to do so's I could read the Bible. I ain't so sure now hit's a blessing. They's hard sayings in there."

In her last two novels, *Storming Heaven* and *Unquiet Earth*, Denise Giardina has drawn upon her youth in a West Virginia coal camp, but these two books as well as her first novel, *Good King Harry*, actually grow out of a still more fertile ground — an imagination rooted in a love of struggle with the big questions. It would be careless and reductive to refer to Denise Giardina as a regionalist; she is simply someone paying attention to her life. Her concern for the political and the spiritual, the philosophical and the day-to-day, emerged in our conversation in August 1993 in Charleston, West Virginia, where she teaches at West Virginia State University. Giardina received her bachelor's degree from West Virginia Wesleyan University and did graduate work at Marshall University before taking her master's degree from Episcopal Seminary in Alexandria, Virginia. *Good King Harry*, a historical novel that allows King Henry V to tell his own story, established Giardina as a writer of considerable insight into the psychological and spiritual forces that motivate human action.

147

In the more recent novels, *Storming Heaven* and *Unquiet Earth,* Giardina brings her gift to bear via characters whose lives are defined by the history of the West Virginia and Kentucky coal mines. She invites readers to "live in the skin" of her characters, not so much to be reminded of painful episodes of American history as to be pushed deeper into the territory of their own lives. Her various awards suggest her success. She is currently finishing a historical novel based on the life of German theologian and martyr Dietrich Bonhoeffer. The following conversation underscores the charm and strength she brings to the work.

▼   ▼

WDB: I read a transcript of your interview with National Public Radio in which you talk about being an Episcopal deacon and a community organizer. In another place you talk about your preference for books that are concerned with spiritual and political issues. And in an interview called "Fighting Back," you say that you had to choose between being a priest and a writer. All of these things spark my interest in this whole business of religion and art or Christian faith and writing and how those come together, if they do. Can you talk about that?

DG: Well, it's funny because it is something that is really bothering me right now. When I first started writing, I was trying to decide how the callings of priest and writer come together. I worked through that then and haven't thought about it as much since. There is a lot of spiritual content in my writing, but it is something that I am comfortable with. Lately I have been working on a novel about Dietrich Bonhoeffer, and the question is starting to bother me again. Writing about someone who was so much involved in being a Christian and trying to understand what that means is a challenge. I am asking myself these questions again. What does it mean to write about a specific faith, especially in a time when most people aren't religious. Actually that's not true. Let's say a time when most intellectual types aren't religious. We have these fundamentalist movements in all directions, which pose a great threat to a lot of the things that I believe in. Two totally opposing forces seem to be in charge — secularism and pietism. I had a conversation with my editor a couple days ago, something I do when I feel blocked. I keep thinking ahead to how a critic's going to read my work. Are they are going to trash it? She just gave me kind of a pep talk. She has to say to me every now and then, "Don't worry about it; just write it."

WDB: Do you think there is discomfort in the publishing industry with the writer who has a religious point of view?

DG: I think in general there probably is; fortunately, not with my editor and not with my publisher. But I think not with just publishers but with the literary reviewing establishment.

WDB: So any overt expression of religious faith that comes through in the writing is going to be viewed suspiciously by the reviewer?

DG: Yes, if the writer seems to be trying to put something over. Christianity, especially, has gotten a bad name. I think in some ways you can wrestle with the other faiths, but when you have a character who says, "I am a Christian," you have a problem. It is almost because Christianity is the dominant faith in this country and those words have been devalued by Pat Robertson types. I mean, all the Christian bookstores and that kind of stuff. There are plenty of Christian bookstores in this neck of the woods. I try to avoid them.

WDB: Do they sell your books?

DG: No. I don't think they would consider me a Christian writer.

WDB: Why not? Because of overt sexuality in the books, or bad language, or what?

DG: Sex, language, and also challenging questions. My approach in writing about religion is to ask questions rather than to answer them.

WDB: There are preacher types in every one of your books — even Oldcastle in *Good King Harry* is the clerical sort. But you don't make fun of them.

DG: No. I guess the most conservative one is in *Unquiet Earth* — Hassel Day. I simply tried to understand him and admit that, if I'd gone through the experiences he had, maybe I would have tended to his kind of faith too. It is terrifically difficult to stay on balance with the subject of fundamentalist Christianity. I have a brother and sister-in-law who are very conservative Christians, and we don't talk about it.

149

WDB: You seem to be able to poke gentle fun at the liberal camp, too. I recall the scene where Miles says of the Episcopalians: "God could bung them people over the head and they wouldn't know who done it." A gentle spoof?

DG: I feel more free to make fun of things that I am a part of myself or that I actually admire. Maybe it is defensive, but if somebody says to me, "You're making fun of Episcopalians," I can say, I am Episcopalian. One reason I am Episcopalian is because I love the liturgy.

WDB: Do you ever look at the passion of the fundamentalists and almost admire it? Energy and intensity, maybe misdirected, but nonetheless convictions strongly held? The liberals give to the bloodmobile and listen to Public Radio and the rest, but don't get anything done. I wondered if that tension is present with you?

DG: Yes, it is. I was involved for several years with Sojourners Fellowship. I got away from that for several reasons, but it was an exciting period for me because it really did combine a more liberal stance and passion. It was kind of like we were omniscient or something. We were trying a new experiment, and it was exciting. I still look back on that as one of the high points of my life.

WDB: When was this?

DG: The late 70s, early 80s. The magazine had been around for five years at that point.

WDB: I wanted to ask you something about audience. Your books leave strong impressions. I often forget plot lines, but particularly *Storming Heaven* and *Unquiet Earth* arouse anger and frustration. These are certainly books that drive a reader out of the comfortable chair. Is that what you are after? To whom are you writing, and what is it that you want to stir up in a reader?

DG: I think I'm writing for anybody who likes to read. With *Storming Heaven* and *Unquiet Earth*, I do think I've had a double audience in mind. On the one hand, I'm writing for people from this part of the world, saying "This is what happened here and this is who we are." I think this region has been so neglected and mistreated and exploited, and people have taken that on themselves and have an inferiority complex over it. And to people outside, I am saying "This is who I am and where I am from, and this is my story. Maybe you'll be interested in this too, even though you're not from here." I try not to limit my audience. I am conscious of both of these audiences.

WDB: How have your friends and relatives responded to your books?

DG: Overall, pretty positive. But my brother has never read them. The only books he reads are "Christian" type books.

WDB: Is that awkward for you — painful at all?

DG: I wish he would. I would love to talk to him about them.

WDB: I'm assuming that these last two books are family histories in some ways.

DG: Some of it is and some of it is stuff I've made up. My parents are supportive. They have read everything I've written. I have one aunt and uncle who are very conservative politically. They didn't used to be so much, but their son makes his living from the mines. He's not a major strip miner; he's a surveyor. They're touchy about the last book.

WDB: What about your response to critics? You refer to critics as being a blocking point on the new book. Are you pretty sensitive to what the reviewers have said?

DG: Probably too sensitive. I've had a lot of good reviews, but I've never broken through, somehow. I've been reviewed in the *New York Times Book Review*, but most of the reviews I get are inconsequential. I've been pretty much ignored. I get a little one-inch paragraph here or there.

WDB: Some critics have accused you of falsely portraying the people and the history of the region?

DG: Yes. They say I exaggerated how bad things were. The truth is that I toned things down. One reviewer focused on what I had written about families being unable to go to their family cemetery plots because the coal company had blocked the way. It's funny because it happened all the time and it still happens. That is not an exaggeration.

WDB: So the reviewers have made you angry?

DG: Most have been polite. I guess I'd just like to be reviewed in the *New Yorker* and places like that.

WDB: The books indicate a bit of a maverick back behind there somewhere. Even on the church issue, you seem to be somewhat ambivalent. All the way back in *Good King Harry*, you spend a good bit of time on the corruption of the church. And I remember the wonderful line from Dillon in *Unquiet Earth,* "I fancy a God who would just as soon level a church building as look at it."

DG: That is sort of my attitude.

WDB: A certain suspicion of what?

DG: Institutional religion.

WDB: Because it tends to a corruption of power?

DG: That is part of it. Also, there is the sense of putting God in a little box. I understand the dilemma, because it is difficult to talk about God without doing that. But the church often trivializes. I've run into so many people who think that the epitome of being a Christian is to not say cuss words. A few weeks ago, I read at the Governor's Scholars Academy in West Virginia. The same dreary thing happened that I'd seen before when I read in Kentucky last summer. I had kids come up and say, "Why do you have to have all those cuss words in there?" They were offended.

WDB: The students?

DG: Yes. They are young and they haven't been exposed to a lot of literature. But that kind of attitude — that that is what being a Christian is. It drives me up the wall.

WDB: You were born in Bluefield near Virginia someplace?

DG: Yes, but never lived there. We lived in a coal camp in Black Wolf in McDowell County, West Virginia.

WDB: Did you go to church in those days?

DG: My dad's family is Catholic, but he never went to church, so my mom pretty much had a free field. She grew up in eastern Kentucky, and there was a lot of prejudice against Catholics, so at that time she wouldn't have dreamed of sending us to the Catholic church unless my dad had insisted. She is Episcopalian now. The coal camps there all had a contract with the Methodist church, so every coal camp had a Methodist church, and that was the only church. So we went to the Methodist church, but our minister wasn't seminary trained. He was a local coal miner who just did this on the side. It really wasn't Methodist — it was just a general Protestant, fairly conservative church.

WDB: My sense from the books is that it was the Holiness church that tended to be more sympathetic with the unions, and the more formal churches like the Presbyterian would have tended to be more sympathetic with the owners.

DG: Yes. In the county seats, anyway, the Presbyterian or Methodist would have tended to be the churches where the store people, the coal company people, the lawyers, and the doctors went.

WDB: Is that another reason why you are suspicious of the formal institutions, because of the power involved?

DG: Maybe. On the one hand, it's not a bad thing to have an institution in the community that represents the spiritual side. But it is important to see that the church reflects the community side itself far too often. Sometimes there's no opposition there at all. I think one common thing between writers and Christians is that both should be always outside a little bit. They both should have a critical gaze toward society. For the most part I don't think the church does that.

WDB: Is this where you come to your interest in Dietrich Bonhoeffer?

DG: Initially it was two things. One was just that he had stood up for something, and I have a soft spot for people who do that. Also, his book *Letters and Papers* was influential for me. The whole thing about "religionless Christianity," which he never got a chance to develop, fascinates me. There is controversy over whether he meant to take it as far as some people take it. That concept interests me. As I read more about him, I became interested in his whole development. He was conservative for a long time. Apparently he was one of those German intellectuals for whom Christianity was simply an intellectual thing. He was that way for a long time. Then he came to the United States and got involved in a church in Harlem.

WDB: When was he in Harlem?

DG: 1930 or 1931.

WDB: And then in the late thirties back in Germany?

DG: Yes. And he started telling people that he really was a Christian. He shocked his students by asking them if they loved Jesus. But he was still coming to grips with what Hitler's coming to power meant. He wasn't one of those publicly declaring his opposition to Hitler. He wouldn't have stayed out of jail as long as he did. It was a gradual thing. And he wrestled with whether or not he should declare himself or work undercover. Some, like Karl Barth, thought he had become a turncoat. They thought he was a Nazi maybe. He had to give up his whole reputation with people abroad. He returned to Germany in 1939 to share Germany's fate. There's the interesting decision. Yes, we set ourselves apart. If we are critical, we see evil and recognize it is a problem in ourselves and all creation. So you can never separate yourself so much that you fail to recognize yourself as part of the problem.

WDB: That's always the danger of the writer becoming voyeur — watching but not participating?

DG: Right.

WDB: Well your writing is certainly about participation. Stories in your novels become avenues to survival. I remember one scene in *Storming Heaven,* the scene where Sam and Dillon and Homer are trapped in a mine fall. One reviewer said that the scene didn't strike her as realistic. I loved the scene; it seemed to me that they did just what you would do. What I like is that they survived by telling stories to one another. And this emphasis runs throughout your books. Jackie, in *Unquiet Earth,* seems to be telling her story as a way of coming to grips. Are we losing this sense of ourselves these days? Is television robbing us of story?

DG: I don't think we are losing our need for stories. I don't think television is an example of a response to our need for stories. More and more people are simply exposed to bad stories.

WDB: Or the same story over and over again?

DG: Yes. Stories that reach the surface but don't go down below. Even things like the fairy tales that we grew up with are now being sanitized. It is like everything has to be trivialized, repeated, and divorced from a moral sense. I think that is a problem of mass culture.

WDB: You often teach writing courses. Are we encouraging our students to be able to tell their own stories?

DG: My creative writing students have mostly been older students, although I have had a few undergraduates who are really good. My students in most classes have such limited experiences that they can't deal with ambiguity. They are uncomfortable with it. They want the Hollywood happy ending and clearcut good guys and bad guys. We read the *Turn of the Screw* and they worked at it, but they were uncomfortable with the idea that you couldn't tell whether the narrator was crazy or telling the truth. They want to know who the good guy is and who to root for.

WDB: You've been back in full-time academics for a while now. How are we doing? Is education the answer, or are we fooling ourselves?

DG: I think it can be an answer, but I think that public schools are doing a lousy job right now. I think a lot of it is that there is so much censorship and a failure to challenge students. When I was in eighth grade, I had a teacher who gave me *Animal Farm* and asked me to do a book report. The teacher took us to the library to pick out books. I wandered over to the romance shelf, and she came up, grabbed me by the arm, and put this book in my hand. She said, "You're going to read this." It was *Lord of the Flies.* So I told my mom about it, so she could take me to the library to check out *Lord of the Flies.* They wouldn't give it to me. They said I wasn't old enough to read that book yet. My mom even said I had her permission. It didn't matter. They had policies, and anyone under fifteen could not get books out of the adult section. So Mom marched me around the corner to a bookstore and bought it for me. I had a mom that would do that kind of thing. But I think a lot of kids don't.

WDB: I like the graveyard scenes in *Unquiet Earth.* Dillon clears the graves. He's the keeper of the family past. What does that mean in the context of the book?

DG: I think it's a connection with the past. Taking care of the family cemetery is a strong tradition in the mountains. Mountain people are simply more comfortable with death. That's another area that's been sanitized in American mass culture. I remember last year a big controversy about whether or not children should see some movie in which the main child character dies. Give me a break. When I was a kid in the mountains, we went to funerals with open caskets. Nowadays, we don't want to see a corpse.

WDB: Since we're talking about mountain folk, how do you feel about the hillbilly stereotype? Here's a group you can still make fun of.

DG: It makes me angry. It makes me angry on several levels. One is, it makes me angry as a writer because it was something I had to worry about when I was writing. I had to wonder if people would think I was poking fun by using regional speech. I've done readings at schools outside this region and had people laugh at passages I meant to be serious. I think that's because of the sound of the voice and the accent. I've wanted to slam the book and go strangle somebody at times. I've had people say, "This character seemed too intelligent to talk this way."

WDB: The assumption is that the accent means ignorance. Tom Kolwiecki in *Unquiet Earth*, the VISTA worker, has to deal with his stereotypes and prejudices about mountain people. He seems to bring almost as much trouble as he does help. He's not a do-gooder. I see him as a serious human being. What do you think about the anti-poverty programs like Save the Children or VISTA? Have these helped or not?

DG: Some of them have helped to an extent. Some of the federal programs create problems for poor people, but I remember when I was a kid, I knew many kids who had rotten teeth. Half the kids I went to school with had grins that were all black. You don't see that anymore. So some of the programs have helped.

WDB: You are often treated as a regional writer — a term that seems somehow inadequate, like "Christian writer," or "southern writer." How do you feel about such labels? Do you resist that?

DG: I do. The only one that I can stand at all is "Appalachian writer," and I don't even like it because it is limiting. People beyond this region need to know that there is an intellectual life here and that serious stories can be told here. And that gets back to the stereotype we were talking about earlier. And the "Christian" label is too limiting as well. When you think of a Christian novel, you think of something from the Bible bookstore down the street.

WDB: I have been discovering that there are many writers out there who, like you, are writing out of a serious spirituality. They often fall abruptly between two worlds, too religious for a secular audience and too secular for a religious one. In an interview, you talked about the South having some theological notion of itself, and of course I immediately thought of Flannery O'Connor. O'Connor seems to have avoided the secular/religious dilemma.

DG: Yes. I like her a lot. And Faulkner. And the Brontës. Dickens I like a lot. I've started to get into Dostoyevsky. I read *The Idiot* recently. I'm reading *Notes from the Underground* right now. And I love movies.

WDB: What about popular fiction like *The Bridges of Madison County*?

DG: I haven't read that. I'm not really interested in that.

WDB: It's been on the best-seller list for over a year now.

DG: It doesn't interest me at all, really.

WDB: Why not?

DG: It sounds like an escapist sort of thing. It's the kind of book that I read when I was in high school and reached a point where I would rewrite the books in my head because they were so unsatisfying. So I decided when I hit about twenty-two or twenty-three that I didn't have the time to waste on those kind of books anymore. I like British writers. I like some of Peter Akroyd's work. I liked *Satanic Verses*. I like *Remains of the Day*. I loved *Howard's End*.

WDB: Who are your friends? You mentioned a sort of awkwardness with the church right now. Where is your network of support? Where do you get your community or the people to help you get through it? Or do you?

DG: I have several writer friends here in Charleston. I get together with a writer's group.

WDB: You need that sort of support — people to read your stuff?

DG: Yes, I do. But it's really difficult. I find the people I care about the most are scattered all over the place. Sometimes I wish everybody could be in one place. I'm really close to a former Sojourners friend in New Orleans and friends I met through him in Mississippi. Then another friend is a priest in North Carolina. I have friends in Eastern Kentucky. Everybody is so far away and all different directions. And it is really rare for me to meet somebody that I feel extremely close to.

WDB: Is this the source of the title for *Storming Heaven* — when you say that heaven is where all the people are together ready to take on Blair mountain?

DG: I dreamed the title actually. I woke up one morning with the phrase going through my head. But I had been reading the Bible. It comes from the same verse as "The violent bear it away," that Flannery O'Connor uses. It talks about sinners storming heaven. I guess this is

157

another one of my flaky theological ideas. I always liked that part of the Apostles' Creed that says Jesus went into hell and then was resurrected. What was he doing down there? I had this vision that somehow it was God extending grace. God doesn't turn away from sin, which is a good thing since we all participate in it. So "storming heaven" is a way to grace. It also ties to the march up Blair Mountain, of course.

WDB: What's most gratifying to you these days with your success?

DG: I guess I feel like I've been doing what I was supposed to do.

WDB: Do you think of your writing as a calling?

DG: Yes. I think I felt that even as a child, felt that there was something I was supposed to be doing. I knew it had some connection with stories. I feel like the ones I've written so far are the ones I should have written. I don't have regrets. I would like to get this Bonhoeffer one done, too.

WDB: You're not thinking past that one yet?

DG: No. I don't think past this one in any way. Maybe something will develop.

WDB: Do you have warnings for people coming to your books? What should people get ready for?

DG: The only warning is maybe with *Storming Heaven*. Some people tell me that they have trouble with the first chapter, with the dialect, and they had to push on past that. I don't know why that is a problem. People should be open to reading alternative language.

WDB: You still believe that tragedy is not the last word, that joy is at the heart of things.

DG: Maybe joy is even too strong a word for me, but there is a sense of hope. I don't think anything ends.

158

ROBERT GOLDSBOROUGH

ROBERT GOLDSBOROUGH

The Whodunit

"Barnabas Bay then launched into a sermon on death and salvation, and although much of it I either didn't agree with or didn't understand, I had to concede that the guy was one high-octane speaker."

Robert Goldsborough, an elder in a Presbyterian church in a Chicago suburb, is the editor of the national journal *Advertising Age*. But his evenings in front of the PC in the basement bring out the other Robert Goldsborough, the writer of detective novels. Goldsborough is best known in mystery circles as the continuator of the Nero Wolfe novels, the original creation of Rex Stout, who died in 1976, having written some sixty-nine stories about the supersleuth Nero Wolfe and his inimitable sidekick Archie Goodwin.

Passing muster with the thousands of Wolfe and Goodwin fans has driven Goldsborough into the details of the weighty Stout collection. But his resurrection work has followed his own interests — publishing, academia, and religion. His 1992 offering, *The Silver Spire*, features the murder of a staff member of a megachurch and draws on sources as diverse as Jimmy Swaggart, Robert Schuller, and Bill Hybels of Chicago's Willow Creek Community.

Other Goldsborough titles, such as *The Missing Chapter* and *Death on a Deadline*, ponder nefarious doings in the publishing industry. *The Bloodied Ivy* pokes gentle fun at stodgy academics in an imagined New York State college that looks a good bit like Cornell University. In all, the seven books of the continued series bring back Stout's Nero Wolfe in all his bigness and Archie, too, with all his savoir faire.

I spoke with Robert Goldsborough in August 1995 about his attraction to the Wolfe stories, the power of the mystery novel, and the challenges facing a writer who is involved in the currents of popular fiction on the one hand and committed to the Christian faith on the other.

▼   ▼

WDB: I enjoy checking in bookstores to figure out where they put your books. Sometimes you're under *G* for Goldsborough; sometimes you're under *S* for Stout.

RG: I have been known to go into bookstores and move books from *S* to *G*. For several years the Chicago Waterstones store insisted on putting my books with Stout's. I would move them, and move them quietly and surreptitiously, you know. I was in there the other day, and I notice I'm in the *G*'s now. I guess they gave up.

WDB: Why continue this particular series, the Rex Stout detective novels?

RG: It probably goes back to my mother's reading preferences. She loved mysteries and read a lot of them. And she tended towards the nonviolent mysteries, the mind-problem mystery. She liked Agatha Christie's Poirot stories very much. But I think she liked the Nero Wolfe stories best of all. She liked that atmosphere in the brownstone and Archie's personality and the fact that they were nonviolent books. The sex in those books is always by suggestion or inference, and the rough language and the violence is minimal, too. There was some violence in *The Black Mountain*.

WDB: Is that the novel where Archie and Nero go to Montenegro?

RG: Yes, they're in Montenegro, someone is being tortured, and Archie goes in and shoots three people dead. I bring it up because it's so out of character. In most of the books there isn't any violence at all. Not too many guns drawn; not too many punches thrown. My mother liked that. She didn't like the hard-edged stuff. She got me interested in the Wolfe stories in my adolescent years when I was probably whining that I didn't have anything to do. And the Stout stuff was very accessible, too, because in those years the Nero Wolfe stories were serialized in magazines, particularly the *American* magazine. When it went out of business, Stout took the stories back to *The Saturday Evening Post*, where they had begun. But this was her kind of writing, and I got hooked on it too. And that closed world features a really interesting ensemble company of characters. I can't think of another series in literature, detective or otherwise, where there is such a large ensemble of people who keep recurring.

WDB: Theodore, Fritz, Cramer, Lily, and the rest?

RG: Yes. I counted eighteen once. But my mother didn't like violence. Even the Raymond Chandler books were over the line. So the Stout books were the kind of thing she could give a twelve-year-old to read. And I have had people tell me that they've given my books to their kids as presents. Stout said that he didn't see the need to use a lot of profanity. There are some rough words, but it's usually "Cramer *spat* a word," something like that.

WDB: Leaving it to your imagination?

RG: Yes.

WDB: The Stout stories are remarkably prim in today's market.

RG: Oh yes. As I've met people in giving talks at libraries and book signings, I've lost count of the number of men and women who have said that they were introduced to Rex Stout books by their mothers. So my case had been repeated time and time and time again. And these are people that were approximately my contemporaries.

WDB: So you have continued Stout's stories but never actually met him before his death in 1975?

RG: No, I never did. About three years before Stout died, I was working for the *Chicago Tribune*, and it was already well known around the *Tribune* that I was a Nero Wolfe fancier. The book editor wanted a Rex Stout issue, and I wrote the essay on why Nero Wolfe was the smartest of all fictional detectives. I got a note from Stout. I still have it. Three sentences, typewritten, and he said something to the effect of: "Dear Mr. Goldsborough, I have your read your story and I am beaming. It is so nice to be remembered in that part of the country from where one comes." I think he was doubly pleased because the *Chicago Tribune* in the 1940s was very reactionary, and Stout had been singled out once or twice in editorials in the *Tribune* as "left-leaning" because of his attempts to form the Authors' League, which Colonel McCormick, the *Tribune*'s long-time publisher, saw as a devilish union. But Stout plugged away for forty-one years. He was writing pretty much up to the end.

WDB: And how many Nero Wolfe novels did he do?

RG: He did thirty-one or so novels and about thirty-seven or thirty-eight novellas.

WDB: And then a couple of Inspector Cramer mysteries?

RG: Yes and one Alphabet Hicks and a Doll Bonner and a Tecumseh Fox. Stout's biographer, John McAleer, told me that Stout had submitted to one of the magazines for serialization a Tecumseh Fox or an Alphabet Hicks story, and the magazines kicked it back and said, "No, no, we want Nero Wolfe." So he retooled the story. I think what he was probably trying to do was what Agatha Christie had been more successful at: keep more than one fictional detective running.

WDB: Miss Marple and Hercule Poirot?

RG: Yes, she had several, although none were as successful as Poirot. I think for the first half dozen years or so that Stout was writing the Wolfe books, he continued to experiment with these others. And then in about 1940 he just threw up his hands and decided to stick with Wolfe.

WDB: So, you wrote the first one, *Murder in E Minor*, as a gift to your mother?

RG: Yes. I had written it two or so years after Stout died, as a lark, really, and then I decided it would make a nice gift for my mother. I gave it to her for Christmas, in typescript. I put it in a nice leather binder with the title stamped on there. Eight years later John McAleer read it and urged me to get it published. He even went to the estate and tried to interest them in its publication; they were chary about it. Both of Stout's daughters were very conservative, and my suspicion is that it was just too soon after their father had died and they felt uncomfortable. Later on, they became unhappy because the backlist of their father's writing was languishing. It wasn't being promoted very well, and Bantam, which by this time had the entire backlist of Stout's titles, knew about my book and suggested that, if a new one came out, it would help stimulate the backlist. The daughters liked the idea. They had liked my manuscript, but said they would only publish it if I agreed to write a second one. They didn't want to gear up the promotional stuff for just one book, and I said okay. And so I signed a two-book contract at the beginning.

WDB: So that was *Murder in E Minor* and *Death on a Deadline*?

RG: Yes, but now it is over. I've become burned out on them. And I suspect the estate felt that I was being more closely associated with Nero Wolfe now than Rex Stout was. And Bantam isn't very interested in doing any more, because I am a midlist author whose books sell okay. They make some money, but not a lot, and they're looking for fewer titles, bigger profits. That's the way the whole industry's going, and I understand that completely. It is not inconceivable that I'd do another Wolfe story, but it seems to be done.

WDB: So, you've stopped it at seven books?

RG: Yes. If I were to do another book, one that intrigues me would be a book on how Nero and Archie met. Stout's books have no history. You just open his first book, and the ensemble is already gathered. You get pieces of background as you read through the series. This is quite unlike the first Sherlock Holmes book, for example, which actually opens with a chapter called "Mister Sherlock Holmes" in which Watson talks about Holmes and his characteristics. With Archie and Nero, you just get on the train while it's moving and begin to pick up little tidbits about them as you're reading the story.

WDB: When you started doing these things, did your friends start referring to you as the mystery writer?

RG: Oh, a little bit, I suppose.

WDB: Were the Stout books a hobby, a sideline?

RG: Well, I never quit my day job. I've always worked. I've been here, with *Advertising Age,* for fourteen years. And twenty-one years at the *Tribune* before that. The last seven years I was at the *Tribune,* I was their Sunday magazine editor. So the first novel was written while I was still at the *Tribune* but not published until I'd come over to *Advertising Age.*

WDB: I wonder how much you've had to pore back over the Wolfe books in continuing the series. I read detective novels and have trouble remembering them a month later.

RG: I'm pretty much like that, too. And there was such a body of lore about Wolfe and Goodwin that I really didn't want to do something stupid. Readers are very sharp. They own these characters. I'm only a keeper of them temporarily. And I've gotten a lot of letters. Ninety-five percent of the letters are positive, because they're just glad to have Wolfe back. Quite a few of them start like this: "I was very apprehensive when your first book came out, but once I started I realized I was at home again with these characters." Some people take issue with certain small things, and if they're right, I'm the first one to say so. I'll write them immediately with a mea culpa. People love to spot errors, and they ought to get credit for it.

WDB: What have they caught?

RG: In one book I had Archie eating a stack of wheat cakes in the kitchen. They were sour buttermilk wheat cakes. He was drinking coffee and having sausage and so on. A guy writes me from Kansas City and says how much he liked the book but adds, "I don't think Archie ate stacks of wheat cakes. I can't remember which book it was in, but I'm pretty sure that Fritz always cooked them for him one at a time so each one was hot off the griddle." And I read this letter and I just shook my head. I had no idea. About a week later, the same guy writes me a second letter and he says, "Dear Mr. Goldsborough, I found it." He'd gone through every book I guess until he'd found the passage in *Mother Hunt* or *Father Hunt.* Sure enough, Archie talked about eating a wheat cake and then Fritz stepped to the griddle to start the next cake. Another time I had somebody cross the hall to go from the office to the front room, instead of go *down* the hall, because both rooms are on the same side of the hall. And two people, two people within a couple weeks after the book came out, one from some small town in

Wyoming and another woman from somewhere in the East, wrote me and said, "Whoa." And so, it's things like that. Some people take me to task, and they're wrong. They say, "Nero Wolfe never did such-and-such," or, "Archie never . . ." I have to point out that isn't totally true. Now I have a databank in my PC at home. Every time I reread one of the old Stout books, I put things in by subject matter. I catalog things like the glove in Wolfe's office. I note the chapter and the book that it's mentioned in, so I can grab it off the shelf and check myself if need be. Or the picture of the waterfall you can peek through on the wall. I note where that's mentioned, and how big that picture is and how high up on the wall. I keep a record of Archie's taste in suits and shirts, and Wolfe's yellow shirts and his yellow pajamas, and all that stuff. I've never been caught on a New York City geography error. I have maps of Manhattan that I've put up on the corkboard, and I even drew in which way the streets and avenues are one way.

WDB: I wonder if mastering all these details mightn't be very limiting, in some ways. You have to know how tall they are, what they eat, how much sleep they need. You are boxed in there.

RG: Yes, it is. The formula is very tight. I do go to New York, two or three times a year for a day, and when I was writing the books I would go to a specific neighborhood and take notes. I even took the Staten Island ferry, which I hadn't done in twenty-five years, so that I could open the book *Silver Spire* with Archie on the ferry. I put him on the same ferry, the *Samuel I. Newhouse*, that I rode over on. So I was comfortable with New York. I've spent enough time there, although I've never lived there. But I never tried to ape Stout's writing style. I wanted the characters to behave and talk the way Stout had them behave, but he was a much leaner writer than I am. He was a genius, really, and I'm not, so, to compensate for that, I used more adjectives as crutches. I never studied Stout's style, because I felt that I would then be lapsing into parody.

WDB: Can you say something about the appeal of the detective story. Is it our longing for pure reason in the universe, or mere escape, or what?

RG: I think it probably is the solidity of the universe presented there. There's not a lot of ambiguity here. This is good versus evil.

167

And I think that in a world that has grown more and more ambiguous in its distinctions about what constitutes sin and evil, the detective story is quite clearcut. I think that's one of the reasons the genre is comfortable for people. At least this is true for many of the traditional detective novelists like Christie, Chandler, Ross Macdonald, and John MacDonald.

WDB: And Dorothy Sayers?

RG: Yes, definitely Dorothy Sayers. You know who is on the side of the angels. You start with a fairly firm position as to whom you're rooting for. And you know how it's going to turn out. The puzzle may fool you along the way; in fact, it should fool you to be enjoyable. Any story that's too easy to solve also isn't much fun.

WDB: I have imagined a study in detective fiction beginning with *Hamlet*. You know, "Foul deeds will rise." "Murder will out." Something's rotten in Denmark, indeed, but it's going to be brought to light. The notion in many detective fictions seems almost Calvinistic. Justice will emerge, and the detective is a God-like agent of justice. I would included *Gambit* in such a study, Stout's chess mystery. The client in that book says to Wolfe, "You can do something that nobody else on earth can do." And often that's the appeal. Somebody comes to Wolfe and says, "You can save my wife," or, "You can save my father from this charge of murder. You're the only one who can do this." Almost like this Christian knight riding in to save the day.

RG: Yes. That is part of the formula, even though Stout was probably agnostic. He was reared in a Quaker household, however.

WDB: Dorothy Sayers says, "The detective story that deals with the most desperate effects of rage, jealousy, and revenge rarely touches the heights and depths of human passion, presents us only with fait accompli. It looks upon death and mutilation with a dispassionate eye. It does not show the inner workings of the murderer's mind." Do you agree with that?

RG: Yes, I do. In most of the traditional detective stories, to spare the reader gut-wrenching things, the murder takes place offstage and the rest of the story is told, not through the eyes of the murderer, but through the eyes of those who are chasing the murderer. In some ways I think the most interesting Wolfe book is *The League of Frightened Men*, which came out in 1935. It was the second book, right after *Fer-de-Lance,* and there is a character in there who is a deranged genius. He was, in many ways, every bit Wolfe's match, which is one of the things that makes the book good. That book gets into the inner psychology a bit and is, therefore, unusual as the Wolfe books go. I think Sayers is right.

WDB: Yeah, she strikes me as really right up, particularly with regard to Stout. I was thinking about Simenon maybe, or Ruth Rendell. Certainly some detective story writers explore the psychological.

RG: Yes. My wife likes to read the Simenon in French. She loves Paris, and she likes the fact that Maigret is in real Parisian neighborhoods. She can picture them, and she gets her Paris map out once in a while.

WDB: Are there other continuators? I'd never really even heard the word continuator before. I know that Robert Parker recently continued something of Raymond Chandler.

RG: Yeah. Parker did *Poodle Springs,* which is Palm Springs. That book is built on a fragment that Chandler had written late in his life. Four very short chapters. Parker finished the book with thirty-seven of his own, so it really was his book. And then *Perchance to Dream,* a sequel to *The Big Sleep,* was the second one. I don't know if he's going to do any more. Whenever Parker comes to town to promote a new book, WGN radio gets us together with a professor who teaches mystery writing and a few others for a talk show. Sort of a "round up the usual suspects" thing. On one of those shows I was talking to Bob about how he had "fuzzed the era." And he said he'd tried very hard to make it time neutral. He made no references to outside world events in *Poodle Springs* or *Perchance to Dream.* You sort of assumed it was back in the forties, but on the other hand, you weren't sure. He did that by intent. Stout always wrote his books as though they were happening right now. In the first books, FDR is in the White House, and in his last book Nixon is in the White House. But the characters didn't age. They sailed through time, which is one of the nice things about fiction, because you can do whatever you want to. But there are other continuators. John Gardner has done more James Bond books now than Ian Fleming did. And a guy in New York has done a couple of Perry Masons to continue Erle Stanley Gardner's work.

WDB: And other people wanted to continue the Stout series besides yourself?

RG: That's what I understand.

WDB: But eventually you had the official sanction of the estate, and a lovely introduction written by one of the daughters.

RG: Yeah, Rebecca. Becky. She lives in La Jolla, California. Rebecca Bradbury.

WDB: In looking over the reviews, I remember that the *New York Times* said, "We wouldn't read Goldsborough if there was more Stout to read." Is that discouraging?

RG: If I got a whole lot of reviews like that, maybe it would have been discouraging. Most of the reviews were pretty good. *Publishers Weekly* kind of sawed me up on *Fade to Black*. They really didn't like it. They had very nice things to say about all the others. Most of the national papers and *Newsweek* and others who have reviewed me were positive. The *Wall Street Journal* did a nice page one piece when I brought Stout back. I remember the guy that interviewed me. The guy said to me, "Nero and Archie are gay, aren't they?" And I said, "No, no, I don't think so." And he said, "Aw, c'mon, c'mon. We're alone here. You can tell me about that." "No, I don't think they are. And that's one of the skills of Rex Stout. He peopled this house with men, but there was never the slightest suggestion of that." And he said, "Aw, I don't know." And I said, "Well, you can believe whatever you want to; all I can tell you is the people I'm writing about aren't." So I've had some fun interviews, and the reviews have been mostly kind.

WDB: Which are your favorite of the Wolfe books?

RG: Well, I think *The Doorbell Rang* is pretty good, partly because Wolfe took on the FBI and Hoover in a time when that wasn't a popular thing to do. I thought that was a good book, and Stout told McAleer that the book pushed his sales up a good bit. *Fer-de-Lance* goes into some anthologies, maybe because it was the first one. I guess I like the earlier ones more. *The League of Frightened Men* I like for the strength of the antagonist.

WDB: I've always liked *Death of a Dude*, where Stout cites a line from *Huckleberry Finn* as the greatest line in all of American literature.

RG: What was the line?

WDB: "All right, then I'll go to hell." I think he's right about that. He knows his American literature.

RG: That book was written after Stout had taken a vacation to Montana, and he had actually cooked a trout. I think the recipe is in the *Nero Wolfe Cookbook*. He had a very nice time in a Montana fishing lodge, and he went home and wrote this book. That's the book, too, where Archie quits, and Wolfe gets on an airplane.

WDB: Did the William Conrad television show put an end to Wolfe on TV?

RG: Yes, it was unsuccessful. It was a summer replacement and didn't do well. The aficionados didn't take to it.

WDB: It always seemed to me when I read those books that the stuff would work in a film series.

RG: Oh, I think it would. With Sidney Greenstreet as Wolfe, it would have been wonderful. He was Wolfe on the radio. Greenstreet did the voice for about two or three years in the late forties. The Greenstreet of the "Maltese Falcon" would be just about right for Wolfe. He was big and heavy, but not gross or sloppy. And Greenstreet had a neutral voice that you thought might be British or even Irish. He spoke very precisely. The man was tailor-made to be Nero Wolfe.

WDB: So how did you find time to write these books? You've already mentioned the research involved. And there's an enormous erudition in the novels. Wolfe is such a Renaissance man. How could you keep up with Wolfe's reading?

RG: I was always digging into popular books, especially biographical and sociological stuff. Wolfe is not so big on fiction. But McAleer talks about his last conversations with Stout. Apparently they spoke of Nero and Archie as if they really existed. McAleer asked him, "What's Nero reading these days?" And Stout said, "He is rereading Jane Austen's *Emma*." That's what Stout said. So in my first book he is rereading it. That one came direct from the grave to me.

WDB: So you kept your day job and wrote these novels at home?

RG: Yeah, mostly evenings and weekends. It got a lot easier when I got a word processor. And they're not long books. They're fifty, sixty thousand words, about two hundred pages. It wasn't at all easy. I think my newspaper training helped in at least one way. I can take short blocks of time and make them work for me. If I have an hour, I don't sit and stare at a screen or a sheet of paper.

WDB: Given your years with the *Chicago Tribune*, do you get invited to speak to journalism classes?

RG: Once in a while. I have at Northwestern and at Northern Illinois University. More often these days I do a lot of speaking for *Advertising Age*. I am the coordinator of our "Best Television Commercials of the Year" competition every year. I put a reel of commercials together and go out to advertising companies around the country. I speak locally at a lot of public libraries that are looking for someone who writes mysteries.

WDB: You were pretty tough on the journalism business in *Death on a Deadline*.

RG: Yes, I put Rupert Murdoch in there and several others from the industry.

WDB: And you used real-life models for *Silver Spire*, too, didn't you?

RG: Yes, I went out to the Willow Creek church. I visited a service there. I never have been to the Crystal Cathedral in Garden Grove, California, but I took to watching Schuller occasionally on Sunday mornings, and used that as a model. When I was at the *Tribune*, we had done a major piece on the Crystal Cathedral, so that helped as well.

WDB: And your religious background is Presbyterian?

RG: Yes. And I read a Schuller biography, you know, and he's mainline. He strikes me as more responsible than a lot of the televangelists, and I tried in this book to make this guy somewhat responsible.

WDB: Barnabas Bay, the preacher in *Silver Spire?*

RG: Yes. And I wasn't trying to be an apologist for religionists, although I'm an elder in the church.

WDB: That's one of the things that fascinates me about the book. I mean, it's 1992, not long after the scandals of Jim Bakker and Jimmy Swaggart.

RG: And I refer to Bakker, Swaggart, and maybe Oral Roberts.

WDB: Yes. But at the same time you're very restrained. You don't blast Barnabas Bay and his church. You don't present him as an Elmer Gantry con-artist sort.

RG: I tried to make some distinctions. I tried to point out that this big superchurch was doing some good things, like shelters for battered women, and so on. But I also, I have a kind of a disposition against that kind of church for a certain impersonality. I'm sure some of that came through.

WDB: You do seem to be lightly satirizing this building of Christian kingdoms that we see with Christian television, Christian music, Christian books, and the rest.

RG: I think there is a feeling, and some of it is certainly justified, that there is so much evil in the secular society today. Christian groups feel that they need to stake out their own territory. We've seen a boom in Christian schools and bookstores. Even a Christian Yellow Pages. They want to start making some very sharp definitions.

WDB: Sort of a separate track?

RG: Yes. Years ago, everyone just said, "We are a Christian country." I wonder if the ACLU and its insistence on strong separations hasn't strengthened the resolve of some Christian groups to go, "All right, so you won't let us put a cross or a creche in front of the City Hall or the Public Library; we'll do something separate." So there is that clustering of various, usually conservative, Christian groups. Catholics always had their own separate world, their own separate church, their own separate schools, even their own separate athletic leagues. They've had a society within the society. Now Protestant groups are doing that on a greater scale. Interdenominational or nondenominational Protestants are creating a subculture within the culture.

WDB: And you're a little bit suspicious, I take it, when they begin to advertise themselves?

RG: Yes, and when they start wielding a lot of pressure on political candidates. I get a little suspicious about that.

WDB: You underscore the power struggles between Barnabas Bay and the members of his church staff. Is that a suspicion of the bigness of the place?

RG: Well, anything that becomes big has internal struggles. There're always tensions going on because people are human. And when you get a multimillion-dollar institution, the divisions multiply. I took it to what some people might call an illogical extreme. Somebody gets murdered. Now, does that happen very often? No. But I'll tell you what does happen with incredible frequency. Two things happen inside the church community: thieving and sex. We read about this reality with some frequency. So, the scandals are there.

WDB: Were you perhaps a little nervous about how your church friends might respond to your writing this way about matters of faith?

RG: I had some trepidation about how they would react to *Silver Spire*, but nobody criticized me or the book. Maybe the reason that none of them reacted with anger was because I treated religion with respect. We all live in a fallen world, and some of the people on the staff of the church fell. And I think there was nothing to quarrel with there. I realized I was being overly sensitive before I was finished with the book.

WDB: And it turns out that Wolfe's knowledge of biblical texts enables him to solve the crime?

RG: Well, we know from Stout's books that Wolfe has at least four Bibles in his library. So I figured that Wolfe would know the Bible. When Barnabas Bay introduces himself, Wolfe alludes to the New Testament Barnabas. Bay says, "Oh, Mr. Wolfe, you know your Bible," and Wolfe says, "It is literature."

WDB: At the end of the novel, when the culprit is unmasked, Barnabas Bay's speech is a powerful statement about fallenness. No satire there.

RG: I did not want this in any way to be a shot at the church. Archie sort of likes the church, remember?

WDB: Yes. And he hears a sermon. He says he didn't understand all of it and didn't agree with some of it, but it's a pretty sympathetic kind of comment. He's not unimpressed. He also meets Cal and Darlene, the greeters.

RG: Oh yes, I've had that experience myself as a visitor in churches. And I had a little girl playing the violin on a big television screen. I got that from Schuller. I watched him one day, and he had a nine-year-old Asian girl playing the violin, and the audience could also see her projected on a giant screen. And I got the idea for the collection where they use pouches passed up and down the aisles from Willow Creek. That's how they do it.

WDB: I wondered about those greeters. They're very briefly in the novel, but they intrigued me. Archie feels guilty because he lies to them. He makes up a false name and all that.

RG: I can tell you exactly where that came from. I was on a pastoral search committee. So I had to visit several churches. And so you go to a church and they ask, "Oh, what are you doing here?" I had that happen to me in New Jersey and in Ohio.

WDB: And you have to lie?

RG: Pretty much. I almost got tripped up once. Four of us went to this church in Ohio, and we split up in the parking lot and went to different places in the church. When the greeters came along, I told them I was from Chicago and with Crain Communications. And someone said, "Oh, do you know so and so?" I knew I was in trouble. I had to think on my feet to get out of that one. It was very much like what happens to Archie.

WDB: I remember Darlene sitting there in the pew with her little greeter's red rose on her dress. Is she a victim of something? I kept thinking, "How should I feel about these people? And how is Archie feeling?" How should the reader respond?

RG: I put them in there for verisimilitude, because I wanted Archie as the alien, in this case. I mean he's unchurched, or hasn't been to church in years, even though he was supposedly raised in a church in Ohio. These aren't bad people, by any means. I think there's a tendency sometimes in a church to almost scare people away with your "Hi!" You can be scared away by the overenthusiasm of the people in a church. I wasn't particularly trying to drive home a lesson there. People will sometimes be a little heavy-handed. They are well-intentioned but come on a little strong. The church in *Silver Spire* is very much like Willow Creek. You get people in the door in a nonthreatening way. Give them a fairly nonthreatening service, and then get them involved in your Thursday night small groups. That is where you really begin to develop the Word and build the faith. I think I even made some reference to that in *Silver Spire*. I have a New York Giants quarterback come and talk to the men. I placed *Silver Spire* fairly near lower Manhattan, near the Village and the East Village, where you have a lot of unchurched people. Not too different, in some senses, from Willow

Creek, which is out in the O'Hare corridor where there are all kinds of singles living in apartment units.

I should mention one letter I got. It is the only time religion, even in a broad sense, has ever come into a letter from a reader. A woman wrote me and said that she was very unhappy with my use of profanity in the book.

WDB: She must write a lot of letters.

RG: She really came down on me. She said she counted thirty-two uses of profanity in *The Bloodied Ivy*. She actually counted. But to her profanity was three words — *damn, goddamn,* and *hell.* Those were her definitions of profanity. Then she said Rex Stout never had to resort to that kind of thing. She closed by saying, "I have my standards, and so did Rex Stout. How about you?" I looked at her letter and thought I was losing my mind. I had gotten home from work; the house was empty. I pulled out at random a Nero Wolfe book by Stout. Then I sat down at the kitchen table, and I went through and counted the *damns* and the *hells* and the *goddamns,* and I listed them and the page numbers and who said them. Wolfe didn't have to talk that way. It wasn't in his vocabulary, and generally not in Archie's either. It was Cramer. It was suspects. It was Rowcliff. And I sat down and wrote her a very thoughtful letter. I really mused on it for a while. I told her I appreciated getting her letter and that I wanted to set the record straight. Rex Stout did use words that I used in the book. I listed page numbers for her. I asked her to notice that I avoid the obscenities, the vulgarisms. I didn't expect an answer to this letter and didn't get one. But I was dead serious about this. She got my back up a little bit. I was puzzled that she would take issue with the use of the words and not be concerned that in every book that Rex Stout ever wrote, and in all of my books, the sixth commandment is violated. I said we're talking murder here — shooting, stabbing, poisoning, bludgeoning, and on and on. It seems to me that in the eyes of the supreme being this is a far greater transgression than saying "damn." That is how I finished the letter. I was really rolling at the end.

WDB: Let's push this a little further. I could have come in here and said I want to interview you about being an elder in a Presbyterian church and an editor for an advertising journal. Is there an incompatibility?

RG: Yeah, I've heard that. Am I selling out? I don't believe that the professions are necessarily mutually exclusive.

WDB: What's the relationship between being a writer of detective stories and a Christian? Are there times when the Presbyterian elder's voice comes in and says "No, don't go down that road; go down this one?"

RG: I am not sure that there are, partly because of the Stout model. If I were to do something that I'd have problems with as a Presbyterian or as a reasonably devout church-going Christian, I would also be running against the tradition of the Stout books. Stout's principles were high. I am not saying they were necessarily Christian, but he had some high standards for what he wanted in a book, and a lot of those things happened to coincide with Christian ethics. Perhaps my being drawn to his stories was not coincidence. I have certainly never been an evangelical or a fundamentalist. I guess I am one of those white bread, mainline Christians. I have spent a lot of time doing things for the church — and happily, I might add. I am in a men's Bible study group, but I can reconcile that with being a part of society. I think I am in the world and of the world. Actually, I think most Christians ought to be. Now that doesn't necessarily mean they're going to write books about people who get murdered.

WDB: So you have found the Stout series compatible?

RG: Yes. But I'm working on some non–Nero Wolfe stuff now, and that creates different problems. I wrote one book about a fictional suburban detective in the Chicago area. I got an advance for it, and then Doubleday decided not to publish it. I am working on a book that is set in 1930s Chicago. A murder story. A newspaper reporter is functioning as a detective. I find I have to use four-letter words in this one. I can't help wondering how some of my fellow parishioners will react if that book gets published. But that's what was called for in a couple of places. I'm not just littering the book with them, but this is Al Capone talking. When I typed that word the first time and I looked at it after I printed it out — I said to my wife, "Honey, take a look at this." She is a real straight arrow. I said, "Does that bother you?" and she said, "No." She said, "That is what belongs there," and I said, "Okay." I said, "It doesn't jolt you?" She said, "No." But I don't want to just recklessly use that kind of thing.

Also, and I'm not sure whether this is good or not; I do think about what people in the church will think.

WDB: So they are in the back of your mind?

RG: It is interesting when you are part of a community like that, you don't want to be ostracized. On the other hand, I'm not writing a sex book. That might send people over the wall.

WDB: It is interesting to see how you've stuck close to your own experience in the Wolfe novels. You tie into publishing industry things with *Death on a Deadline* and *The Missing Chapter*. And *The Bloodied Ivy* is set in an academic landscape.

RG: Yes, I was a little farther afield there. I did have a couple of friends read the passages about faculty meetings.

WDB: And you've moved the setting out of New York City?

RG: It is Cornell. But Ithaca's too far away, so I moved the Cornell campus to a fictional spot. I wanted Archie to get there in an easy day's drive, and Wolfe could even get up there. In fact, in the original manuscript, Wolfe didn't go to the school. My editor said, "I think Wolfe ought to go up, just so he can react to contemporary American college students." So I had to create a scene in which Archie gets tossed in the slammer, and it angers Wolfe so much that Saul drives him up to the campus.

But the other reason I put the school where I did — exactly where I did — was that I wanted a student to say, "We are exactly halfway between West Point and Vasser and our male students have nothing to do with our female students. They date girls at Vasser. Our female students don't like the male students — they date cadets at West Point." I put the school where it is just so I could use that line.

WDB: But you get the academic jealousies and the power struggles so precisely.

RG: Good, good. Someone else said that, too. My mother used to work for a college. She wasn't a faculty member. She was in the library and then she was in the development office. At dinner she'd say, "Well, you're never going to believe what happened over at the college today!" It was like things festered among these people. I was amazed at the junk floating around in the lives of these brilliant people — a lot of jealousies and a lot of territorialness.

WDB: I wonder if there isn't something of an instinct toward satire in your work? You scold the publishing industry, and the advertising executives really take it on the nose. And religion, of course, in *Silver Spire*.

RG: Yes, no question, I like to have fun at the expense of these things, but also it isn't all just flip.

WDB: You're also saying, maybe there's something wrong?

RG: Yeah, with the newspaper business, with organized — hyper-organized — religion. Certainly the advertising industry. And universities do take themselves awfully, awfully seriously.

WDB: Would it be a fair surmise that your books created a rejuvenation in the sales of earlier Stout books?

RG: Yes. I believe the publisher did feel that I gave the other books a lift. But Stout's sales were often up and down. He never achieved the kind of success of an Agatha Christie or somebody like that, but he always had a very loyal audience. It was deep but not wide.

WDB: How has all of this hit your family? Do your kids come home and say, "This is my dad; he writes stories about murder and mayhem?"

RG: Oh, a little bit. But I think they have always been pleased about it.

WDB: Did you become obsessed with Archie and Nero?

RG: Yes. Sometimes when I'd be walking to the train from my house, I'd find myself turning things over in my mind about them. And my wife said, "You know, when you go down in that basement and sit in front of that screen, it is like you are transformed — you are actually in the brownstone." It helps to walk around Manhattan a lot.

WDB: Are you like Archie or like Nero?

RG: Temperamentally, I am like Archie. Archie likes the city. I like big cities. He likes to walk around the city. I'm not quite as cocky as Archie is, but I'd like to be. Archie is very popular. Jacques Barzun once said, "If Rex Stout had done nothing more than create the character of Archie Goodwin, he would have the everlasting debt of the American literary world." I think the real reason a lot of people read the books is because of Archie's observations and cheekiness. He's kind of a smart aleck, but he's also a good guy.

WDB: And that brilliant ability to recite any conversation he's ever heard, word for word.

RG: Yeah, and the smartest second banana in the history of detective books. He ain't no dummy. There's a book where Wolfe sends him out on an impossible task. He's to go to Atlantic City on the train and bring a woman and her daughter back to the house. And he does. And when he walks in the door with these two people, Wolfe stands up. And Archie says, "He wasn't standing up because two women walked in. I knew why he was standing up. He was saluting me." All of us would love to be saluted by a man like Nero Wolfe, just once.

JON HASSLER

1977 — *Staggerford*
1979 — *Simon's Night*
1981 — *The Love Hunter*
1985 — *The Green Journey*
1987 — *The Grand Opening*
1990 — *North of Hope*
1993 — *Dear James*
1995 — *Rookery Blues*
1997 — *The Dean's List*

JON HASSLER

Happy Man

*"If you let sunshine stand for the goodness in the world and
you let rain stand for evil, do goodness and evil mingle like
sun and rain to produce something?"*

Like a character in one of his books, Jon Hassler voted for Franklin
Pierce in 1976. The man and his books cut to the heart of things with
wit and laughter and a good bit of wisdom, too. This Minnesota
Catholic has been discovered by those who read for serious pleasure,
and, after years of rejection slips, Hassler is enjoying a wave of
popularity. Andrew Greeley is right to label Hassler "a superb storyteller as well as a man of deep and powerful hope and enormous
literary talent."

Staggerford and *Simon's Night*, Hassler's two novels of the late 1970s,
display his gift for characterization. (The plots, he says, are always
difficult.) With good reviews in hand, Hassler proceeded to write
several more well-crafted novels through the 1980s. And suddenly,
everything was out of print. None of the books had been promoted
extensively, one suspects because the novels refuse to beat the drums
of popular fiction. What follows is a most unusual story in book

publishing these days — a book buyer's revolt. As booksellers began to demand more Hassler to satisfy their angry customers, a sales representative from Ballantine got into the picture. Now Hassler's nine novels and two young adult novels are on the shelves.

Hassler's stories feature moral dilemmas and the stuff of real life. He treats aging and romance and marital fidelity in small-town settings that might be most anywhere. And he considers the role of religion as well. Agatha McGee, a character in three of the novels, struggles over the changes she sees in her beloved church. Frank Healy, in the ambitious 1990 *North of Hope,* reflects upon his commitments to the priesthood as they conflict with his love for Libby Girard. Faith, like doubt, is part of the fabric of the world Hassler weaves. And finally, there are the affirmations of grace. Hassler's novels resound with the conviction that we will come through; somehow, we will come through.

Jon Hassler says he is a happy man, and the laughter, present in all of the books, shows up most remarkably in *Rookery Blues* and *The Dean's List.* The new book pokes fun at stuffy academics and jabs at the romance novel genre as well as opening the typical Hassler questions about relationships, faith, and morality. Hassler has recently gone public about his battle with Parkinson's disease and has announced that he is working on his memoirs. We spoke before his reading in Ann Arbor in August 1995.

▼   ▼

WDB: So it's New York to Memphis to Ann Arbor to Madison? The book tour. Does it help?

JH: They tell me it does. It does establish these connections with booksellers as well as readers around the country. It's a funny thing: when I began to write, I'd write a novel and send it off. Now I go out and read it to people.

WDB: A *New York Times* reviewer in 1990 or so said that you had been "published halfheartedly" and "branded as a regional author." What do you make of that designation "regionalist"?

JH: Everybody's a regionalist; it never bothered me any.

WDB: You have to be from somewhere?

JH: Yes, right, exactly. I mean, you have to have your foundation someplace to be universal, you know. It never bothered me because I am definitely regional. It bothers me only if my readers are regional. If I only can be read by people in Minnesota, that's limiting. But the "halfheartedly" is accurate, I think. I was at Athenaeum, and they were very small at first, and they didn't get my work out. Everything of mine was out of print by 1986. That's when Ballantine picked me up and put it all back in print again.

WDB: I talked to a book distributor who told me that she had handled orders for your new novel, *Rookery Blues*. She had ordered three hundred copies sent to the Nashville, Tennessee, area and something over a thousand to Fort Wayne, Indiana. How do you account for such a disparity? Is it simply word-of-mouth in a particular area?

JH: Yes, I think it is. I think it grows out from a center somewhere like that. Of course, I have quite a following around the Twin Cities. I recently autographed in the Twin Cities. In nine visits I autographed 1,320 books. Those are big sessions. So that's gratifying, of course, to see all those readers out there. Then I'll go to someplace like Milwaukee, which I did for the first time on the last book tour. I went to two bookstores; they couldn't get everybody in the bookstores! It was just a great turnout. Then I went to a store in Chicago, and there were eight or ten people. So you're right — there are pockets.

WDB: In *Rookery Blues*, maybe more than before, you satirize the publishing industry. You give us a slick editor, Emerson Tate, trying to get a romance novel out of the poor slob of an English professor, Neil Novotny.

JH: What pen name did I give him, Cornelia?

WDB: Yes. He thought it was going to be Neil Niven, and then it turns out the editor wants a woman's name on the cover.

JH: And his colleague accuses him of selling his vision. Part of the fun of *Rookery Blues* was watching Neil's book being transformed into a romance novel: "a gamy formulaic book full of words," somebody calls it.

WDB: Have you felt some of that pressure to write the page-turner yourself, to write what seems to sell so well?

185

JH: Never. I've just watched other people do it. I don't say they've sold out, either. Some of those folks are doing the best writing they can do. I have no right to complain. But I thought it would be funny to have some guy so desperate for publication that he'd sell out like that. I don't know if that's based on anybody. He was a figure of fun for me. He's the most inept teacher too. Most of the mistakes he makes in the classroom are mistakes I've made along the way. I remember the day I brought a student to tears by criticizing her favorite poet, just like Neil does in the novel.

WDB: The students accuse him of being too fascinated with death poetry.

JH: Yes. And he lets them choose their own, and before they read their choices, he lectures on the fourteen weaknesses of bad poetry. Then he calls on a young woman who says, "You've just destroyed my poetry." I did that one time.

WDB: This was at a college in Minnesota?

JH: Yes. I've stayed in the state but moved around a good bit. I was born in Minneapolis, and then moved to a small town when I was six months old. That was to northern Minnesota, a town called Staples, where my father had a grocery store.

WDB: And that provided the material for *Grand Opening?*

JH: Yes, except the store is actually modeled on one in a town in southern Minnesota where we moved when I was ten. The first store was a chain store, which he only managed for the company. And then he bought his own store in this little town called Plainview. I call it Plum in that novel. That's my boyhood book. I went from there to St. John's University, where I teach now. After being away for twenty-five years, I went back in 1980. In the meantime I taught ten years of high school. The last six of those were in a town called Park Rapids, which I had in mind when I wrote *Staggerford.* And then I went to Bemidji State College, where I loved teaching, but I didn't have a doctorate, so they pitched me out. I finally found my level in Brainerd Community College, where they only wanted good teachers. My existence at Brainerd was very peaceful and permitted me finally to get around to writing at the age of thirty-seven. I published *Staggerford* when I was forty-four. After twelve years, Brainerd grew stultifying.

I was invited back to St. John's, where I was glad to go. I'm still there part-time.

WDB: The whole teaching thing runs through from *Staggerford* on in one way or another. Miles, the high school teacher in the first book, and of course Agatha in three books.

JH: I just finished my fortieth year of teaching, so it's no wonder.

WDB: You do get in your shots at the academicians, "ackcomedians" you call them in one book. And the last two really poke fun at departmental shenanigans and administrative boneheadedness.

JH: How about the administration? Pretty dumb, huh?

WDB: Yes. Those scenes at the president's house are laugh-out-louders.

JH: Good.

WDB: What's the serious side of this? Where are we in education these days? Do you still take a lot of sustenance from the students, or do you feel discouraged?

JH: Both.

WDB: You feel the doom that Agatha sometimes feels in the three novels where we hear her bemoan the state of academia?

JH: Oh, yes, definitely. She's the negative side of me. She says it for me. I think we are losing ground, actually. I can remember doing poems with high school students in the late fifties that I can't do with college students now. They don't have the reading background. It's hard for kids to read these days. I worry about that.

WDB: You think there's a general demise of what used to be called liberal arts education?

JH: Yes, I do. And my students at St. John's are good students. They're competitive, they're smart, but they have no background, really. And a lot of them are so insensitive to literature. I try to tell them that literature can be a comforting presence throughout life. It has been for me, certainly. And some of them believe me, maybe, but they don't read much. They don't go on to read much as adults.

WDB: That's Simon Shay's line in *Simon's Night*. He talks about how we've forgotten to teach that literature gives pleasure. It sounds like you try to do that.

JH: I do that. I had a student at the end of last semester who told

187

me how my course reminded her of how much she loved to read, how much she liked literature. She said she's been so busy reading it during her college years that she'd forgotten how much she loved it.

WDB: I'm tempted to apply the label "satire" to your work, but that's probably the wrong word. Do you prefer "humorist," or "Catholic novelist," or "Christian novelist"? These labels get thrown around.

JH: I appreciate any label; I'm a writer, and whatever kind of writer they want to call me, I've earned it, I think. I think I'm a satirist. I think I can be funny, although a friend of mine said I used to be funnier. And Catholic, Christian, Regional. Sure, I'm all of those.

WDB: What about comparisons to that other famous Minnesota writer, Garrison Keillor?

JH: I can see the connection. We're both writing about small towns. I think he used one of my stories on his show once. After *Green Journey* came out, the *News from Lake Wobegon* the next week was about this woman who was in love with a priest. And she wrote him a letter and said she was coming to see him, and the priest panics. Straight out of my book. So I wrote him. And I said we'd been fishing in the same stream so long, it's no wonder we got our lines crossed. He said he was unaware of my book. Our subjects are pretty much alike, I guess, but I think that our treatment is a lot different. His writing is more burlesque, I think.

WDB: Yes, your humor is very different from Keillor's. Catherine Bailey says your work is a body of "life-affirming fiction," and Robert Narveson says the plot of *Grand Opening* is about "the triumph of Christian love." I think that a part of your popularity must be attributed to something fairly rare these days: the assumption that faith, religious faith, is one of the realities at work in human life. I mean, it is a part of so many of the characters in your book.

JH: Yes, it sure is.

WDB: Is that something your readers write you about?

JH: I hear quite a bit about that. At an autographing just last week, somebody told me that *Dear James* taught them more about Catholicism than they'd ever learned before. I was on a radio talk show recently, and a man from Duluth called in to say that he was Lutheran, and he had always been curious about Catholics and what he called "this torture of celibacy for the priests." He said he never understood it till he read *North of Hope*. That's very gratifying.

WDB: So my sense is that you see faith as impacting upon the stories you tell. It's not something that you manipulate necessarily, but you seem to think it's a natural part of things?

JH: I do, because the people I write about often have it. Now there's not a Catholic in *Rookery Blues,* as you noticed. So, I don't know how this book and *The Love Hunter* conform to that vision. I think *The Love Hunter* does. I didn't think much about faith issues in *Rookery Blues.*

WDB: There's certainly a kind of moral and spiritual struggle going on in a character like Connor, who has fits of deep remorse.

JH: Yes, right.

WDB: But I read some place where you say you're through with priests.

JH: I don't know if I'm through with them; there just aren't any in this book.

WDB: Was this book, then, a conscious departure from the earlier ones?

JH: No it wasn't. When writing my books, I follow my instincts entirely, and I just didn't feel like getting into it.

WDB: Do you think in general there's a suspicion of writers who write seriously about faith? Annie Dillard tells me, for example, that to be classed as religious is a death knell.

JH: I think that's right.

WDB: You think publishers are wary of too much religious stuff?

JH: I think so. I think certain people in publishing fear it; I think certain booksellers fear it. I don't know if fear is the right word, but they're suspicious of it. I happen to have an editor and a publisher who produce books on angels, and the history of God, and the like. They don't seem to flinch at all to the subject, so that's good.

WDB: I wonder if this fear in the publishing world has led to the strange phenomena we see in the local mall. There's Waldenbooks at one end of the corridor and the Family Bookstore at the other. What do you make of that? Would your books ever be found in the so-called Christian place, the Christian bookstore, or the Family Bookstore?

JH: I wonder. I'd be surprised if the people patronizing those

Christian bookstores are very widely read. I don't think I'm even in the Catholic bookstores. But then there isn't much fiction in the Catholic bookstores.

WDB: That's the point that Andrew Greeley makes in his article about you. He says that nobody's reading what Catholic novels there are today.

JH: Yes. He was very kind to me.

WDB: Who is your audience?

JH: A woman, to begin with. She's probably never written to an author before. Many letters start with "I've never written to an author before, but. . . ." There's something in my work that prompts them to pick up a pen and write to me, which I like, of course. I get maybe four or five unsolicited letters a week from people all over. And they say the most heartwarming things. And then people turn up at these autographings. I can tell by their smiles that they like me. And they like my work. That's a really gratifying thing to experience. And they're from all walks of life and all ages. Mothers and daughters and grand-daughters share my books. A granddaughter came up to me the other day, weeping, telling me that her grandmother was reading my book when she fell ill, so the granddaughter finished reading it to her right before she died. There's something in my books that comforts people or consoles people.

WDB: Is it consolation having to do with aging, in many instances? It seems to me many of your books treat the general subject of aging. Maybe that's particularly because of Agatha's presence in three books and Simon in *Simon's Night* and the grandfather in *Grand Opening*.

JH: Maybe it's Agatha that does it. But I think it's not the aging so much as the trials I put these people through. And then they come out the other side.

WDB: So it's the affirmation? It's the hope?

JH: I think so.

WDB: At least one of your novels has been made into a movie. Is there more of that coming?

JH: Well, four production companies have just turned down *Rookery Blues*, because it's not simple enough for the movies. They want one plot with one climax. Too many subtle ups and downs here, they say.

Nor is there anything else in the offing. I wrote a play of *Simon's Night*, which was successful around the Twin Cities. Someone else is writing a play of *Grand Opening*, which they hope to perform next summer in the Twin Cities. But as for movies, no, and I don't know if that movie of *Green Journey* was successful. It was shown on NBC as a movie of the week and then repeated a couple years later, and that's the last I heard of it.

WDB: And they had Angela Lansbury as Agatha, this Agatha that you say represents a side of yourself. Is that the more fastidious, perfectionist, worried-about-the-state-of-the-world side?

JH: Exactly, and the side looking backward.

WDB: Now what's the other side? Is there a character that represents that side?

JH: No. That's me, I think. I haven't needed anybody to represent me on that side. I think the other side of me has no opinions about much of anything. Pretty dull. I mean, I don't lead a very exciting life or anything, like Agatha does. In some ways, Agatha came from my problems with the changes in the Catholic liturgy. I was so upset by those.

WDB: So she represents your working through the modernization of the church?

JH: Yes. When I was writing *Staggerford*, I sent her to church with that old Latin missal. I had her refusing to shake hands. Occasionally you can work out your frustration that way with fiction, I find.

WDB: There are a couple pieces that discuss this so-called Catholicity in your writing — names like Walker Percy and Graham Greene come up there. One of the articles I like best quotes Flannery O'Connor, of course. She said, "A Catholic novel is simply the novel that represents reality adequately, and it's going to look strange because no one's doing that anymore." Do you agree that fiction based on such topics as the fall, redemption, and judgment are strikingly unusual, and, more importantly, should your fiction be located there as writing that does still fall into those categories?

JH: Yes, I'd be pleased to have my fiction categorized there. And I can think of others. William Trevor, whom I like very much. And Kaye Gibbons in *Ellen Foster*, I suspect.

WDB: John Desmond says that yours is "a fiction of second chances." So often, the villain, say Wallace Flint in *Grand Opening* or Gary Oberholter in *Rookery Blues,* goes unpunished. There's the fellow in *North of Hope* who plummets through the ice. We knew he was going to get his, but more often their punishment is the private hell of their own creation. Is it fair to say that forgiveness, the possibility of grace, is a major part of your storytelling?

JH: It seems to be; I don't know if I ever intended that, but I think it's true in the books as I look at them. I'm not good at talking about themes in my work. I don't know what they mean really, until I talk to somebody like you. And I think you're right; I think there is a good deal about forgiveness. I guess the classic case is at the end of *Dear James,* where Agatha doesn't come down hard on Imogene but lets her have that library job. I didn't know how to end that book. I said to my editor, "Do you suppose Agatha might forgive her?" And he said, "Agatha's better than the rest of us." Then I wrote it that way, and it works. People are struck by that. I got a letter from a Catholic bishop who said that Imogene should have been punished. She was let off the hook too easily. "Why did you let her go?" A bishop. Isn't that great?

WDB: So there's affirmation, but there's certainly doubt as well. In *Staggerford,* Miles suffers from a malaise of the soul. You manage to make doubt a believable subject. Do you set out to do that, or is it again something that just happens?

JH: I never set out to do stuff like that. It just happens along the way. You see, I discover how my books unfold day by day as I work on them. I have no intentions from the start.

WDB: Did you get letters about the ending of *Staggerford?*

JH: Letters, yes, and even phone calls!

WDB: Angry ones?

JH: You bet. I didn't want Miles to die. I cried when that happened. But this was a premeditated death. I knew from page one he was dead. I knew that this was the last week in a man's life. I wrote it that way the first time so the reader knew it too. Then I rewrote it to see if I could re-create the surprise. And evidently I did, judging by the reactions. And I used to try to explain why. Then Waco happens. I thought, "My God. There. Now I can just say Waco and people will understand."

WDB: That craziness does in fact break out?

JH: Oh yes, when things are chaotic like in Waco. More recently, instead of explaining it, I simply say: "Miles is too good for this world. He's a sacrificial lamb; he's the quintessential teacher; he gives everything he has."

WDB: Catherine of *Grand Opening* is another of your memorable creations. She reminds me of Carol Kennicott from Sinclair Lewis's *Main Street*. Was any of that conscious?

JH: As I worked on her, I saw the similarity. In some ways, *Grand Opening* is *Main Street* brought up forward about fifty years.

WDB: The reader really picks up on Catherine's fears of being destroyed by that small town.

JH: Yes. She was based on my mother, who never did care for Plainview. We left that town a week after I graduated from high school.

WDB: And what a place, a small town "at odds over the love of God." Was that your experience?

JH: Yes, it was the town I grew up in. My own father was defeated for the school board elections by the Lutheran majority. So I put that in the book.

WDB: So it was Lutherans versus Catholics? That was the landscape?

JH: Yes. Half and half. The children got along fine. But I sensed a real antipathy among the adults.

WDB: And your Catholics often argue among themselves. I remember Bishop Baker, who likes to be known as Dick, and his debates with Agatha in *Green Journey*. I suppose he represents all those forces of modernism undoing the church.

JH: Yeah, but the other side of me liked him better than Agatha.

WDB: Agatha seems to loosen up a bit in that book. Is that a part of what you're up to with Agatha? Trying to bring her low — make her see herself better?

JH: Am I ever. I was trying to give her a bigger problem than herself. I had written a couple of short stories about her besides the *Staggerford* novel. The pattern was always the same. She'd come up against a problem and solve it, and that was it.

WDB: She's even more inflexible than the church.

JH: Right. So I thought, if I gave her a really big problem, we'll look and see how she handles that. So I had her fall in love at the age of sixty-eight. Obviously that is too big for her. Although the movie had a resolution, the book is inconclusive. She and James are chummy and writing letters at the end of the movie. Agatha came from my mother more than anyone. I think I was always trying to tell my mother to loosen up. She was pretty rigid. But she was a wonderful person. She had such a great sense of humor and such sensitivity. And yet, as she grew older, I saw her harden. She loved Agatha. She loved those Agatha books. I was revising *Dear James* at my mother's deathbed as I sat there day after day. I had revised *Green Journey* at my father's deathbed eight years before.

WDB: So you really mark your own life by these books?

JH: Yes. It's interesting that Agatha was there with me at both of those deaths.

WDB: What about *North of Hope?* That book seems a long way from Agatha. Some critics said it was your most ambitious book. Is that true? Was it harder to write?

JH: It's true. It's true. It's more intense than any other book I wrote. It's colder. It's longer.

WDB: Even more labored than, say, *Rookery Blues* or *Dear James?*

JH: Yes. *Rookery Blues* has a very intricate plot, yet it came much easier than *North of Hope.*

WDB: Did you get a lot of letters about Frank — the dilemma of the priest who falls in love?

JH: Yes, I did. I hear from people. Somebody last night in Madison, Connecticut, raised her hand in the audience, and said, "I love Frank Healy. What's he doing now?" I said, "I often wonder myself. He and Libby are still in touch. I think the novel points to that at the end."

WDB: I wondered as I read the novel how much a contemporary reader would relate to this drama of a character restraining himself to keep a vow. In the same way that I get a little annoyed with Agatha, I got a little annoyed with Frank. I wanted to say to Frank, "Lighten up. Loosen up."

JH: People have felt that way about Simon, too, with that marriage vow of his that was twenty-three years old. People say, "Oh, why didn't he forget it?"

WDB: You make a drama somehow of these vows that people keep, but obviously it's working. People are buying the books.

JH: They sure are. I can relate to it, so that's why I write it. I'm hoping readers can, though I don't know how much longer they can. And I must say I find the Catholic Church begins to look shabby to me today. I think of the quality of seminarians today, which is apparently on the decline. I go to church and I see a drum and a guitar and somebody singing through his nose. It all seems sort of shabby to me. I just had to get that off my chest.

WDB: Your saying that makes me think of Sister Judith, the wacky liberal in *Dear James*. But your portrayal of her turns out to be almost sympathetic.

JH: I generally end up liking my characters, even the dolts. I can't help it; I have become used to them. I have to gotten to know them.

WDB: *Dear James* is also interesting because it has a miracle in it, or maybe it's a miracle.

JH: It is. It's the only miracle I've ever put in a book.

WDB: You make explicit the theme of the need for forgiveness and connect that to the violence in Northern Ireland. With all that, I wondered if it went over as well with readers?

JH: Not as well as *North of Hope*. It went to maybe twenty thousand in hard cover, while *North of Hope* was over thirty thousand. Maybe *Dear James* is off-putting because it's about an old lady.

WDB: Well, *Rookery Blues* is about everything. You've got painting, music, fishing, teaching, striking, and more.

JH: That comes of waiting so long to write it.

WDB: *Rookery Blues* is notable in its portraits of domestic interplay, say between Leland and his mother, between Connor and his daughter. And a happy marriage, a strikingly happy marriage.

JH: Isn't that something? It's about the only happy marriage in any of my books. I was so happy to discover Annie. I love her. Every time she appeared in the book, it livened up, you know.

WDB: But am I right if I say Peggy is the center of the thing? She's the drama? Is it Peggy that brings healing into all those lives?

JH: I think so. She leads the band.

WDB: In between all these novels of your own, what do you read?

JH: John Cheever was the one I read to learn to write. Recently it has been *Stone Diaries*. And I loved *Shipping News*.

WDB: What gratifies you at this point in your career? You seem to take great joy from the letters and even the readings.

JH: Yes, I have to say they are gratifying to me. Everything in life pleases me right now. I've got a wonderful life. After years of struggling to write between classes and on weekends, I have a nice balance between teaching and writing. You're looking at a happy man.

WDB: What's annoying? What's galling? Anything you wish you had more time to do?

JH: I wish I could be at home writing my novel right now, instead of traveling. It's ironic that after all those years of struggling to write, the only thing keeping me from writing is writing.

WDB: The question of influences is always tricky. You've mentioned Cheever and the small-town Minnesota experience. What about the Bible or the church?

JH: Not the Bible, but the mass, certainly. And the ritual of the church.

WDB: And it sounds as if your mother insisted a good bit of the right kind of reading on you?

JH: I don't think she ever dictated what I read. She was a great encourager. She was a librarian and a teacher, so she always made sure there were books around. My father was also a reader. So I grew up with these readers as examples. I saw the enjoyment they got out of it.

WDB: You've published two novels that get classified as adolescent literature. *Jemmy* and *Four Miles to the Pine Cone* have survived a long tenure in paperback. Is that something you did and then just stopped doing?

JH: I like both of those books. I get more reaction probably from *Four Miles to the Pine Cone* than anything else — teachers who tell me that students who don't read books will finish that book. *Jemmy* I wrote as an adult novel, but it was marketed as a young adult novel. So I didn't pull any punches or anything as I wrote that. That's a good book, too. I was very pleased. Between novels I have tinkered with another one, but it hasn't really worked, so I've put it aside again.

WDB: Well, what do you say to the person who shows up tonight

196

and comes up and says, "I've never heard of you before, and where should I start?" I mean, are there particular books that you mention? Do you like to start at the beginning?

JH: I say start where I started: *Staggerford*. It's pretty accessible. Probably the most accessible.

WDB: What does your publicist say about *Rookery Blues*? Do you have the sense that the publishers are pleased or hopeful?

JH: They're excited about the possibilities of this book, even more than *North of Hope*. The wholesaler in Minneapolis ordered thirty-five hundred in three days. And I'm doing an interview with *All Things Considered* which should help.

WDB: I hope people buy this one. It is a playful book with oomph. And the storytelling there is marvelous.

JH: Yes, I made fewer wrong turns in that story than in any other I've ever written, I think.

GARRISON KEILLOR

1977 — *GK the DJ*
1982 — *Happy to Be Here*
1985 — *Lake Wobegon Days*
1987 — *Leaving Home*
1989 — *We Are Still Married*
1991 — *WLT: A Radio Romance*
1993 — *The Book of Guys*
1995 — *Cat, You Better Come Home*
1996 — *The Old Man Who Loved Cheese*
1997 — *Wobegon Boy*

GARRISON KEILLOR

You Can Take the Boy out of the Country

> *"In school and in church, we were called to high ideals such as truth and honor by someone perched on truth and hollering for us to come on up, but the truth was that we always fell short."*

Almost two million listeners set their Saturday evening schedules by him. The initiated can talk about the Whippets and the Sidetrack Tap with a knowing exchange of intellectual humor. He is the celebrity of the Public Broadcasting System, the hero of the liberal remnant, Garrison Keillor. His fans among the L. L. Bean–clad, upper-middle-class trendniks know that Lutheranism, or some sort of -ism, lurks in his background. They know he comes from Minnesota where there are cows and snow and strange small-town folk. And they pack theaters around the country to watch the live production of his radio show, *A Prairie Home Companion*, every Saturday night. They've been at this now for twenty years.

Our most renowned humorist and social commentator since Will

Rogers or maybe even Mark Twain, Keillor works steadily to produce around thirty live variety shows each year for over three hundred public broadcasting stations. Devotees of the program know how often Keillor veers into the religious arena, drawing upon his knowledge of midwestern churchgoers to underscore the serious and the hilarious. The listener gets the sense that Keillor knows a good deal about "God's frozen people." Maybe, we sometimes think, he's been one of those people himself. We talked in November 1994 in Keillor's Manhattan apartment in a room lined with books beside a window that overlooks the Hudson. A long way from Lake Wobegon. But not so far, either.

▼   ▼

WDB: Since I began this project, I have been running into you everywhere — responding to the sex survey in *Time* magazine, the narration you did on the Ken Burns Civil War series, the *Face the Nation* appearance. It seems that you have almost become a national icon, if not consultant. You must be the most famous G. K. since G. K. Chesterton. I even ran across you in the Lands' End catalog. They printed a letter from a woman who was thanking them for sponsoring your show but then went on to say that she and her husband had named their child Garrison in your honor. How do you deal with all that? How do you keep churning out stories — somebody says over two thousand hours of stories in twenty years. You've got to be as prolific as Faulkner. I saw your piece in the *New York Times* last week, the Op-Ed piece. Where does all this energy come from?

GK: I don't feel very productive. I feel as if the material is very gawky, and I don't really want to go back and look too closely at what I've done in the past for fear that I'll be mortified and I'll lose heart. I do think I am lucky, though, to be working and to be as avid about writing and about radio as I am. When I was a teenager, I assumed that people petered out somewhere in their thirties. I felt this very strongly when I went off to college. I had a sense that twenty or twenty-one would be the peak of my life, the time when I was most agile intellectually. I assumed the time of enthusiasm, loyalty, and curiosity was very brief, perhaps no more than ten years. I suppose that is the reason that people feel gloomy when they come to their landmark birthdays at the decades, the thirtieth, the fortieth, and fiftieth. I didn't feel gloomy at mine, however. I felt gloomy at my fortieth, but at my fiftieth I felt tremendously lucky, having rescued myself from retirement from *Prairie Home Companion* and having steered the revival of this show safely through the reefs and back to what it was supposed to be. I think I simply made some right choices when I was young, and one continues to reap the reward for these choices. I decided that I was never going to work for a living, that I was never going to do anything I didn't want to do. This didn't seem like a very reasonable career move, but I have pretty much kept to that. Every so often I violate it, but mostly I do exactly as I please. That's a wise thing for a young person to realize, that one's most precious asset is one's enthusiasm, and that we must husband this enthusiasm, not wasting it in causes we don't believe in. You don't want to serve in some position as a way of eventually getting yourself into a place where you can then do as you like and what you are crazy about. You really want to start right away. Luckily, I chose radio because you don't have to serve a great long apprenticeship in radio. You didn't when I started out in it because nobody wanted to go into it. Radio was a collection of sad sacks, boobs, and nerds, and you could forge your way right up to the front of the line. That is not true in television. Television for some reason looked very attractive to people because they grew up watching it. I had not. I grew up listening to radio. I am probably the last person in America who could say that.

WDB: So *Prairie Home Companion* just keeps the cycle going? The investment flows out of what you love to do?

GK: Yes. Anything that you want to talk about you can do. The audience for the show is an audience that shares certain qualities that are valuable to a writer. They are a very patient audience and I think a tremendously cheerful audience. You don't get floods of threatening mail every time you step across the line. They are people who by and large have pretty good lives, and this show celebrates them. I hope so, anyway. But they also have a lot else going on for them, if you know what I mean, so they don't look at it in some strange or spooky way.

They don't treat me in some sort of spooky way. I see really famous people sometimes who hesitate to go out in public. They simply can't because they will attract the attention of sad and troubled people. That doesn't happen to me. It is good for a writer to be able to just walk around.

WDB: What day do you start working on the script for this weekend's show?

GK: It varies a great deal. This show came very late because of Thanksgiving and because I was down in Washington on Tuesday. So I had to sandwich a little bit of writing on Tuesday morning and a little bit on Wednesday morning and Thursday was gone and then I wrote from 7:30 in the morning on Friday until 1:00 A.M. and then got up at 7:00 on Saturday and worked another eight hours before I went down to rehearsal.

WDB: But that's not a chore? You just have the energy for that?

GK: Some of it is a chore, and some of it is a little scary. Sometimes the monologue, the story from Lake Wobegon, does not really take shape until about noon on Saturday. If I were smarter, that would scare me to death.

WDB: Aren't there times when you wonder if it is going to happen this week, or do you just know it will come together?

GK: I never considered not doing it, but it just gets hard. So the monologue on Saturday was weak and poorly constructed. But still, as poorly constructed as it was — it wasn't even a story at all — listeners probably could find something in it. The listener could reconstruct it. Listeners, given a few strong images, can make something better for themselves.

WDB: Where do you go to hear stories these days? I know you used to go to small Minnesota towns and hang out in bars and hear stories. Do you have ways now that you listen?

GK: No. I am sort of in a drought as far as listening to other people talk.

WDB: Does celebrity status play a part in that?

GK: I'm sure that it does. But I also think that to hear stories requires one to have a certain relationship to the teller, and my relatives are very wary of telling me about their children and their lives. I don't blame them. I do think, however, that I have been ethical about not embarrassing my relatives and disguising them so that they could deny the stories. I think it requires one to lead a little slower life than what I lead. I am in a period of dreadful business, really and truly awful. It is not good for anybody.

WDB: Are you suspicious of the celebrity, of the success in any way? Obviously you haven't walled yourself off like a Salinger, but is there any way in which you are dubious of your success?

GK: It doesn't exist for me. That's all. I fully expect it to end badly and horribly. I have constant and terrible premonitions. I don't worry about it because I assume the worst. Every now and then in New York there are stories of the fortunate, the privileged, suddenly crashing to the ground, and these stories have powerful resonance. The murder of John Lennon continues to have great power for people. Thirteen or fourteen years later, I still think of it when I pass by Seventy-Second Street and see the entrance to the Dakota. I happened to be at the White House on November 22. I was at a dinner, and the other people at the dinner were perfectly cheerful and bright and laughing and talking. But it is hard to be in that room and not think of what had happened in that house that night in 1963 when they came back from Dallas. This is a story that every American over the age of thirty-five shares.

WDB: You talk about the Buddy Holly story that way, too.

GK: Yes. They were on a bus tour, and they were on a terrible bus. They were at the mercy of small-town promoters. Nobody had much experience in putting on rock-and-roll tours. Here he was one of the most successful recording artists in America, but he's still trucking around the Midwest in the middle of winter in a bus that reeked of bus exhaust, and they are playing one-nighters far apart. So in exasperation he charters a plane to fly out of Mason City, Iowa, to avoid eight hours riding in a bus, trying to sleep in seats that do not even recline. The man is trying to fight his way out of a dreadful tour, and he gets a very young pilot who misreads the instrument panel — the horizon indicator. There were two kinds of horizon indicators, and they worked opposite to each other. One shows the attitude of the plane to the horizon, and the other shows the horizon's angle, and you read them in an opposite way. So when this pilot, flying by instrument in the snow, thought he was ascending to his left, he was descending to the right. He flew the plane directly into the ground.

WDB: You give me a little sense of yourself as a pessimist there. I had thought of you as content, happy.

GK: I am! I'm very content. But one has this ominous sense of the temporariness of all things. Of course, growing up in the faith, it was certainly drummed into us. We knew we were not to be conformed to this world. One of the great preaching points of the evangelists when I was a child was the sinking of the *Titanic,* which was the same story. The dazzling life of the wealthy and privileged suddenly came to an end through human arrogance — the arrogance of the captain of the *Titanic,* who ignored warnings and did not cut his speed.

WDB: You've already alluded to your background in a distinct moral and religious culture. One of the things that we've heard in the replay of the recent Republicanization of America is that it is a call to a return to moral virtue — that voters are trying to send some message about decline. We hear phrases about culture wars, and I wonder about your reading on all that. The whole business of our falling away from something in this country that voters are trying to bring us back to, does that make any sense to you at all?

GK: One can read it that way. To me the Republican Party is morally and intellectually bankrupt, and I'm very sorry about that because I believe there is a need for at least a two-party system. But the Republican Party is to my mind beyond the pale. It is a great shame to have a party that dare not speak with even an ounce of compassion for poor people. This is a part of their demagoguery, and if you are unable to speak in public with any compassion, with any feeling or sympathy for broken people, you are morally unfit for public office. I mean that. This is a criminal party. I think it is a demagoguery to promise ever more draconian punishments for crimes such as drug selling, to tie hands of judges (through rigid sentencing guidelines) who might be tempted to show mercy. This is evil. This is deeply evil. Democrats have been forced to play this game to some extent, too. But this is a corruption of American politics. I am truly ashamed of religious people who have signed up. I am truly sorry that fundamentalists — not all,

I'm not even sure a majority — but certain very public figures have signed up for this. This truly is a betrayal of their own faith. This is not what Jesus called us here to do.

WDB: Several years ago in an interview, I think during the Reagan administration, you referred to this cynical use of fundamentalists by the political right. Do you see that continuing? Has there been a cynical manipulation of our fear of moral decay?

GK: Absolutely. I think that Newt Gingrich, for example, who has been very high lately, has no real grounding or base in the faith. He is not a man of faith. He is a politician, and he has found it convenient to use this rhetoric because it gives him something he lacks. It gives him conviction. Politicians need that. Most of them supply it themselves. Some politicians cannot supply their own conviction. They want to exercise power, but there is nothing they really are themselves in their hearts convinced of. I think he clearly is one of them. Gingrich is the very sort of politician whom he himself decries. He is there for life. He is not a citizen legislator. He has only one aim and object in life, and that is to hold office. I think that his courting of fundamentalists is completely cynical.

WDB: You allude to the Gospels in your talk about compassion for the poor. Maybe we should get to the question of your own background and your attitude toward it. I listened to the gospel song you performed last night and wondered if you sang it with some ambivalence. Years ago in an interview in *The Wittenburg Door,* you said your Christian beliefs subtly emanate from everything you do. *The Christian Century* says, "Faith is in the midst of his marvelous tales." Is this still true? Your monologue in Madison, Wisconsin, a week or two ago focused on the lessons of the Thanksgiving holiday — human responsibility, reaping what you sow. Last night there was a story about guilt and a closing admonition to grace. Is there a sense in which that religious background is still playing at a distinct and observable level?

GK: I hope so. I am sure it is. What else is there to tell people? It is only that I can't imagine I would ever seek adherents to the faith. I don't want to try to direct people toward the Lutheran church. I don't even want to direct them toward Christianity. We have a considerable segment of Jews who listen to the show, especially when we are in

207

New York, people like the sister of my piano player. She is in rabbinical studies. She likes the show and the monologue. The monologues are about midwestern Protestants and Catholics, but they still work beyond those groups.

WDB: Is there some ambivalence when you sing a song like "Softly and Tenderly Jesus Is Calling" on the show?

GK: "Softly and Tenderly Jesus Is Calling" is not a trumpet call of the faith; it is not a declaration of theology. It's a very emotional, altar-call hymn, and I think that one could sing that song with great conviction at life's worst moment. When your faith is at its lowest ebb, such a song might even mean more to you.

WDB: And you grew up among the Plymouth Brethren?

GK: Yes. They originated in the south of England. Plymouth was where one of the first assemblies was organized. A man named John Darby was one of the founding fathers in the early nineteenth century. They were learned men, many of them, and they left the Anglican confession because they wanted to conform to the precepts of the New Testament. They wanted a more primitive church organization, and they wanted to throw out the pomp, the liturgy, the creeds. In the end they simply created a more complicated, unwritten liturgy. They stressed the priesthood of all believers, so there were no ordained clergy, except the full-time workers, Laboring Brethren, who were supported by all the assembly. These had to be called by the Spirit. There was no central hierarchy or denominational structure. In reality, the simplicity made everything much more complicated. So there were some who struggled for years with their call. My uncle, late in his life, announced that he had a call and wanted to go out into the work. Support was often meager for Laborers, and the politics became much more complicated. The divisions between groups were passionate, and the disputes were over tiny, tiny points of doctrine. These arguments caused immense harm and grief to people. So these were people, like Mark Twain says, who were "good people in the worst sense of the word." I think it is possible, however, to lead a spiritual life within such a group. I remember my Aunt Eleanor and some of my other aunts whose passion for the Morning Meeting and the breaking of bread grew as they got older. It became more and more precious to them. The Brethren ideas of separation became especially difficult, however, for some. I have met people who grew up in the Brethren and who are very bitter about it. I am not one of them, and I don't know that I understand the people who are.

WDB: I think you have more sympathy for and more understanding of fundamentalism than any public figure in America today. I remember in *Lake Wobegon* where you say growing up among the Brethren was "like growing up with six toes, you'd just as soon keep your shoes on." What did you get from that background? Did these folks pass along their earnestness, their love for words?

GK: Well, they were very serious about studying Scripture and reading texts, very closely. Some of the Laborers could come and spend two hours in a discussion of a few verses. It got your attention and was deeply absorbing. And you did get to hear the King James Bible in an utterly normal way. It was revered, certainly, but it was regarded as the stuff of every day. It was the daily bread; it was not literature, and I think that to regard it as great literature is to hold it at arm's length. But it is literature, of course, so we were accepting great literature as everyday food. That changes you, and it's quite different from regarding television comedies as your everyday food.

WDB: So the cadences and rhythms of the KJV are still with you?

GK: I'm sure they are.

WDB: I know the celebrity business has made attending church difficult. But you still think of yourself in relationship with the church. And you're not affronted by language like "born again"?

GK: I have gone to church pretty regularly. I travel more than one ought to if one is going to be a part of a church. When I do travel, people always invite me to go to their church, but I don't like to go because I don't like to be treated like a famous person. I find that offensive. You're not supposed to have a minister stand up in front and gesture to you and have you stand up and have people applaud. I went to a Lutheran church in New York for a while, and it was comforting in a way. Walking through the doors, you were in Minneapolis. When I first moved here, I found that moving. So I went to that church, and then they asked me to do a benefit. I shouldn't have agreed to do it, but I did. They managed to fill the church for the show.

I was up in front of the church, working hard, a two-hour, one-man show, and I thought to myself, "I can never come back to this church without feeling strange." I ruined that church for myself as a place where I could peacefully go on Sunday morning.

WDB: One critic claims you maintain biblical values even though you have a deep suspicion of the institution. I don't hear you saying that.

GK: No, I'm not suspicious of the institution. The church doesn't need to satisfy some high standard for me. What I feel bad about is when churches do not serve their own people. I felt that the Brethren did not serve their own people so well, and their theology was not in the end as powerful as the psychology of the group. That which was truly loving and generous was always at a disadvantage. I walked away when I was twenty years old. The difficulty is for those who remain and struggle with it. Many of my family are still in it.

WDB: Do you think there is such a thing as a Christian writer?

GK: The writer may be a Christian but I would hesitate to call the writings Christian writings. I don't believe in that. "Christian fiction" is a terrible term. Christian bookstores are, in my experience, a ware-house of horrendous art and dismal writing and really dreary music. I wouldn't go in one on a bet. The Protestant church in America has not by and large created much artistically that anyone would be proud of. And I am completely biased against the so-called contemporary Christian music, based on having heard a little bit. To write songs about the Savior and to cast them in such personal terms that they have the sound and the feeling of a romantic ballad is to me a travesty, almost blasphemous. Victorian hymn writers certainly gave us a lot of pretty sticky hymns, but at least they're hymns that people can sing together as a congregation. I don't think that the modern Christian songwriting is worth anything for more than fifteen minutes.

WDB: I wonder how your storytelling ties to your Brethren heritage. You have spoken often of your uncle, whose stories didn't just come to a point but came to a point of contemplation. And Peter Scholl says that the drama of redemption is at the root of many of your stories. How does the storytelling come in here?

GK: We heard stories, of course, from early childhood. The story of Job and the story of the prodigal son were the two most powerful stories that I heard. I went to a Baptist church in Louisville a few years ago, and the preacher gave a sermon that consisted entirely of the telling of the story of Job without any explication or exegesis. He simply told the story from beginning to end. I thought it was one of the best sermons I had ever heard, and there haven't been that many of them. Most of the sermons I have ever heard in my life could easily have been dispensed with and the congregation would have been better for it. The sermon is, I think, one of the terrible failings of the church. And they're doing it to their own people. They're punishing the faithful with this querulous exercise in piety, the terrible harangues that nobody is entitled to deliver.

But the story of the prodigal son is a perfect story, and I'm sure that it's my story, except that my story is more difficult. Because when I went to the far-off country and fell among evil companions, I didn't spend my substance; I gained much more substance. So it takes me longer. I grew up with those stories, some of them difficult to understand. The parable of the talents, for example, and the stories of great vengeance and bloody triumph in the Old Testament. But narrative is the most difficult form of writing, and it holds the writer to a higher standard than rhetoric, exposition, argument. Politics would be enormously elevated in this country if we required politicians to abandon argument and to tell stories. Reagan was a great, dishonest storyteller, a very sentimental storyteller, but he had no standard of truth whatsoever; he believed his own stories. He was editing his own life. He wanted so much to believe them. I think his own life was painful to him. He took the easy way. And it is when religious people require us to do that, to pretend to a simpler life than we really have, that is when the church is bad for people.

WDB: Don't you think that might be the source of some of the bitterness that you alluded to a moment ago? Some people look back at the church experience as that which demanded falsity and self-righteousness. Now they see the wreckage that introduced into their lives.

GK: The world requires pretense, though; the world requires self-righteousness. It isn't only the church. The church is a very human institution. But when you're there on Sunday morning, you want it to be different. You don't want it to simply be a human institution.

211

WDB: *Christianity Today* did a profile of you just a few years ago, in which the writer, Gordon McDonald, said that he wished you had found a way to stay closer to home. Have you wandered so far from home?

GK: In some ways not. I'm sure I'm every bit as suspicious of strangers as I was brought up to be. And I certainly am every bit as dubious of success and privilege as I was brought up to be. The people I grew up with tended to be dour. And I tend that way too, I'm afraid. I don't know what one does with that. When I was in college and read Dante and saw that one of the circles of hell was reserved for those who refuse to be joyful, that rang true for me. But it was not what was preached in the Brethren. The psychology of the church is more powerful than what God actually tells us in his word, and the preference seemed always to be for a great excess of sobriety and for silence. The Brethren tended to produce silent young men, young men who could all come trooping into a room and hardly ever exchange a word. There was suspicion of joking around. So that's an unfortunate legacy. I would rather be among people who don't have that burden. I would rather be the only person in the room who has the burden, and then feel a little buoyed up by my companions.

WDB: You have Val in *Lake Wobegon Days* say that "excessive fervor is better than none at all." Do you ever envy the energy of those fundamentalists?

GK: No, I don't admire the zeal of people who I think are betraying their own message. I don't envy people who spend their lives preaching their own gospel. I think that it's a terrible thing to be a preacher. It's a very hard life. I don't envy someone like Jimmy Swaggart, who has been caught up in his own contradictions a couple of times. I don't envy Billy Graham, although I think he's had a pretty good life. He has avoided some of the troubles of many other evangelists by being careful about money, from the very beginning of his ministry, and saving himself from accusations of splendor and extravagance. But I think that it must be an impossible life for a Christian to be an evangelist. It's a terrible, terrible price to pay. But growing up in that world gave me a reverence for language. God spoke to us through his word, not in pictures, but in the King James Version, which was an everyday part of my life.

WDB: I am sure that among the fundamental tenets of the Brethren background was something about providence. It seems to me your work is fairly strewn with hints about miracles and considering the lilies and paying attention. I remember the lovely story about the dropped storm window. As you look back over your own life, as you think about the work, what do you feel about the drift of your own days? Are there nuggets of meaning? Is it going not anywhere but somewhere? Is there "Amazing Grace" humming along in the background, both in your writing and in your life?

GK: Yes. I think so. I feel sort of awkward telling you about it. Most of my life doesn't make sense, and the parts that do seem awfully fortunate. Being so busy I think seems to introduce permanent confusion into one's life, but other things seem to be very lucky. Whenever you find your audience, you have been terribly lucky. That may be the thing that seems to an outsider to be almost automatic, that, if you did a show, of course you'd find an audience. That isn't true. I did a show down in Washington at Wolftrap. It was our last show of the season about three years ago. You really look forward to the last show. The season gets hard. You look at a season week to week. I don't plan too far in the future. I don't think about the fact that I have to do thirty-two shows and I have to write them all and they have to be done at one-week intervals. So you come to the last show and you feel this great exhilaration, and the big empty summer is yawning in front of you. We were at Wolftrap, outdoors. We were about ten minutes before showtime, and I was looking at the audience, and it started to dawn on me that the first ten rows of this amphitheater were empty. There were a few people in the very front row and then about ten or twelve empty rows. It really bothered me. We had about five thousand people way up on the hill. About five minutes before we went on the air came this amazing parade of men in black ties and women in minks and gowns. They had been out at a garden party — probably eight or nine hundred of them — and they came trooping into these seats. I recognized that Wolftrap had pulled this horrible trick on me. They had taken eight hundred seats and sold them for an ungodly amount of money as a fund-raiser for themselves, and I now had a dead audience in front of me. This was the worst audience I have ever stood

213

in front of. They didn't care about the show. You could hear the laughter coming from out on the hill, and the applause from out on the hill, but these rich people just sat down there. Rich people are the worst audience you could ever hope to find because they've been everywhere, they've seen everything, they're completely blasé, and they have no need of entertainment. They have far more amusement than is good for them. Nothing you could ever do on stage would interest them in the slightest. About half of these people left during the intermission. No, more than that, just about all of them. It was terrible, just dreadful. You find this often when you're in this line of work, and you find it in different ways. Sometimes you are unable to connect with the people that you want to talk to and who want to hear you. And that's a killer; that just is a killer.

WDB: You said once that it's just a hobby that got out of hand. You seem surprised at the way it's all gone.

GK: Yes, it's not supposed to last this long.

WDB: In *WLT: A Radio Romance* you say,

After a year, they have broadcast more words than Shakespeare ever wrote, most of it small talk, chatter, rat droppings. Radio personalities nattering about their pets, their vacations, their children. Dreadful. The thought that normal healthy people didn't have better things to do than to sit idly absorbing it all — the daily doings of Avis and her cheery friends, and little Corrine warbling "My North Dakota Home" and LaWella's recipes for oatmeal cookies, the cowboy bands, and the Norsky Orchestra, Grandpa Sam telling the story of Squeaky the Squirrel, and Vesta droning on earnestly, plowing through Louisa May Alcott — it was eminently dreadful, he thought — *I hope to high heaven people don't listen to all this!*

That's a nice paragraph. Is this a bad time to be a writer, given that sort of comment on media in general?

GK: Yes, I think so, because there are a hundred times more airwaves than there used to be. I think there are ten times as many magazines. Publishing has just absolutely exploded. So you walk into a bookstore and it's just packed with titles, most of which you would never want to take a second look at, and the same with radio and television.

WDB: Most of it is temporary, faddish?

GK: It's very thin, very thin soup, and most of the writing is so very juvenile and so self-centered. Great writers always gave us a picture of a much larger world. They were never prisoners of their own skins. Even Emily Dickinson, the most socially isolated writer in America, even her writing is never self-conscious. She is never sitting in her tiny room narrating her own feelings. She was obviously a writer who loved words. She was a joyful writer. I think if Emily Dickinson were writing today and publishing poems, she'd be completely lost. I don't think that out of our time there will be three or four or ten writers who stand head and shoulders above everyone else. There's a great vast patch of weeds. I wish that John Updike would. For me, he stands head and shoulders above the others.

WDB: There is a deep theological bias running through Updike's work, too, a theological understanding.

GK: He's a very Christian writer. No one would consider him one because he writes about adultery as if he might have committed it himself. But radio, at the moment, is in a paroxysm of right-wing call-in shows.

WDB: Rush Limbaugh, G. Gordon Liddy. . . .

GK: Yes. They have taken over the low-rent part of radio, the AM stations that were losing money, and so it's like porno shops moving into a quiet town after businesses have abandoned it. But our show keeps chugging along. We haven't really had any complaints.

WDB: Is it harder to be a satirist? Are there too many targets?

GK: There's so much to satirize. And what is the center from which one writes satire? It's a writer's responsibility to write satire, and it's a failure if you don't do it. There's simply so much in America that is dreadful, ugly, and inhuman that one has to take off after.

WDB: I think it's Reynolds Price who says he has difficulty understanding how a Christian could be a satirist. You would say on the other hand that there are things which the Christian must notice, atrocities which must be addressed.

GK: Yes, I think so. I don't see how a writer could abandon the

215

idea of satire. One might fail to rise to it, but I don't think one could turn away from it. Some of the most devout writing I can think of is writing that has some satire in it. Writing that is called devotional writing I find by and large pretty dreadful. There's a writer out in Minnesota who writes very devotional things about nature. I suppose he imagines that he's following in the footsteps of Thoreau, but Thoreau is a deeply satirical writer, very cutting. For some reason Thoreau couldn't write anything other than what he wrote. He couldn't seem to describe people as individuals, he couldn't seem to write dialogue. He wasn't even that good at describing nature. I don't think from reading *Walden* that you get a very clear idea of where he was, what it looked like. But you certainly know Thoreau.

WDB: You get the power or the impact? Is that what we come away with?

GK: Yes, and he was fierce, uncompromising personally. No one would have wanted to live with him; it was good nobody had to.

WDB: Have you read Kathleen Norris's *Dakota*?

GK: Yes, I have. I don't care for her writing. She's trying too hard, somehow, to let us know that she feels every day the profound spiritual beauty of the high plains and that none of us can. This is what I get from her.

WDB: Some kind of "elitism"?

GK: It's a weird kind of elitism. She is, I think, almost without humor.

WDB: You say that books about humor are false books. Who are the good humorists now, where do we look?

GK: Well, I think there's a great long list of them. You have to seek them out. Roy Blount has a fine book, *A Book of Southern Humor,* an anthology. But his preface to the book is an amazing piece of writing. I just got a copy of that today. It made a big impression on me. He also has a nice joke in here about a man, when asked if he believed in infant baptism, says, "Believe in it, hell, I've seen it done." Let me see, I think I can find this great paragraph. Ah here it is! Page 31.

What makes most Southern humor rot? Not meanness — Sut Lovingood is rough as a cob, Mark Twain damned the human race, Faulkner said a good book was worth any number of old ladies, didn't anybody mess with Memphis Minnie, and Katherine Anne Porter once praised Eudora Welty for "her blistering humor and her just cruelty" in "Petrified Man." Nothing is less enduringly savory than narrow-mindedness that tries to pass for geniality. Whereas a tang of meanness may be a preservative — vinegar for pickling real fellow feeling and love of the world. Mean as in biting, mean as in common, mean as in signify.

Nothing's funny unless it smacks of delight. But what surely leads to spoilage in Southern or in any other humor is condescension — or as Porter put it (describing what Welty eschewed), "that slack tolerance or sentimental tenderness . . . that amounts to criminal collusion between author and character." The Southern humorists who put me off are those who rest their crabby/maudlin appeal upon the assumption that certain of their characters (for instance themselves) are just about the most precious *thangs.* . . .

Too much Africo-Celtic blood has been shed for Southern humor to be good *and* cozy. The precious thang in any kind of writing is slippery exactitude.

I like that. Of course I take that to heart, too. That slack tolerance, or sentimental tenderness, that collusion between the author and characters — and of course he's right. But in the pietistic upbringing of people in the Sanctified Brethren, we were meant to be sentimental about the faith and to eschew that kind of meanness or that exactitude, and that's what I am offended by in Christian bookstores. I see that sort of gluey sentimentality everywhere. Family values, I think, is the occasion for a lot of pretty bad writing.

WDB: Has there been a cynical use of the family values jargon by people like Dan Quayle?

GK: Quayle was accusing a *Murphy Brown* episode of being sentimental about single mothers. I think he was right about that. It really was a dishonest episode; they were not representing this experience honestly.

WDB: When you finish a book, do you sort of file it away, or do you have memories associated with books?

GK: I have memories associated with all of them, sure.

WDB: Do you think things like, "This book came at a difficult time," or perhaps associate the book with what was going on in your life at that point.

GK: Absolutely.

WDB: Someone writing about *Happy to Be Here* says, "There's no anger, no righteous underfur, no corrective purpose." Does that sound right; do you think of that as happy and light?

GK: No, I don't think that book is entirely happy. I think that story, "Drowning, 1954" is anything but a happy story.

WDB: In my own reading of *Happy to Be Here*, I am struck by how you really find your audiences' stories in some way. I think Walker Percy calls it giving people a "sensation of recognition." Are you conscious of that connection?

GK: No, because I don't know the reader in the end, and so it's better if I don't worry about the reader.

WDB: You just assume that that connection will happen? You just say, "If I tell the truth of my own experience, then whatever happens, happens?"

GK: Yes, I think that the audience does not really enter into the book until maybe at a later stage. Certainly when you're editing your work, you have to be aware of readers, but earlier on you're only aware of your power as a writer and more aware of your terrible limitations. One has to get through that oftentimes pretty horrible first draft, and you find you've created all of these problems for yourself. So you have to resolve those first. You have lurched off into directions that you were not qualified to go; you have committed absolutely flatulent, flabby, self-righteous things left and right and all over, and you have to get those out of there. You're aware of what you do well. So you naturally want to follow that, but you also want to push yourself into rooms that you have a harder time with. But I'm working on a book now that is working out differently for me than other books.

WDB: A novel?

GK: Yes, about people from Lake Wobegon who go to Europe.

WDB: Like *Innocents Abroad*?

GK: Oh sure, yes. Though I have not gotten them as tied up with

218

Europeans as I suppose I should do. The book has taken an entirely different direction, and they find that travel loosens their tongues. Getting away from home on this trip, with like-minded people, puts them in a confessional mood, so they sit around tables in European cities, outdoors in cafés, and they tell stories at great length, intimate stories. I'm not sure how plausible this is.

WDB: It sounds like the Lake Wobegon material is still at the heart of your work.

GK: Yes.

WDB: Even with *Book of Guys* and your other successes, people still refer to you as the writer of *Wobegon Days?*

GK: Yes, quite. My publisher would rather I did not do a book like *Book of Guys* or *WLT*. They don't do all that well. But I wanted to do them.

WDB: Why would your publisher not want you to go beyond the Wobegon material? Because it changes the way you're viewed by your audience in some way?

GK: Yes. I think that successful writers, commercially successful writers, are writers who find their road and they go straight down it.

WDB: When I first read *WLT*, I was struck by the bawdiness. It seemed to be a departure in some ways. Yet, I found both the history of the radio and the humor marvelous.

GK: It may be bawdy compared to what I've written. I don't think that anywhere in it is a description of people making love. There is great anticipation, there's a certain amount of youthful necking, and there's references to such frivolity, but it stays pretty innocent.

WDB: What about *Leaving Home?* That seemed to me to be a book about parenting somehow. I don't know why it struck me that way.

GK: My son would have been about eighteen at the time and going through quite a difficult time. He and I found it very difficult to be in the same room together, found it very difficult to talk. But he got through that period fine and without any harm to himself.

WDB: Is there more anger in that book? I remember that introductory letter where you talk about shopping malls spreading like fungus. Many of the stories seem to feature frustration and disillusionment.

GK: I think that I unloaded a little bit on Minneapolis and St. Paul in that foreword because I had been so preoccupied with my little life and work. I really had been closeted with *Lake Wobegon Days,* and I hadn't noticed how ugly parts of the Twin Cities were, how really ugly. A kind of sprawl had set in. And these are things that should never be said at home, so I said them and I think made a lot of people there angry. It was a mistake to have written it the way I did. Minnesotans don't like you to be saying that sort of thing.

WDB: But you're back there for twenty or so shows a year?

GK: Yes, a lot.

WDB: And that's okay?

GK: Oh, I don't mind. That's fine. I think we just have the audience that we have. There may very well be people who are angry at me there. But that doesn't bother me in the least. I have bought eighty acres of land in western Wisconsin. It is a beautiful piece of land. I have never owned land before, other than the land on which a house sat, never owned a house until I was forty years old. This place has a lot of meadow and a hardwood forest and a lot of birches. I grew up among birches along the Mississippi River. I actually moved in a couple of old Swedish immigrant–built cabins, so when I moved back to the Midwest and established a home there again, it was to live in the woods. When you live in the woods, you're not that aware of how your neighbors feel about you, I must say.

WDB: What about *We're Still Married?* Somehow I associate that book with the art of writing. I've used it in composition courses. What's your memory of that book?

GK: It was a book that I put together when I first came to live in New York in 1987 or so. I liked the stories. I liked the stories an awful lot. I thought it was a generous book. It covered a lot of territory for one collection. I guess now I would probably cut it down, cut it by about a third. I like the little letters in it; they were talk-of-the-town pieces for the *New Yorker,* and I was criticized for putting them in. Some reviewers felt that I was just hauling everything out of the drawer and sticking it in a book. I don't really think I was. Maybe I wouldn't take out a third. There are a couple pieces I would discard.

WDB: Do you have a working relationship with an editor who could make such suggestions as those, or are you pretty much on your own?

GK: I'm afraid I run my own ship.

WDB: What about *Book of Guys;* was there anything in particular that motivated that book?

GK: I had maybe six or seven stories to begin with, stories I thought I could build on. It took me a couple of years. It started out with Al Denny, the self-help author who goes off on a lecture tour and forgets where he lives.

WDB: What's the reaction to that book?

GK: I think that it has been taken as a piece of men's literature. I thought it was more like a spoof of men's literature. But, taken as a work of men's literature, it never found the audience that it wanted.

WDB: I like that part in "George Bush" where you talk about a social shift toward "barbarism." Do you still have some sense of that new barbarism that you refer to there, a kind of "you have it, I want it, I'll take it" mentality?

GK: We are certainly in the midst of it. The barbarism that I am troubled by is the barbarism of journalists and radio/television performers and commentators who fail to take responsibility for their own work and who seem to feel that their work is part of a larger zeitgeist. They seem to think that they are not responsible for the things they say, the truthfulness of what they say. They say they are simply giving the public what it wants. I find that bewildering. I think that there's a dissatisfaction with reporting on the part of writers and perhaps also the audience that really is deeply troubling. It should be troubling to anybody that we find opinion and gossip sexier and that we're very impatient with genuine reporting. We're very impatient with information, with facts; we're very anxious to cut to the chase. This is a kind of barbarism.

WDB: Are you often misquoted in your own encounters with journalists?

GK: No, the problem is that when you entrust your words to someone else, they seem to want to quote you at length at your dreariest, but accurately. They quote all of the most tedious stuff you say, at great length, and somehow your brilliant jokes, even when quoted accurately, seem flat in somebody else's hands. You say some light-hearted frivolous thing in a conversation with a reporter, and it's quoted more or less accurately. But in print it's not frivolous or light-hearted. It's horrible. You've said this horrible thing. Taken literally, it's so horrible you promise yourself you will never, ever do this again. So I try to remember that an interview is not a conversation.

WDB: What do you make of the critical studies published by Judith Lee, Michael Fedo, and Peter Scholl? Do you find yourself interesting in these books?

GK: Well, I'm honored of course that people would want to plow through as much material as Judith Lee and Peter Scholl plowed through, and I found the early chapter of the Scholl book to be interesting on the development of Lake Wobegon. It helped me recall what happened. But to the extent that they shade into biography, then they seem to me to be wildly wrongheaded. The Fedo book is really a non-book. It was an exploitation book, written very quickly. I think he wrote it in thirty or forty days. It's just mainly rewriting from some newspaper clippings. Nobody really wanted to talk to him because they suspected him of wanting to write an exposé. The book is really crippled by the fact that nobody who knew me wanted to talk to him, and I asked them not to because I thought he was a dreadful writer.

WDB: I've avoided the Twain stuff, because that comparison is overworked, I guess. But I remember your show from Hartford where you broke his billiard ball. You show a marvelous respect for him. What do you think of his connecting sorrow and humor? Wasn't he a profoundly unhappy man, particularly in the last ten or fifteen years of his life?

GK: I don't think so. I mean, he was a man who was hit awfully hard. First the deaths of two daughters. Then the sadness of his wife, who seems to have been really, truly disabled by grief and who was in a great period of darkness in her later life. But Mark Twain really enjoyed his life. Mark Twain loved sitting and writing in that little gazebo in upstate New York, in Elmira. He loved to perform; he loved being famous.

WDB: Loved walking through hotel lobbies?

GK: Yes, he loved to be admired, and there never was a writer who was so publicly admired as Mark Twain. He traveled around just eating it up. He got to do London and Australia and all the length and breadth of this country. Mark Twain loved to be interviewed and reporters loved to interview him. So I don't see his life as being sorrowful despite those terrible blows. He had a very healthy instinct for self-preservation. He went West to escape the draft, found out how to earn a living writing for newspapers, though he'd never been trained for it. It was a new industry, and he wrote those pieces from the Sandwich Islands that made his name back East. Then he came back and exploited it, unlike Bret Harte, who was always mournfully seeking himself, and who distrusted his early success and was a troubled man. Twain was not troubled; he went straight to it. He had a fine business sense until he came up against the typesetter. But he had a terrific publishing sense.

WDB: You don't think his mom's Presbyterianism was in some ways working in him? Isn't there a tide of woe flowing beneath his humor? In your own experience you talk about that sort of cataclysm that you're always aware of. Isn't there some connection between a sense of potential sorrowfulness and what makes humor work?

GK: Yes, I'm sure. It's only as the humorist picks up this burden that he or she becomes an interesting writer. Even if you don't write directly about it, the issue is there. I admire a writer like Dave Barry, because he's very diligent and he's very funny. I think he is. But he's a writer who can't delve into his own life. Someday I'll write my memoirs. I probably should do it sooner rather than later. That's the test of a writer. You owe the public an account of your own life, or so it seems to me. I'm not prepared to do it yet. I have been avoiding it. But it certainly is what a writer owes the public.

WDB: You do think about that, about writing your memoirs?

GK: Sure, because I have been privileged to lead a certain life that nobody else got to lead. So I would want other people to have the benefit of it, insofar as is possible without hurting too many people too badly. I want to be able to do it.

WDB: So you have the new children's story — *Cat, You Better Come Home* — coming soon, and there's the novel you're working on. And the memoirs in the back of your mind. And the show just goes on. What else is on the burner for you?

GK: I just go along with it. I've written another children's book called *The Old Man Who Loved Cheese*. It's another long poem. I'm co-authoring a book for young people about a musician. I'm still working on a movie script.

WDB: Wasn't Sidney Pollack interested in a film version of *Lake Wobegon?*

GK: Yes, he still is, but now they're going to make a television movie of *Lake Wobegon Days* for ABC. I'm also editing the *Oxford Book of American Humor,* which is a daunting task.

WDB: What do you make of the fascination your work has received from Christian camps? So many articles about your work have appeared in *Christianity Today, Christian Century, The Wittenburg Door,* and other journals of that sort. Annie Dillard tells me to be too closely associated with the religious camps is a "death-knell." Does the attention make you uncomfortable in any way?

GK: Well, it does. It does because one doesn't want those people to be disappointed, and of course they would be, the more they counted on you and the more they looked up to you and the more they hoped for you.

WDB: You mean the more they're going to sort of expect you to be a spokesman for them?

GK: Yes. The more they expect you to be a champion. The role of the champion of the faith is not a role that belongs to any one of us. But I enjoy feeling that they are a part of the audience. Where does Pastor Ingqvist go for confession; where does Pastor Ingqvist go to be on retreat? He certainly doesn't go to those of his own flock. If Pastor Ingqvist wants to have a retreat, which he ought to have once in awhile, he should come live on the west side of New York, come East. This would be a great experience for him and his wife. They should go to a lot of movies, and they should walk around and listen to people talk. They would find that they are from a very rarefied neighborhood in America. It would be a good place for him to take a break from Lake Wobegon. If he is lucky, he might run into an exiled Minnesotan. There he would find somebody to whom he could unburden his heart. Someone who had grown up in a similar place and who now is out here. He would be the sympathetic stranger that all of us want to find. He won't find that sympathetic stranger in his own congregation.

WDB: There's a way in which you, as a writer and a performer, are a sympathetic stranger for people like Pastor Ingqvist now?

GK: Yes, as a writer and even more directly as a performer, but you don't want those people to admire you for being a sympathetic stranger. It's hardly an admirable line of work. You want to be admired for having stuck with work that was really hard and having finished it. But the audience isn't supposed to know how difficult it is, you know. It's not part of the deal. And, of course, humor is tricky business. It works by surprise. Looking for it, you kill it. Nothing looks funny.

WDB: Does it feel awkward to you that you are the subject of seminars and people are teaching your stories in university classrooms? Are you suspicious of what they might be doing in the classroom with your stories, or do you feel gratified by that?

GK: No, I would be gratified, of course, because you're happy to have your work read. It's meant to be read, and of course the work itself is only a medium to something else. It's only a stage for some kind of classroom discussion to take place, and the imagination and curiosity of the students and the teacher, I suppose, to some extent, are the main things, and that carries them off in whatever directions they choose to go. It's not that the work itself is the object. I don't think it is; it's just the route through which they choose to go on to whatever it is they really want to talk about. But in scholarly writing, there is often a great deal of thrashing about, without much effect. You are acutely aware of this when you read scholarly writing about your own work; you are much more sensitive to bullshit when it's about you than when it's about a dead guy. Many of the stories, you know, were really pretty simple and were written under great pressure to do the honorable thing and support one's wife and child.

WDB: I remember your "Gospel Birds" story, and it epitomizes something that I've been after in your work. For me, you're laughing there a little bit, and you're satirizing there a little bit, satirizing pretensions like the world's smallest evangelist and preachers with gospel birds, and so forth. But at the same time, it seems to me, you're considering the possibility of grace even through such a craziness. There is a magical moment that grows out of that performance. A genuine moment of grace, a genuine thing happens there. It seems you're considering the whole possibility of grace. Even in *Lake Wobegon Days*, there's miscommunication, there's death, but you end with revival. Is this a fair summary of your work? Some light does shine? Will things be okay in the end?

GK: Well, I don't know that they'll be okay in the end. That's up to other people than me. No, things probably won't be okay in the end, but at least we may see a bit more clearly, see through the glass darkly. We may understand; our understanding will be more complete. That's what we want. That's why we need the Sanctified Brethren. But I don't want to give up my freedom of conversation, either. I do not want to have such strictures placed on expression that it is impossible for us to talk as human beings. I do not want to subscribe to a discipline that requires me to be a plaster saint. My people took very seriously the admonition that one should not be a stumbling block to one's brother and that you should "let not a word proceed out of your mouth. . . ." I can't remember the rest of that verse; I put that out of my mind. "Let not a word proceed out of your mouth that is not edifying." That's it. The avoidance of unedifying things as the ultimate value makes us lead very strange lives.

WDB: You keep coming back to that desire to tell the truth.

GK: Well, I don't know. As far as the show goes and monologues go, it does take place on a program that's meant to be entertainment, and so one hesitates to make other claims for it. In October I took some reporters on a tour of places where we had done the show in the past twenty years. It was odd to go back and visit all those stages again. Some of the theaters were so much smaller than what I remembered; it just was almost claustrophobic to be in them. We went to the Orpheum Theater in downtown St. Paul, which has been locked up, I think, ever since we left. It was musty and seemed like it was about to fall apart. It was dark, and we brought a couple of lanterns in. It's like we were going into a cave, like a cavern with all these seats that had been empty for almost ten years. Ghostly place.

WDB: But this helped you to reflect on your career in some way?

GK: Yes, I think so. It is an evanescent line of work, I guess. I've been around far too long, though. It is no great asset having a humorist in your midst. Humorists eventually become the butts of their own jokes. All told, people would rather have a good romantic novelist. And that would be better for tourism, too.

Photo by Karen Tam

PEGGY PAYNE

1988 — *Revelation*
1991 — *The Healing Power of Doing Good* (with Allan Luks)
1997 — *Doncaster: A Legacy of Personal Style*

PEGGY PAYNE

Writing and Revelation

"Sometimes God makes his presence known and we don't want to know."

Peggy Payne's 1988 novel about an ordinary minister's extraordinary encounter with God continues to work. Now available in paperback, the book tells the story of Swain Hammond, a Presbyterian cleric whose routine is quite dramatically disturbed when he tells his parishioners that, while barbecuing in his back yard, he heard the voice of God. When the congregation figures out that their young pastor is not speaking metaphorically, the fun begins.

A native of Wilmington and a 1970 graduate of Duke University's English department, Peggy Payne came to her first novel as a veteran freelance writer and journalist. Since *Revelation*, she has published *The Healing Power of Doing Good* (coauthored with Allan Luks) and is currently at work on a new novel, *Sister India*, which grew out of a stint in India on an Indo-American Fellowship. The trip to India also inspired another nonfiction work, tentatively titled *This Way to the Burning Place: A Ganges Pilgrimage in a Violent Time*, a personal look at the paradoxical rioting in the holy city that Payne saw during her stay.

The *New York Times* cites Payne's "serviceable style" in its praise of her novel, and we talked in May 1991 of style and the difficulties of moving from nonfiction to fiction, of the special challenge of writing seriously about religious matters without sounding religious, and about the revelation some books can be.

▼　　　▼

WDB: Let's talk about your career before *Revelation*.

PP: I started freelancing in 1972. I graduated from Duke in 1970 and worked for the *Raleigh Times*, covering education and science. I was on the education beat when the school desegregation occurred, so that was a real lively time. It was wild then, no sleep for about a year. Then I went freelance in 1972. I'd had in mind always to be a self-employed writer. My family has always been self-employed, and that struck me as a normal thing. I wanted to write, so I wanted to sell my stories. I started working for myself and doing a little of everything. I was still doing some education stories, but I found out that there was not a real lucrative freelance magazine market. And travel interested me. There's a lot of market for travel stories. So for years it seemed to balance between travel stories for newspaper travel sections and political stuff.

WDB: Straight nonfiction features?

PP: Yes, where to go and what it looks like, how it feels, a thousand words, a few hotel prices, that sort of thing. And then I'd come back and I'd be covering the state legislature, which I did for a while for the public network for North Carolina. I was on a three-night-a-week television show talking about state politics and the bills that did or did not get through that day.

WDB: You were an English major at Duke?

PP: Yes. And I really didn't mean to get into writing about politics. I really liked to write, but there it was. There was a market for such writing. So I covered the legislature for eleven years. And I was a stringer for the Norfolk papers. They needed somebody to cover North Carolina government, but they didn't need a whole bureau. I did a couple of stories a week for them. And then I did the public television stuff for a couple of years. I also have done a fair amount of work with general interest feature stories for magazines. I wrote some travel for the *London Times* once, and I've done some pop psychology type stuff, as well.

WDB: Have you become involved in politics yourself as a result of the beat you worked?

PP: Well, as a reporter, I couldn't. And I've only been a few years out of it. It took me a couple of years to realize that now I could get involved. It just didn't dawn on me. I was so much in the reporter's mode of bumper stickers, buttons, vote, and nothing else. Now I'm starting to get more involved myself. And that has happened partly as a result of a nonfiction book I'm writing, with a collaborator. It's on altruism, and it's called *The Healing Power of Doing Good*. I'm working with Allan Luks on that. Allan had done the research and teamed with me as a writer to do the book. I basically approved of the notion, but I had been still in the reporter's mode, and this book has kind of loosened me up. The whole point of the book is that by doing volunteer work, by doing any small thing for somebody else, you improve your own mental and physical health and spiritual well-being on every front; you in fact feel better. Ironically, I was spending all this time writing this book and having lower back pain, too, and I thought, "I really should do some of this volunteering." So now I'm doing more, and I think I've gotten to be more of an activist.

WDB: So, after all of this, why the switch to the novel? For sixteen years you did freelance and journalism and then suddenly a leap into fiction?

PP: I wrote a few short stories for a class in college. But I couldn't figure out what it was you put into a story. And I wrote maybe two after I got out of school. But then, money got to be an issue. It's hard enough to break into nonfiction, and I was having a horrible time struggling with that. So a combination of not knowing quite what to do in fiction and the pressure and interest in the nonfiction stuff. And I just didn't bother with it for a long time. In a lot of ways I think *Revelation* is the story of my being dragged into writing fiction in spite of my intentions not to do it. I know I had protested too much over the years. I had said to my friends who wrote fiction, "Why do you do that? That's crazy. You'll never make anything on it." "You're wasting your time. You may not even sell it." I said some really obnoxious things, and I've been reminded of that in recent years.

WDB: So *Revelation* insisted itself upon you?

PP: Yes. I mean it really felt like a conversion experience. I was so unwilling to do it. I had spent so many years struggling to get comfortable and satisfied with my success in nonfiction. I did not want to start over and learn a whole new business.

WDB: You do see the novel as starting over?

PP: Certainly. I had advantages. I wasn't afraid of paper, and I was used to typing eight hours a day. Also I had a track record with publishing, and that helped. I thought I'd just walk down the hall at the publishers and hand the fiction manuscript in at a different office, and that would be fine. And that was not the case. I wrote probably thirty short stories first. And then I wrote about a hundred pages of a novel that really wasn't very good, and I just threw it away finally. I wrote another novel, one not published, but one for which I have hope. Actually, I like it. It's got some problems for marketing because it falls between the cracks between a young adult and an adult book.

WDB: It's called?

PP: *The World's Best Dreamer.* It's about a fifteen-year-old girl. I thought I was writing an adult book, but it's not quite adult-feeling entirely. So I need to get that straightened out.

WDB: I'm fascinated with this notion of *Revelation* as a conversion. What I found fetching the first time I came to the book was this business of the liberal minister, the liberal church, and the sudden encounter with God. Then the congregation figures the preacher is not joking or speaking metaphorically, and everything breaks loose. Did that idea just sort of come out of nowhere? Or do you know of a situation like that?

PP: No, I don't. I really think that the closest thing was my sudden urge to write fiction popping up in the context of my already being a writer, and I'm saying "No, no, no."

WDB: So, it's gone with the nonfiction for years, and you're settled into a routine, and suddenly there's this new demand?

PP: Yes. And that particular idea came after I'd been a few years into writing fiction and publishing short stories. I'd had no big break-through and I was frustrated. But the actual idea came when I was reviewing for the *Raleigh News Observer* and reading *A Late Divorce*, by an Israeli novelist. It's not a religious book particularly. I mean, it's about a messy divorce late in life. But it was set in Israel, and that started something churning in me. Bob, my husband, was standing over in the kitchen doing something, and I said, "Suppose a minister heard the voice of God, and it was just a disaster." And the church that I've been a member of for years, although I'm really not active there right now, tends to be a social activist kind of church.

WDB: A give-to-the-bloodmobile-and-watch-PBS sort of place?

PP: Exactly. And I simply thought about what would happen if the minister got up there and announced, "Let me tell you all something: hey, I heard the Big Banana for sure." I would think that he needed some therapy. And that struck me as an incredible irony since, after all, we're there to talk to God. So I thought I'd fool around with that. And, of course, I am that congregation, so I'm not making fun of them.

WDB: I was going to ask about that. No satire intended?

PP: No. I am absolutely in that congregation and very sympathetic. But that idea grew from just the one sentence: "Suppose a minister heard the voice of God and it was just a disaster for him." First I wrote a short-story version of *Revelation*, which is called "The Pure in Heart," and that's been published now. It was cited in *Best American Short Stories* the year that it came out, so I was pleased. I thought that was the end of it. I went on with the novel I'd been working on. When that was finished, I was really ready to write another novel right then. And I didn't know what about. I didn't have a clue.

My husband sometimes has all-day workshops on self-hypnosis here at the house, and it's something I was interested in watching. I was interested in seeing him work, and I also wanted to take a day off. I decided to stay out here one Monday when Bob was working with trance states and join in. And what happened was really a big deal for me. People were flopped on the floor, lying down. Bob was encouraging us to relax. And what came to my mind was a series of images that I thought of as something like a box of slides, where every now and then one slide or another would just fall down and flash on

233

the screen. And they were all stupid, nonsensical, and I thought of them as the first three frames that you pop off to be sure film is winding. You know, people's feet or a lightbulb, something weird like that.

But some of those slides have been showing up for ten years or more. And what I imagined when I drifted off into a trance was that I was walking from here at the house down across the pond to the mailboxes. And it was real; it really felt almost like I was doing it. I got there, opened the mailbox, and it was stuffed with envelopes. And each one had a marking on it of a particular slide. And I hadn't even set out to think about those things really, but they were just in my mind. And so I had this stack of them to open up, and there was a message inside about each one. Five minutes later, I could not remember anything but two of them. One of them was an image of me sitting in the lobby of a hotel in Paris and reading Adam Smith's *Powers of the Mind*. Now is this weird? And I had sat there and I had been reading that book, probably ten years earlier, and the note with that one said, "This is about waiting." I didn't make much of that. The other slide that I remembered was the one that led me to write *Revelation*. It was a complicated picture which had no linear logic to it. It was a collage of India and Jerusalem, both places I had been. And I was extremely attracted to India and still am — I'm probably going back in a couple of months. And it was a scene in one of those parts of Jerusalem where it's walled, covered streets at an intersection where vendors sell soccer balls and dates, you know, a mixture of Kmart and Bible school. And in this picture I was disembodied, just eyes. And as I watched, this row of Indian women came walking through, each one in a sari, like a jewel of beautiful colors. And as they came toward me, each one turned her face away from me, and something like a veil passed between us. It makes no sense. But what the piece of paper said was, "You tried so hard to turn away from being a minister" — which I did. About ten years before that time, I had had a big upwelling of desire to be a minister, and I had fought that down. And then the fiction thing came to my mind, and I said, "I'm going to beat this too." Somehow I knew I'd have to go write the minister novel then. I came back to awareness. Bob was giving the cues to pay attention again and wake up refreshed. The next day I went to the office and typed chapter 2.

WDB: Was it exuberance you felt, or something of a burden — "I've got to do this"?

PP: No, just businesslike. It was good to have it settled. It felt right. It really felt right. And I didn't feel exuberant. I just did it.

WDB: I was planning to ask if you ever wanted to be a minister. There's something in the book that tips that off somehow.

PP: I grew up as a Methodist. My family was Methodist, and I always went to church. That was just part of growing up. When I moved into the Triangle here, I went occasionally to Memorial Baptist church, maybe because of the minister's liberal politics. Actually, he was fairly traditional theologically. I didn't see him as doing anything radically different. It was an interesting mix of the familiar and the social activist agenda. And I liked it, and I liked the congregation, too. And so I kept going back occasionally. And then in my midtwenties, I was getting more and more interested. All of this may begin to sound like another New Age story, but that's really not what I mean. I was writing an article on ESP research, and I was interviewing some of the leading parapsychology researchers who were at Duke. And then came my closest thing to a religious experience. I was coming back from an interview, and I just felt overwhelmed, emotionally overwhelmed. I felt, "It's all true; it's all true." And I had to pull off the road because I was so agitated and excited. And it was not specific. It was no more specific about Christianity than it was about teleportation or something. But it just felt like a real strong affirmation of "There's more than you see."

WDB: Of spirituality?

PP: Yes, of spirituality.

WDB: So is that when you began to think about ministry and seminary?

PP: It crossed my mind. Then I got really involved in a church, and it was very important to me. It was very sustaining and exciting. It felt like being in love, and that stage lasted about two years. I think it was also affected by the fact that I got a divorce during that period and that I was in need. And the congregation was a very warm, welcoming group. That was certainly a part of what was going on, both on a social and spiritual level. So all of those things came together. I was on the worship committee. I wrote a series of Lenten services, and I did a service myself. Lots of things. I stayed active.

WDB: You obviously draw on that time period in *Revelation*. You even have sermons there, sermons you maybe wanted to preach?

PP: Yes.

WDB: But basically you seem to have found the church to be warm and supportive?

PP: Very much so.

WDB: So you really have no ambivalence about the church as you talk about it in *Revelation?*

PP: I don't mean it as satire at all, no more than I just normally make fun of myself and my own work.

WDB: What about some of the sharp lines like "Church people love trouble" or "It's the kind of place where you can yell fire and nobody will flinch?"

PP: Well, I think those are true, but they're true of everybody.

WDB: You certainly touch on the stodginess and some of the dangers of tradition. But you haven't been cut by the stained glass?

PP: No, absolutely not. I'm not somebody who feels damaged by religion at all. I've run into it, but I don't feel that.

WDB: Most books that talk about the church seem to underscore injury. Lots of us have been crippled by religious experience. One of the ways *Revelation* veers away from the usual treatment of religion is in the last chapters. The book ends with the congregation embracing Swain Hammond, their visionary pastor. In my experience, they'd be more likely to kick him out on his ear. You must have great faith in the church?

PP: About the potential being tremendous, yes.

WDB: And in some ways, the miracle of your book is the church doing a good thing, isn't it?

PP: That he doesn't get thrown out? Yes, I guess you're right.

WDB: In some ways the miracle that he'd been praying for all the way is wrought in an odd kind of way in their response to him.

PP: That's true.

WDB: What about the reaction to *Revelation?*

PP: Well, I was pleased. I flipped through some reviews last night. I hadn't read them in a couple of years. One thing I thought was that there are almost as many reviews as there have been readers, you know. That's not true, but it seems like it. I thought, "Wow! This is a lot of reviews." The reviews were good, with two exceptions — one of which was my home paper. The *Raleigh News and Observer* gave it a mixed review. It wasn't really horrible, but it was mixed enough that you didn't really want to wake up on Sunday morning and see that right here at home. And the other not good one was from *Southern Magazine*. The rest pleased me; I mean they raised critical issues and things to wonder about and argue about, but I thought they were basically positive, and the stuff that was brought up was interesting to me. It was very satisfying. People wrote letters to me. I got a lot of letters.

WDB: Had that ever happened with your nonfiction?

PP: No. That was a new thing. And I answered all of them. That was important to me. People told me about their own churches, their own religious experiences.

WDB: So these were a lot of religious people who wrote you letters?

PP: People like me, actually. I don't think there were lots of people who came from a fundamentalist background, because these folks would be put off by the book. I actually saw one minister pick up the book, look at some of the language, close it, and walk away.

WDB: I've wondered how a conservative Christian audience might respond to *Revelation.*

PP: I don't think that's my audience. These were people like me. People who would be surprised by a spiritual event. And the reporters who interviewed me seemed actually to have read the book. I assumed that nobody would, but several did. And several talked to me about how it affected them. There was one radio reporter who did a half an hour interview with me. He said that he had read it and was so upset by it that he threw it at the wall two different times. And I thought, "Is this bad?" He was a real solemn-faced guy, not very lighthearted. And I finally understood that it meant a lot to him, and he was identifying with the main character.

WDB: I wonder which times he threw it at the wall?

PP: Yes, I don't know.

WDB: So there has been hoopla? You had to do interviews and book signings and all that sort of thing?

PP: Yes, there was lot of that. I don't do a lot of it now. I did. For about a year and a half I didn't write much. I was promoting the book, and I was enjoying it. In some ways, it felt like I was rewarded for the long solitude. I loved it. I finally slowed it down because I need to finish another novel. And you could go on forever, you know, chatting about the last one. But I enjoyed meeting new people and just being out there for a change.

WDB: This book jacket compares *Revelation* to Frank Capra's film, *It's a Wonderful Life*. Was that your analogy?

PP: No. I had never seen that film. I was surprised at the reference. I think they're talking about the mood of the novel. They didn't say that I was inspired by the film. But I watched it, after I read the blurb, and I liked it.

WDB: I wondered what they were after with that comment, because there's some tough stuff in this book.

PP: Yes, there is. I suppose they were talking about the happy ending thing, and the idea that each person can serve as a minister to another and make a difference. Swain does discover his true ministering finally when he'd given up all the rest of it.

WDB: Yes, in that powerful scene where he goes to sit with the cantankerous old woman. But while we're talking about your main character, I wondered about the psychological goings on — the scene in the graveyard, for instance, where Swain Hammond reconciles with his dead parents. And I thought about your husband's practice and the influence of his career as a psychologist.

PP: Yes. The book is dedicated to my husband. He's all over it. But we don't talk about psychology much in clinical terms. I mean it would be a natural, but we don't exactly do that. I am fascinated by what he does. I read most of his stuff, sometimes get more excited about it than he does, I think. We have an ongoing interest in the psychological and hypnotic and the possible spiritual sides of that. I have had an interest in psychology for a long time. It was not anywhere near as well-informed as it is now. Having an in-house guru is kind of handy, but his influence, which is tremendous, does not take the form of a particular what-is-this-character-thinking kind of thing.

WDB: It's more a shared point of view?

PP: Yes, a shared point of view toward life even though we have some strong differences, and I think that's interesting too. I mean he's very spiritual and nonreligious. He's very, very nonchurch. He's not at all interested in churches and organized religion, but he's quite interested in Buddhism and the martial arts, and in all those disciplines which bring together spirituality and trance induction activities. He's also interested in Native American stuff. I'm drawn to that old-time religion and where it hits parapsychology.

WDB: Well, you live here in a veritable hotbed of old-time religion. I stopped at the little church just next to your place here. There's old-time religion there, I'll bet?

PP: Sure. I actually based a character in *Revelation* on a former minister there. Her name was Ossisa May Brown; she was probably 6'4". She's really something. And she stuck in my mind.

WDB: I love that anecdote about the minister picking up the book and glancing at it and closing it. Was this in a bookstore someplace where you just happened to be standing there?

PP: It was at a signing. He had just wandered in. He was very polite, and he didn't say "I don't like this language." We had been having a pleasant conversation, then he just sort of flipped through and closed the book and disappeared. And that, of course, was the end.

WDB: We've gone down this road a bit already. Might not a religious audience be uncomfortable with the book, whereas a more secular audience might be uncomfortable with its religious subject, so that you get sort of between the cracks?

PP: I think there's some truth to that. Although I think there is a large potential audience. I mean I think again it's the NPR crowd.

WDB: Can you see a fundamentalist audience gaining anything from the book?

PP: Yes, I do. I really think that's possible. It would require some broadmindedness about the fact that the minister doubts in the first place, about some of the language, and about the explicitness of the sex. There was one review written in a denominational magazine which

239

argued for people reading this book even if they might be offended by it. It was so decent. It made me feel wonderful.

WDB: The sexuality is another thing I'd like to talk about. Is it Updike who says people go to church because they want to live forever, and they go to bed with one another because they want to see what it's like? There's a certain amount of that sort of religious longing in *Revelation,* especially in Swain Hammond.

PP: Yes. This reviewer I mentioned, Jill Baumgarten, said in her review that the church in general is shutting off and turning away artists. Christians, she said, are afraid of any portrayal of the dark side and the ambivalence. They want no bad behavior, just the sanitized version. And that's not what you're going to get from serious artists. And so we are losing all of that power that we could have to our advantage.

WDB: Swain Hammond, your character, apparently feels torn between duty and honesty, between doing what he wants and doing what he thinks is expected. It's an old theme in American Literature — Huck Finn and Hester Prynne and the rest. Was that in your mind at all?

PP: Not consciously, but it's an issue, so it's no surprise that it's there. I'm constantly dealing with the workaholic issues. I don't think of it quite so much in moral terms so much as in production terms. As a kid, it was a different feeling. As a child I had a hypersensitivity to moral issues, and a heavy burden of guilt over nothing, and I finally shook that one, but I also think that you don't totally shake anything that's been that big of a deal.

WDB: Well, this book is a lot about guilt, too.

PP: It probably is. You're right, it is. But I don't ask myself everything; some of it just flies onto the page.

WDB: Swain Hammond strikes me as homesick and restless in some spiritual way. He wants it all to make sense. Are you suggesting through your novel that beneath our dressed-up, formal approaches to God, what we really want is this authentic encounter, some experience that will give us a sense of clarity and focus?

PP: Swain had a lot going all right in his life. He didn't have major complaints except for the fact that he was cutting himself off somewhat. He was too inward, perhaps. And he wanted there to be something else, but like all of us, he was a bit vague about what that something else might be.

WDB: What fascinates me about Swain's longing is how it connects to a universal longing for a sign. I grew up among literalists who took every biblical jot and tittle very seriously. They called themselves the people of the Book. "We speak where the Bible speaks and are silent where the Bible is silent," they said. And though I'm long away from there, I still look over my shoulder at their enthusiasm, their passion, their energy, their clarity about life, and it has a kind of forcefulness. Sometimes I miss that. Yet there are doubts about which I must be honest. Do you know what I'm saying; does that dilemma ring any bells for you?

PP: Yes, I absolutely understand.

WDB: And I think that's finally what attracted me so much to your book, that dilemma working itself out in Swain Hammond. He is theologically liberal and yet longing for black-and-white clarity and for energy and passion. We disdain the fundamentalists on the one hand and we're jealous of them too.

PP: Oh, absolutely. I feel that way. I feel this little tilt toward Catholicism, sometimes, toward that entire rich structure of answers and ways to think and things to wear — I mean the whole shooting match. Of course, answers are attractive, you know. And that whole tradition is so colorful.

WDB: So Swain Hammond finally hears the voice of God and everything goes smash. Instead of clarity, he gets disaster. Why play it that way?

PP: Because I think it works that way. Somehow in getting to the good stuff, you've got to deal with a lot of problems. And probably because for me it was so hooked into the I-must-write-fiction thing, which caused so many problems. But I also think it's true that lurches of progress in internal life are not just great surges into glory. I don't think it works that way. You go through a period of wrestling with something and then realize six months later that you in fact have gotten a better handle on it. So, the good news is a delayed reaction.

WDB: What about the way the Bible comes into your book?

241

PP: Some of it came easily, but I don't know the Bible well. I know it about like anybody who was raised in a church. I still have my Bible that I got when I was five — King James Version. It's a little white Bible where I wrote "from Santa Claus" on the inscription page. That's the one I'm still using; it's in my office. And I used the concordance to check out a few things, but basically I used Scriptures that are pretty familiar. I interviewed one minister for a couple of hours. He was the Baptist chaplain at North Carolina State University. He talked to me about his personal experiences in and attitudes towards the ministry. Then I called the minister at my church to check out what is the standard line on a particular piece of Scripture. I can't even remember it, but it was an ambiguous sounding verse, and I didn't want to use it in one way if everybody else who ever went to a Protestant church understood it in a different way. So I wanted to be sure. And he confirmed what I thought.

WDB: You seem to have a feel for the scope of the ministry — hospital visiting and other demands. Have you done some of that?

PP: No. I mean I know they do hospital visits.

WDB: Well, the whole thing with Jakey, the young boy who is blinded, you really get the anxiety of those hospital visits Swain Hammond makes.

PP: I did think about doing some visits myself, and I realized that I would not be good at hospital visits. Actually, now I'd be better at it. At the time I first thought about being a minister, when I was twenty-five, it would have been disastrous. I've gotten a little more relaxed and easier going than I was then, and probably I could handle it now. But I thought about those things in particular because those things are how I couldn't be, the personal counseling, the bereavement, and all of that.

WDB: So Swain's tension about the business of ministering reflects your own contemplation of the job? And I like the business, too, of Swain Hammond talking about himself as an impostor. I sometimes get that sense in the classroom, that somebody's going to come in and drag me out and apologize to the students and tell them how this was all a mistake. Your character has that sort of insecurity. Early on, he says:

God was supposed to unlock whatever it is that keeps Swain
Hammond so tied up. Sometimes he feels as if his arms are tied
to his chest with barbed wire. And all around him, everywhere
he goes, people are reaching over him, touching each other.

Is this about our guardedness within the institution, the church? Or
just about our universal longing for connection?

PP: That was purely personal. I remembered having done multiple
drafts of that section, and people kept saying to me, "He's so aloof,
he's so unreachable," and people have called me aloof all my life, and
I was getting less and less amused. And I finally decided that the whole
book was aloof; it wasn't just the main character. And I knew I could
not deal with the character without changing myself. And I went into
therapy in a group because there'd be other people there to deal with
the issue of my walled-offness. I'm the sort of person who, if I walk
into a party, I can see people say, "Should I pat her on the shoulder?
I don't know. Would she like that?" I could see people who ordinarily
would hug somebody would hesitate at me. So I was urgent to get this
book fixed, but it was actually that personal.

WDB: Well, it's fascinating the way it works itself out in the text.
At the end, for example, when his wife is pregnant and everybody's
wanting to touch her, and Swain is jealous, it's as if he wishes they
would touch him. Yet that aloofness remains. And somehow, despite
everything, at least one person is listening — Gladys Henby. Right?

PP: Yes. I didn't think hard about Gladys. I suspect she's influenced
by the fact that the church is so much dominated by older women.
They're also in a position of supposed powerlessness. You know, lesser
clout. I think that's partially my comment on the way that's not how
it is or should be. I think it's partly the last shall be first, and it's
partly, "Who says this lady is last?"

WDB: Do you sometimes get that sense of isolation that a preacher
feels as you write? "I'm throwing all these words out and who really
gives a rip?"

PP: Sure.

WDB: Swain Hammond gets his burning bush experience, but you
always keep poised the question of whether it really happened or not.

Maybe it's a mental collapse. That's clearly important to you, doubt and faith in mixture?

PP: Yes, it's not jabbing me in the side all the time, but it's all still there. I know that. Sometimes I think, "Who could believe all this?" But I don't think it with any angst. I think there's something powerful pulling, but there's no way to know for sure. I want to believe something, but I'm very nonspecific about it. I don't feel enormously Christian. I'm going to have to say that I feel sort of open to many possibilities and that I'm more Christian than other things, partly because it's the familiar tradition, but that I could just as easily be in another tradition. And I think they're all partly right and partly wrong. Your view depends on what seat you get on the bus.

WDB: I keep coming back to Jakey. When I think of the doubt and darkness in *Revelation*, when Swain Hammond prays for the blind boy, I get the sense that God missed a chance. You affirm much in your novel, but you insist on inexplicable tragedy, too?

PP: I think that may be my major issue; at least it seems so now. I'm reasonably close to finishing another novel, tentatively titled *Parasol*, in which the issue is evil. It's about an artist who is stalled because she will not face her own dark side. And she's so afraid of what's going to come out that she's lost the ability to paint at all because she can't, just like the woman in that review says, because you can't decide in advance to do a sanitized version and come out with a live version. Half of herself is engaged there. And I wonder too how it's going to be if that book comes out. You never know what can happen. *Commonweal* is probably not going to review it this time. This woman briefly becomes a prostitute. And it's dark. I consider it to have a redemptive ending, but I'm finding not everybody does. Yet it's coming from the same place that *Revelation* did.

WDB: It's trying to speak the truth?

PP: Yes, and it's trying to deal with the mixture that we are.

WDB: You resist the Christian fairy tale. Do you ever go into the so-called Christian bookstores, or do you know much about that world of fiction?

PP: I've been in there, and one of them even carried my book. I pitched it to them. I mean I think it's a real Christian book. I really do.

WDB: What about some of the writers who work from a more-or-less Christian position?

PP: I've reviewed Walter Wangerin. I liked him. Dan Wakefield and I stay in touch. He's been so kind about my work. Somebody gave him an anthology which had my short story about Swain in it. He went to the trouble to call to ask if I was turning that story into a novel. He proposed it for the Unitarian annual fiction prize, which it didn't win. And he has helped me. He wrote letters to publishers to encourage them to look at *Revelation*. He's written a couple of grant recommendations. But my main encouragement still has to be my parents, who made it all right to be a writer. They didn't say, "That's a weird thing to do." And my high school teacher, Mildred Modlin. She's in the acknowledgments. She told me I was a good writer at the time when I needed to hear that.

WDB: *Revelation* certainly puts you in the company of those who write out of issues of faith. Somehow, too, it's a book about blindness of many sorts. Jakey's blindness is only the most obvious, I guess?

PP: Jakey came from the fact that my office was on the route for a mobility training course for a school for the blind. Every day I saw blind children going by, learning to use a cane, and that's very stirring. It became part of me. I didn't plan that to occur in the book at all, but it cropped up. So I learned a little more, went over to that school and went out with some kids doing the training, and I interviewed some children who were blind.

WDB: I recall Swain's phrase for Jakey as one "doomed to a look of permanent disappointment."

PP: I think blindness is my worst fear, and that's true for lots of people. And I think it's an interesting parallel to the idea of not seeing in other senses. In the book I'm working on now, there's a character with a vision problem. But more than that, she has a problem of not being very perceptive in other ways.

WDB: There's also the fact of Jakey's youthfulness that seems to disconcert Swain Hammond. In fact, he's very nervous about children and troubled about the possibility of having his own. What's going on there?

PP: I don't have kids, and it was time to make the final decision about that at the time that I was writing this book. I was thirty-seven or so, and I'm not especially good with kids.

WDB: So part of Swain's sort of hesitancy is your own?

PP: Oh yes. I got bogged down on the manuscript at one point and decided I would just throw in an event. Usually I go with what comes, what seems to just rise out of the material, rather than sticking something in. But this time I decided to make Julie, Swain's wife, pregnant and see what would happen. It was not a planned event for any of us. But the possibility of having children has been a big issue for me. At the time I was writing this book, I realized in a nonverbal way what I was missing. It was almost like my animal self was grieving. I really didn't want to add children to my life, but my physical self was alerting all other systems that this is not what we had in mind. I really had this strong sense of a wounded animal saying, "You are not treating me right." And that version of me was supposed to get to have children. So I just sat that one out. And partly I was helped by writing the book; that was a way to focus my thinking self on the whole issue.

WDB: Another issue evident in the book is God's unpredictability. God is invited in dramatic ways and doesn't do a thing — a blessed thing or a damned thing — however you want to look at it. And then there are these moments when he's suddenly there at the barbecue grill or something, the completely unexpected moments. I mean, is that sort of mystery something you were after?

PP: Yes. I think that's how it happens.

WDB: Are you trying to suggest to your readers that we keep our possibilities open? That we never know when something extraordinary or miraculous might happen?

PP: When I was in school, the most interesting question I ever had on an exam was "Was Bismarck an opportunist or a master planner?" And I've asked myself that on a number of occasions — not about Bismarck in particular, of course. I wonder about that for both God and Swain. It doesn't look like planning is the whole answer to this. It doesn't look like there's anything predictable about spiritual life at all.

WDB: So you're something of an optimist? You stay open. You keep listening, paying attention, staying awake?

PP: Yes, an optimist and an opportunist.

246

WDB: About this business of loosening up and trusting life — some of your early readers suggested that you make Swain less aloof, and you got to thinking about that in a larger way. This character needs to learn to dance. It's a struggle for him all the way through, isn't it? He never really does loosen up completely?

PP: Not really. He'll be slightly different after it's over, I think. It's not a radical change. He'll always be who he is, but I think it's going to be looser.

WDB: So there's still barbed wire there?

PP: Yes. But my feeling was that the novel ended on a good day for him. And it's not the answer to everything, but it's a genuine turning in a good direction.

WDB: Are there other writers, women writers in particular, that you turn to?

PP: Well, I haven't thought of them as women writers in particular. My particular brand of feminism has always been trying to ignore it. But I've gotten more conscious in recent years. I think maybe ignoring the gender differences isn't going to work.

WDB: So you are conscious of yourself as a female artist?

PP: Becoming more so, yes. And this is new for me. *Revelation* is written from a male point of view. I did not think about that. It was fine. It gave me some distance from the material. And I thought of it in that way. But I went to a women's studies conference at Duke, and Caroline Heilbrun and Carol Gilligan were the speakers. I was very impressed. And I had read *Writing a Woman's Life,* and that affected me. I've always felt strongly about equal rights, but I haven't felt pushed into it much until now. My mother is a very strong model for a powerful woman, and I've always thought that's how it was. And she had a career, so there were so many things that the women's movement brought up that had never been an issue for me. I just assumed that women were very powerful. So I skipped that stage. And now I'm becoming conscious of the possibility of a female point of view as a definite and different contribution. I've always read from every direction and not hovered over particular artists for long periods of time. The chief exception to that is Henry James. I've just reread *Portrait of a Lady* to teach it. I read it once in high school and fell in

247

love with it. I read it again in college and felt the same way. And I just read it again a couple of weeks ago, and I'm so pleased to find that I'm drawn to it still and I understand my attraction to it better.

WDB: James sort of drifted to my mind a moment ago when you talked about the way you compose, the way you let it rise out of the writing itself, which is, of course, what he says. He would see a scene — Isabel Archer standing there at the fireplace, that moment of recognition when she realizes that Osmond has had a relationship with Madame Meryl — and he started the book by wondering what would happen. Do you write that way?

PP: Yes, I do. And I didn't even think of connecting that with James particularly. And I've just read his notebooks for the first time in preparing a series of lectures, and it was satisfying to find that connection. I've received a fellowship to go to India and give three lectures on American writers. I actually want to go to India to work on a novel about a lapsed Southern Baptist, a scientist, who has grown up in the river baptism tradition in a rural, old-fashioned Baptist church. He goes to India to study water quality and is fascinated by the daily immersions he witnesses along the Ganges River. That's what I'm going to do next. To get the money, I had to come up with some deal with the university. And I wrote and offered various lecture or workshop possibilities. The head of the English department wrote me back and said they didn't want to hear anything about contemporary southern fiction. He said they would like to hear about *Moby Dick*, *Portrait of a Lady*, *Herzog*, and *Farewell to Arms*. And I'm chiefly qualified by being American, I guess. I majored in English twenty-something years ago, so I'm really boning up.

WDB: So you have lectured on the southern novelist. What about that? Do these radio shows and reviewers talk about you as part of a so-called southern voice? If you write in the South, then Faulkner has to come up and Flannery O'Connor has to come up?

PP: I take the point of view that I was describing earlier about the women writers — I just don't think that much about it. I think that it does affect life for a writer, though. Partly because there is a strong expectation apparently of a particular southern tradition — often referred to as "grit lit." And some of the reviewers pointed out that my book is not about the world described in many of those books — the small town, down home, front porches. So I feel like any southern writer is going to be partly defined in terms of how they do or do not fit into that. I really like the tradition, however. It's not quite the way I do it. My own background is not in the country, and my writing reflects that experience. And I just don't worry about it. I really like what other people are doing.

WDB: As *Revelation* ends, we hear Swain Hammond proclaim that "God's as real as a station wagon." Sometimes? All the time? I mean, that's more what he wants to believe than what he believes, isn't it?

PP: Yes. It's something he believes part of the time.

WDB: It's what we all want to believe?

PP: Sure. He's unsure, but he's in there pitching.

WDB: When he delivers his final sermon, he says he's come to the conclusion that we really can't communicate anything important about our experience of God to one another. And he says his ministry just turned out to be his search for God. Do you feel that way about spiritual issues finally?

PP: No, I think we can communicate about spiritual experience, but not the way Swain had in mind. I think we can keep people company in a way that encourages their spirituality. But it's a very indirect thing. It's planting seeds and trying not to do harm.

WDB: And the last word in the last paragraph of *Revelation* is the word joy. That's your sense of the last word — beyond the tragedy there is a kind of affirmation?

PP: Yes. It's a matter of tuning the machine. I feel like I haven't adjusted the knobs right sometimes, haven't gotten the signal as clear as it ought to be. It's so easy to be worrying and fussing about so many things. And I do feel like it comes down to joy when we get there, when we get the knobs adjusted right. I always feel slightly unqualified to say that because nothing dreadful has happened to me. I mean, if I were paralyzed from the nose down, I don't think I'd believe that. I don't know if I would. When I say something like that, the thought crosses my mind, "But what do you know? You got it easy."

WDB: Can you give advice on writing, or do you just have to have the knack?

249

PP: Lots of drafts, for me, lots of drafts. And I feel strongly about getting feedback and listening to it and rewriting. I rewrite endlessly. And I get several readers. And I want to be read, I want to be understood, I want people to get what I'm saying finally. So I put myself through numerous criticisms. I'm going through that now. I really thought I was just about through with this new book, and I got two responses that indicated to me that some stuff really wasn't clear. So I do feel very strongly about the value of criticism and wanting to listen to it and use it. At the same time, I have to keep my balance and not get personally discouraged by critical stuff so that I can't use it. It took me a long time to feel that I had stories I wanted to write.

WDB: So the move from nonfiction to fiction is a way of loosening up, but is it more difficult than the earlier stuff?

PP: Well, it's harder in some ways, but it's immensely more satisfying.

WDB: And more personal?

PP: It sure is. I mean I far prefer to do fiction. Even though it's so tremendously difficult to do.

WDB: Any way to summarize all this?

PP: I don't have a one-sentence theology. I think it comes out as who to trust and how much to trust myself. I'm not always clear on my own beliefs about God. I'm primarily interested in storytelling. I'm not willing to say what I don't think is true. One person in my writing group kept wanting me to change a scene. It seemed to me that we just had a disagreement. We simply differ on the point; he wanted the scene to have a moral. I rewrote it all right, but only to make my position clearer. But I also feel I have some overall set of things to say and, even if I don't think about them, they will emerge in the stories.

WDB: So you resist labels like "Christian novelist" or whatever, but there's something bubbling there that's going to come into the books?

PP: That's it.

WALTER WANGERIN

1978 — *The Book of the Dun Cow*
1983 — *Thistle*
1984 — *Ragman and Other Cries of Faith*
1985 — *Book of Sorrows*
1986 — *Orphean Passages*
1986 — *Potter*
1987 — *A Miniature Cathedral and Other Poems*
1988 — *Miz Lil and the Chronicles of Grace*
1989 — *The Manger Is Empty*
1990 — *As for Me and My House*
1991 — *Elisabeth and the Water-Troll*
1992 — *Mourning into Dancing*
1993 — *Little Lamb, Who Made Thee?*
1993 — *Branta and the Golden Stone*
1993 — *Reliving the Passion*
1993 — *Measuring the Days*
1994 — *The Crying for a Vision*
1996 — *The Book of God*

WALTER WANGERIN

Man of Letters

"I use the forms they understand: drama, poetry and essay, fables, letters, memoirs, any form whereby the words may cry the Word."

Since he first leapt into our libraries with his bestseller, *The Book of the Dun Cow,* in 1978, Walt Wangerin has persistently perplexed those who deal in labels. Formerly the Lutheran pastor of Grace Church in inner-city Evansville and now writer-in-residence and sometime professor at Valparaiso University in Indiana, Wangerin has produced poems and children's books, essays and short stories, sermons and newspaper columns, and more novels. Some of his readers speak of *Miz Lil and the Chronicles of Grace* or *Ragman and Other Cries of Faith,* while others focus on *The Book of the Dun Cow* or *Book of Sorrows.* Maintaining a herculean lecturing schedule, he has still found time to do the hard work of disciplined writing, most recently producing *The Book of God* to kind reviews and high volume sales.

Walt Wangerin's stories and meditations ring with a deep regard for the real lives of people and a rooted faith in the providential actions of a benevolent God in those lives. But the faith never comes easily, and his writing is a quest for the meanings in things, he says. Wangerin spoke with me in August 1995 at his farmhouse in Indiana about the responsibilities of the artist, the attitude of the church toward art, farm tractors, writing for children, and the grace of the stories that have come his way.

▼   ▼

WDB: I first heard you speak at a conference in Wisconsin in 1992. I remember seeing you in a little room pacing back and forth as you waited out the moments before your speech. The energy was obvious. People who write about you often refer to your passion and intensity. Where does all this fire come from?

WW: I've always lived with that intensity. Most of life struck me hard. I think I was just born with a tympanic response — a vibration. My father was a preacher. And I know that he speaks with some energy. But I outdo him. I outdo him because my father structures his presentations rather more conceptually. I do it more dramatically. My mom has always lived at a dramatic level. That can be frightening to a child. She was charged in everything she said and did. She was able to translate her feelings into an intense language. She speaks in poetic language, in metaphor, in hyperbole, by nature. And I think that's part of why I do.

WDB: You grew up listening to your own father from Sunday to Sunday?

WW: I did. There were long patches, however, when he was something besides a preacher, when I would listen to someone else. And I grew up a reader; I felt everything I read. So there was internal passion. Later, ministering myself in a black parish, I developed and refined a speaking style that reflects that culture.

WDB: You've made a drama of your personal life. You've written about your parishioners in Evansville and about your own family. You reach back to childhood memories and make much of them. Is there risk in dealing this closely with the details of one's own life?

WW: I have no doubt that life is dramatic. Artists try to communi-

254

cate that drama. Some better. Some worse. That's what a short story is. It's communication of our human experience a bit edited, boiled down, or imagined, invented. Whether one is a writer or not, we are in a drama. I believe that this continually unfolding drama has God as protagonist. The drama becomes metaphor, a way of explaining what happens. I teach my students that writing requires paying attention. Be attentive. Develop an attitude toward existence, an awareness. And this requires honesty. I require it of myself. But it's a helpless thing. I have paid attention. And I'm bound to tell about what I've seen. When I close my eyes and remember my childhood, the memory isn't just visual or oral. It's three dimensional. I know where I was and how things felt and what they smelled like. It's no great achievement of my own. Given the choice, I would have said "No, thanks. Let me be a farmer." Sometimes it's just too much. So I require of my students that they pay attention because that's what's necessary for writing. But I don't praise myself for having paid attention.

WDB: So writing is something one is born to, but the hard work of developing the craft comes in somewhere too, doesn't it?

WW: Oh yes. From grade school on, I read much, and I did want to write. Even now as I try to translate my own experience into art, which is what I think I do, I hope I do it so well that people think I'm telling them straight off, like it has simply spilled from my mouth, from my experience. And yet it's been edited. And that's tricky business, trying to edit and be true to the experience. It is possible, as an artist, to obey the craft more than we obey human rules of politeness and kindness. I have to draw the lines. Things in my own life that I'm going to write about, I will shape them myself. And that's a treasure, a gift. And a risk. Having said that, I have been very fortunate. If I wanted to include my children in a story, it is a principle of mine to ask them if it was okay. And they always say yes. The first thing is that they knew they had a choice. I think knowing they had a choice relaxed them.

WDB: Did they ever complain later on?

WW: Only once, and now my daughter doesn't even remember whatever it was that she didn't want mentioned. The second fortunate thing is community. I grew up in the church. We as a family grew up with grace, and I grew up as a preacher. So when I would tell my children's stories, it never was like telling them out of the house. It never really was like hanging our laundry up in public. It was like telling them within the house among people who loved them. And so I don't think my children ever felt embarrassed by it. Preaching is, among other things, a chronicling of the life of a community. That's why I called one of my books *Chronicles of Grace*. Fortunately, I had learned rules like when you tell those stories the sinner is yourself. Almost always in those stories, there's a sinner. Stories have sinners; that's why they're good stories. Almost always it was me. Humor is a grace. It's absolutely a grace because, if people laugh, willy-nilly they make commitments to what's going on. They make good commitments, too. They covenant. Laughter is a kind of a covenant, a spiritual covenant. If it was gentle humor, then they liked it. And so, we grew up together.

WDB: But now your family is grown, and you no longer minister to a small church family. Where do the stories come from now?

WW: I continue to write columns, but they are to a broader community — five million people. And so there's little intimacy there. It's a little more generalized to talk about them or name them. So, yes, I'm in a new place. The only thing I would say for now is that my writing tends to be more invention these days. The substance isn't necessarily tied to memory.

WDB: Does that make it more difficult?

WW: Somebody asked me when I left parish ministering what would I use for stories. And I always answered, I'll make them up. The point being that a storyteller will always tell stories, will always find a story to tell. If experiences can't be as experienced, then you'll make them up. So the issue is, of course, from what barrel are you going to draw the apples.

WDB: Your stories have often been categorized as Christian in some way and have then been sent over to the Family Bookstore. What do you make of this sacred/secular distinction that dominates the publishing industry?

WW: Let me tell you about my dealings with Simon and Schuster with my novel *Crying for a Vision*. The novel does deal with spiritual issues, but when I talked to one of the editors at Simon and Schuster, she just talked about this religious focus. It set my teeth on edge. Not because it's not a religious book, but because I don't like her definition of religious. And thus we get B. Dalton and Family Books. If those stores represented two poles on a continuum, one would be at peace. But they do not; they are two shops that don't talk to each other. And I'm sorry for both shops. I'm sorry we just don't love books anymore. Historically, even up to the last century in England, a handful of people wrote books for a handful of readers. Only a small group of readers read at a level of subtlety, recognized the literary qualities of the books they read. Today in our country, we boast of our high literacy rate. But we have ceased to acknowledge the fact that there is complexity in literature. It is still a small group that has been willing to learn the subtleties. There's no one to blame. But as a consequence, we merge the whole idea of books. Literature has lost its place. So we sell to the masses, people who can read words, but who have themselves made narrow choices. And we sell by category, by classification. And because sales, not literature, have taken over the industry, those who genuinely wish to write literature are embarrassed by it. I'm embarrassed for my publishers when I say I'm writing art, because it makes them squirm. They don't want to sell art. Because art is unclassifiable. But they classify me anyway. In classifying me in this procrustean way, they cut off my legs. I don't like it.

WDB: So it is all market driven?

WW: Sure. Somebody decides you are to be classified as religious. So my whole kit and caboodle got moved over to HarperSanFrancisco. I scarcely realized in those early days what that had done to my career. And I don't think that they even realized, or cared, what they had done to my career. They had narrowed my audience.

WDB: *Little Lamb, Who Made Thee?* must have given the classifiers fits?

WW: You can imagine what they thought of the title.

WDB: I hear they wanted to change it to *Little Lamb, Who Made You?*

WW: Yes, they had no glimmer of the allusion to Blake's poem.

WDB: And they had to find a category?

WW: They just don't know. They are moved by the book. They like it. But then when they get ready to sell it, they scarcely look at the complexity that's inside of them. I finally have to put my trust in God. And I mean this in the most childlike way. I simply write stories. I resist the labels: religious writer, fantasy writer, children's author, theologian, memoirist, and all that. Labels create a false anticipation. They impose laws on the reader. It is a presumption of a bookstore or a publishing house.

WDB: Is it difficult to get around the minister thing? Is there some assumption that, because you are an ordained minister, you will logically write religious stuff?

WW: Yes, exactly. I remember a *New York Times Review* that said I'd written a pretty good book for a minister.

WDB: Do you miss those Jesus Revolution days, the early 1970s, when you worked in a bustling inner city? At least you weren't caught up in the vagaries of the publishing industry.

WW: I don't and I do. I was scared all the time. I miss it, but I would rather not be thirty again.

WDB: How much has the Evansville period shaped the work you do today?

WW: It has not been a defining thing. But it is certainly part of me. Much of my sense of the dramatic and my sense of timing as I speak to audience probably goes right back to that time.

WDB: You've reached a stage in your career now where academics read papers on your work at learned conferences. What is it like to have your work reviewed, analyzed, and the like?

WW: Insofar as the interpreter obeys rules of interpretation, I'm very happy. Most academics do that. Not all. Which is to say, I'm glad to find that my work has gone beyond me. And I'm pleased that people of genuine insight and experience find so much more in it than I do. I'm very grateful. But I want to hear it as an objective person, not as though I need to respond. I'd rather just listen than have somebody say, "Well, what do you think about the interpretation?" I can't argue it. The only time that I really dislike it is when the rules bend, when the rules of interpretation are forgotten by somebody who has a hobbyhorse to ride and is using me to fulfill something outside of my work. They twist the work. And academics do this too. And I get angry because they ought to know better. Feminists now will approach works of literature from a viewpoint which shears off whole elements of that literature because it doesn't fit. Likewise deconstructionists. It's an arrogant presumption that they have the last word in what literature is, and their last word destroys what I'm thinking when I sit there writing.

WDB: The author is somehow unimportant?

WW: Yes. There are always those who think they know me because they have read my writing. I'm not bothered by them; I just know they're wrong. Many people read my books and think the books detail my experience wholly. This is a weird thing, but I will be true to my experience and I will present it to them. At the same time, there is a universalization that always goes on in true writing. And this brings a veil down over me. I'm one degree removed. I am not only revealed; I am also veiled by my making myself a universal thing. This is something of what fiction is when fiction is genuinely art. At that moment of writing, I'm not there anymore. So readers make a fundamental error when they think they have discovered me by reading my book. I'm on the move. The person in the book doesn't really exist anymore.

WDB: So when somebody comes up to you at a book signing and begins to talk to you, you often realize they have assumptions about who you are?

WW: Yes, and that's okay. I gave them these assumptions about who I am. And those who think they have fallen in love with me, or hate me, because of what they have read of me, scarcely know that they have fallen into love or into hate with a fiction. Even though the story is totally true. I wasn't writing letters to a friend; I was writing art.

WDB: Is there any way that your huge success with *Book of the Dun Cow* almost hurt your career?

WW: It got me wrongly defined, I suppose. But so did *Ragman*. And the book was such a jaunt. It was such a joy to have discovered a story that I not only could tell but one that told itself.

WDB: How long did it take?

WW: Six weeks. Writing day and night. I carried it with me wherever I went. I had typewriters in various places. And I would sit down all morning and write in one place, then I'd do some work, and then I'd be somewhere else writing in the evening. Only once did I go down a false path. And I knew exactly what it was. It was relatively early, about a fifth into the book. The prose suddenly felt false. I pulled back, listened for the pulse, and the whole pleasure of this flow of words returned. But that one book doesn't define me. I grew up reading Samuel Johnson, who wrote whatever he had to write: a novel, poetry, broadsides, articles against the king, and the like. I guess that's always been my notion of the writer, a man of letters.

WDB: I've seen several occasional pieces of yours; one in particular, a speech called "Tacking toward an Aesthetic of Faith," addresses this business of what art does. There you talk about writing as prayer. Can you elaborate?

WW: I do think that writing is a request of the deity. The writer names things that have gone unnamed since creation. I think that's an artistic affair. And this naming must take place in conversation with God. The writer is going into an unexplored region.

WDB: It's not just that you have a conversation with your characters, letting them inform the direction of a story, but there is also this other voice coming in?

WW: That joins in, yes.

WDB: You also say that "the object of a writer's faith is absolutely crucial to the transcendent value of the writer's art." So you argue that what a writer believes is inherent, is fundamental, to the story?

WW: Yes! How else does the writer make sense of anything? Without faithfulness at the core, what the hell are we doing? Something else. There is always something at the core. Maybe it is selling yourself, or making money, or telling people what they want to hear, "tickling the ears" as the prophets would say. These things, if standing at the core, represent faithlessness. If all you're doing is giving people what they want, you may create an enticing thing. Those writers who write with great skill and no faith are dangerous. Now some people will hear everything I say in context of Christianity and will think that I am talking about Christian faith. I'm not. Whoever is responsible for Homer's works, for example, had a profound faith. Sophocles had a profound faith.

WDB: What does it mean then to express one's Christian faith in a poem or express one's Christian faith in a story? Clearly, you don't sit down and say, "Well, I'm going to write something for a Christian audience; therefore, I need to have certain pious things in here."

WW: No, I don't sit down and say, "Now this is Christian." I just don't. Sometimes, as with the story "Ragman," I am thinking of a specific audience. I wrote that story for one person. And this was a person who was asking, I thought, a very Christian question and was not getting an answer. But artistically, I just do my best to tell the truth. If I want to preach a sermon, I preach a sermon. I do that all the time. That's what I meant about being a "man of letters." I will write sermons, and I'll know when I do. And they're overt. That's one kind of writing. When I wrote *Crying for a Vision,* I tried to tell the truth, a true story.

WDB: What would false writing be?

WW: There are people writing today who are producing material which others want to read. Some write romances for those who wish to read romances — Christian or not. Some write fantasy, and so on. I simply say that we shouldn't call it art. It only sins against art if we try to elevate it to that level. When it is what it is, I don't mind.

WDB: If it's defined as popular fiction, that's one thing. If it's defined as art, that's another?

WW: Yes, or when its presence somehow overshadows art. When you think of what people could be reading, that's when you get excited. Much of this fiction produced these days is sedative. It benumbs us and reinforces stereotypes. It doesn't move us to new levels.

WDB: Particularly in the area of so-called Christian popular fiction, the Christian thriller and all, I wonder about the handling of Scripture. Your work visits and revisits Scripture. You don't merely retell; you revisit. How important is Scripture in this project of being true?

WW: Scripture is the story, the defining story. It is how I know the universe. Scripture is endlessly fruitful and rich, a single story in many forms, but a single story. And it is a story that happened within our history. It's one of those few times where God put a toad into the water of creation and disturbed it. And we're in that water. No other disturbance has the same quality as God disturbing these things. None.

So it's not as if I'm sitting with a Bible in my hand drawing really good material for stories; I dwell in that story.

WDB: Is a belief in providence one of those core assumptions of the artist who happens to be a Christian?

WW: Yes and no. You presume that human experience has meaning. Those who despair presume that it doesn't. Despair is to be without a future because you recognize the futility of the present. That's one way to define despair. And there are many Christians who are that way. But my presumption is that there must be meaning in what happens. Good or Bad. Writing on that assumption is a seeking after meaning. It is an incredible search for something you don't know. But hope is at the center of it. It isn't this modern picture of the artist who merely keeps on telling us over and over again that life is meaningless and what asses we all are to think that it had meaning.

WDB: Michael Malone, the novelist, categorizes most modern literature as sophomoric because, as he puts it, the cynicism is "too easy."

WW: That's right. It is. It is the shattering sense of meaninglessness we get in adolescence. But eventually, we begin to use our wits to search for meaning. We get older. And writing is about that process, the seeking, the trying to name. I don't think it's merely providence. I don't think it's just providence in terms of God simply designing all that's happening. That doesn't cut it. I like the notion again of drama with God as protagonist and us as antagonists. I'm using the Greek notion of *agon*, a wrestling. It is something that is developing. It isn't all developed. And God's existence is above and beyond time, and the whole framework of my existence doesn't mean that God knows how things shall develop, despite His absolute design. So the writing is like a wrestling match. It is Jacob wrestling with God; that is a defining metaphor for what goes on all the time.

WDB: So mystery is fundamental?

WW: Oh, it is. And the motion from not knowing to knowing, that continuum of mystery, is never overwhelmed. So the writer doesn't just photograph what is. The writer enters the mystery, wrestles with it. This is life, too, of course. We all do it everyday without thinking about it. The artist enters into a mystery with great awareness.

WDB: Sometimes you address the church in your writing. You say, in fact, that the job of the pastor is "to image the church to the church." Is that a prophetic sort of role? Is that one of the roles of the man of letters?

ww: Definitely. Prophets prophesy to the people of God, and their prophecy is generally incidental to the rest of the world. It was meant to call the people of God to change. Self-appointed prophets in our country, especially the Christian ones, often seem to think that they are called to prophesy to the whole country. Now, we have these Christians who think they can tell presidents what to do. They think that they can also control voting and give instruction in morality. Let's just take abortion, for example, an act I believe to be immoral. But that gives me no right to dictate, to prophesy to the whole secular world. My only right is to become the righteousness I want in the world.

wdb: To model an alternative community?

ww: Yes. Be alternative people. And to be public about it. The Christian Coalition wants to go through the legal system. We go through Congress. We go through the Republicans. We're shaking our finger at them. We're saying, "We Christians, as Christians, will not put you in office." Now I agree with their platform. I think abortion is murder. But I get very upset with people who have the arrogant presumption that they may be Isaiah and Jeremiah to the world, whereas Isaiah was Isaiah to Judah only. Because there was a covenant already in place that they could talk about. Can I be prophetic? I just was. There are those times when one must be direct. The prophet is not indirect. And I suppose some of my stories may have prophetic qualities, but that is not why I wrote them. I really don't want to be a prophet, and given any other ultimate alternative, I wouldn't do it. When I was writing columns in Evansville newspapers, I used the phrase "If I can and I may, then I must." That means, if I have the ability to say things that must be said, to speak of the breaking of covenant, then I have the responsibility.

wdb: So the church is going wrong in getting mixed up within the power structures?

ww: People won't like my saying this, but I think we've become secularized. Even our interpretation of Scripture is more modern than traditional. We're like scientists poring over the words. We don't dwell in the stories. The roots are in the Enlightenment, in empirical science.

WDB: What do you say to your students, then, who have found the church to be wrongheaded, unnecessary, or irrelevant?

WW: Right now it feels to many people that the church is wrong. It's in such turmoil. I think the turmoil is a good sign. The whole church is struggling with issues: feminism, sexuality, and the rest. That wrestling is a good thing. I don't know what will evolve from this, but I think the body of Christ will emerge. Students, you know, are at that age when they want to kick over the traces. I don't mind. I did the same thing, but I will bring before them the presence of the church and ritual. The church through the ages has recognized and honored art, either directly or indirectly, by taking art into its rituals. I would tell students that the church has acknowledged art and in many ways shaped itself according to the artist. Our liturgy shows it. We use the human senses to talk of mysterious things. That's one thing I would honor in the church. Unfortunately, the church doesn't honor art the way it used to. Lutherans are willing to honor music. They don't honor language so much, because language is ambiguous. Artistic language always is. They're okay with visuals, stained glass and so forth, but they don't like some of this dramatic stuff. They are wary of fiction because fiction is a lie.

WDB: I know you continue to have significant interaction with many people, with students for example, but I wonder if the role of writer is more isolating than the role of pastor?

WW: As writer you have no more access to human experience than anyone else, maybe less. As a pastor, you have access to a rich community. Human beings trust you. They invite you into their most dramatic lives. Who'd invite a writer in?

WDB: And the importance of community is a resounding theme of your work. *Book of Sorrows* even suggests that the community, the saints as it were, has the ability to suppress the evil represented by Wyrm.

WW: Certainly a healthy community can confront evil. Evil does very nearly destroy the community in *Book of Sorrows*. I think the community has the ability to maintain the structures of peace and purpose. It is hope. But it can be destroyed. And a community can kill itself. When we fail to honor one another, then the community is no more. I heard the other day that this is the first time in history that we have seen our own children as economic competitors. People don't have children because that would mean a descent to a lower income bracket. It is this worrying over individual rights that destroys. It's something right now the church needs to speak about.

WDB: In *Book of Sorrows* and *The Book of the Dun Cow*, the central failure is to miss what you were meant to be, miss your purpose. When the villainous Cockatrice arrives, the canonical hours are done away with. The hours are not marked and purpose is lost.

WW: Yes. And also the holiness of time and orientation, in every sense of that word.

WDB: Do we live in such a time now?

WW: I think we always have a potential of losing the holiness of time.

WDB: And the rhythms of grace and forgiveness?

WW: Yes. What is the important time now? What is the fullness of time? Elections. Right now we are looking forward to an election. Everything aims that way.

WDB: You remind me of Garrison Keillor in your disdain for politicians. In fact, I've seen you compared to him. Is he an influence of sorts?

WW: I listen to him. He has that penchant for drama we've spoken about. I appreciate him. I have learned about oratory by watching comics on television. These comics are often great storytellers with an extraordinary sense of timing. Keillor's timing is extraordinary. And Richard Pryor. Bad as his language was, he was remarkable at literally creating other worlds and then walking through them.

WDB: Who else do you read and listen to?

WW: The speakers I've turned to are people like Jesse Jackson or Martin Luther King. Although I would never construct a speech like King, I've learned much from his use of dramatic progression, intonation, the rise and fall of the voice. They have influenced my verbal presentations and, of course, that has crept into my writing as well. I always hear what I write. Careful readers will sense that. Now I find that my style is changing. It's becoming much more spare, much less elaborate.

WDB: Do you get letters from readers?

WW: Not so much from the fiction. There I'm writing people into an experience. But they're not sermonic. I get many more letters in response to *As for Me And My House* and *Mourning into Dancing,* the nonfiction.

WDB: Did you read Norse myth somewhere along the way?

WW: Oh yes!

WDB: The Midgard serpent?

WW: Certainly. That's an element of my fiction. Norse myth is cold and melancholy. And there's no compromise. Whereas the Mediterranean myth is laid-back. There is certainly a relationship between the *Prose Edda* and *Dun Cow.* That's where I learned the power of point of view. I remember the chills of tension that Snorri Sturluson could produce with his shifting point of view. I knew what would happen to characters before they knew. In *The Book of the Dun Cow,* there's a scene where Lord Russel, the fox, has awakened late and the hens have run away. He goes rushing toward the river and comes out on a rise, and he sees the dead hen and the chicks. And then he sees Pertelote and Chauntecleer talking. That's a direct take from Sturluson. I knew what I was doing.

WDB: What gives you the most pleasure these days?

WW: Besides my tractor, you mean? Well, I have the pleasure of parenting and trying to obey the seasons. I'm still trying to learn how to live, how to obey that which I cannot control. I have seventeen acres here, and I've learned much by working on it, obeying it, watching it regenerate.

WDB: You continue to produce stories for children. What's the special challenge for writing for children?

WW: You have to remember not to talk down to them. Often people think what you do is drop it two or three levels to talk to children. That's backwards. In terms of genuine artistic craft, you raise three or four levels to talk to children. And that's because you have to be briefer, more elemental. I get angry with those books that talk to children with their tongue between their teeth. Compromising and patronizing. Even the very successful Disney films like *The Lion King* are often reductions. We reduce things to that which we think children can handle. The challenge is to tell a story that children can walk through easily, even though it's also to believe that children live very well with mystery. They don't have to have everything explained to them. Adult writers think they have to explain everything. They don't use words that are difficult. They don't use structures — sentence structures or narrative structures — that are difficult. We forget that children walk through mysterious worlds all the time. They are always meeting things that they do not understand. And either they come to understand them or they just accept it and go on.

WDB: And some of what they accept is dark, too. You talk about Matthew coming in at night with the nightmare. You can take him downstairs and show him there isn't a burglar, or you can enter his imagination.

WW: Exactly. That's it too. You enter it in order to walk with them to some conclusion rather than saying it doesn't exist. And that's very complex stuff. And many adults, even those who read it, think that what you're doing is hurting their children. What they're doing is thrusting their children companionless into the world.

WDB: Virginia Stem Owens wrote a fine essay about your work for *Christian Century*. Talking about *Book of Sorrows* and some of the stories for children, she says you were able "to break news of suffering," that you had said to children, "Yes, there is a wound in the world." I remember a scene in *Crying for a Vision* where there's something in the salt lick. And the wolf licks his own life away. One can imagine a child recoiling at that. Yet you pull it off.

WW: Because I love the children. If you don't love them, you'll give them a horror to horrify them. But if you love them, you tell them the truth. And you know that doing it will move them toward you. This is where I get upset with writers who are very good but do not love those to whom they are writing. I don't think Shel Silverstein loves the children. He plays with them, and that's okay. He gives them good games to play. But I don't think he loves them. I think he spends more time being sad about himself.

WDB: Part of the hard truth children have to know is sacrifice, isn't it?

WW: Oh yes, it is. That's elemental too. That gift of free choice is that gift of sacrifice on God's part. I can't define love apart from sacrifice. This world can. I must not.

WDB: And that strikes me as a principle that runs through your work that is antithetical to our culture.

WW: Absolutely.

WDB: Our message is generally about loving oneself?

WW: Self-esteem. That's our answer. Cruelly abused and oppressed, we are to have self-esteem. That's no answer. The single moral principle that everyone agrees upon these days is individual rights. Think of Jesus coming into Jerusalem on Palm Sunday with all the people hailing him. He must have been on the verge of tears, because not one of them knows what he is about to do. That great quality that brings him there is the very opposite of what they're hailing him for. That sacrifice is the beginning of the crucifixion. At the core of love is sacrifice. And the beloved may not even know it. If anyone is forced into a sacrificial act, that's not sacrifice. Then it's oppression. There has to be choice.

WDB: Warren Rubel says that *Book of Sorrows* is about overcoming evil within as opposed to *The Dun Cow*, which is about overcoming the evil without. Do you like that?

WW: Yes, I've heard that. As soon as you say that, however, you've begun to conceptualize what should just be story. But I did make that choice. I didn't think about it with *The Dun Cow*. When I was done with *The Dun Cow*, it was fairly evident we were looking at an external evil, and the little evils, the foibles. But when I thought about what I would do next, I knew it had to be the evil within. I even called it *The Book of Lamentation* as a working title.

WDB: And the evil within is pride?

WW: That's a way of defining it. It certainly is a way of defining Chauntecleer's thinking. Chauntecleer is like the good person who begins to presume. He presumes that his goodness has heroic value. And so he separates himself. As I wrote that, I really thought I was writing a fable for the best of our readers today. Not the worst of them. Not this crap you read. For the best of our readers. This is the danger of goodness. This is Abraham Lincoln's danger. This is Robert E. Lee's danger.

WDB: That goodness is remarkably vulnerable to corruption?

ww: To think that we are our own salvation.

wdb: In *Little Lamb, Who Made Thee?* you address Dorothy, your sister-in-law, who has Downs Syndrome. You say to her, "God honors hearts more than brains." Is that a way of expressing your own weariness of the pride of intellect?

ww: I think I was really just thinking about Dorothy. And, perhaps, of how we elevate certain parts of the human being and diminish other parts. The only way we seem to be able to measure the value of a person is "How well do they think," and then "How much money do they make?"

wdb: Are you closely connected to a fellowship here?

ww: Several, actually. The university itself is a very good community. There are so many artists here. I work with a jazz band. I am doing a hymnfest with our outstanding organist. All sorts of things like that. A musical of *The Book of the Dun Cow* has been commissioned. And *Dun Cow* may even be made into an animated feature film.

wdb: So there's a potential for a larger audience?

ww: I suppose, but the pleasure is in doing it, not in what will happen thereafter.